"Riveting . . . Rother presents a fascinating study of one woman's evil and greed—that ultimately leads to murder. An emotional and gripping tale from beginning to end."
  —**Aphrodite Jones**

"Once again Caitlin Rother gets to the heart of a very compelling story. A must-read for true crime fans."
  —**Robert Scott**

"Caitlin Rother hooks you from the prologue . . ."
  —**Suzy Spencer**

"A chilling account of murder and its aftermath by an author at the top of her game."
  —**Fred Rosen**

## LOST GIRLS

"A close look at a killer . . . a deeply reported, dispassionately written attempt to determine what created a monster and predator . . . a cautionary tale and a horror story, done superbly by a writer who knows how to burrow into a complex case."
  —*Los Angeles Times*

"Well-written, thought-provoking . . . if ever a 'true crime' deserved a book-length study, this is certainly that crime."
  —*San Diego Union-Tribune*

"Rother addresses the complexity and difficulty of managing paroled sexual predators. This book will be popular with fans of Rother, Ann Rule, and other popular true crime writers."
  —*Library Journal*

"This thoroughly reported and well-written book draws a terrifying portrait of a man who was sweet and cuddly one day and a crazed killer the next."
  —*San Diego Reader*

"Impressively reported in a forthright narrative . . . a pitch-perfect study of avarice, compulsion and pure California illusion."
—**Ron Franscell**

"We've finally found the next Ann Rule! Caitlin Rother writes with heart and suspense. *Dead Reckoning* is a chilling read by a writer at the top of her game."
—**Gregg Olsen**

"A true-crime triumph . . . Rother solidifies her star status."
—*The San Diego Union-Tribune*

"Rother is at her best. . . . This gruesome story is fast-paced and will grip any lover of the true crime genre."
—*North County Times*

"Rother brings a journalist's careful attention to detail in this chilling look into the mind of a psychopath."
—*Coronado Life Magazine*

"A mesmerizing story."
—*Orange Coast Magazine*

# *POISONED LOVE*

"A true-crime thriller that will keep you on the edge of your seat."
—*Aphrodite Jones*

"Absorbing and impeccably researched . . . a classic California noir story of passion and betrayal and death, with a beautiful, scheming adulteress at the center of the web."
—**John Taylor**

"With integrity, class and skill, Rother weaves this complex story seamlessly in the page-turning fashion of a suspenseful novel."
—**M. William Phelps**

"Chilling . . . Rother paints a portrait of the culture that raised Kristin, hired her, was lured by her beauty, and now must share in the dire consequences."
—**Kevin Barry,** producer for Oxygen Network's *The Kristin Rossum Story*

"A lively and immaculately researched book."
—**Carol Ann Davis**

# I'LL TAKE CARE OF YOU

## CAITLIN ROTHER

PINNACLE BOOKS
Kensington Publishing Corp.
http://www.kensingtonbooks.com

PINNACLE BOOKS are published by

Kensington Publishing Corp.
119 West 40th Street
New York, NY 10018

Copyright © 2014 by Caitlin Rother

All Kensington Titles, Imprints, and Distributed Lines are
available at special quantity discounts for bulk purchases for
sales promotions, premiums, fund-raising, and educational or
institutional use. Special book excerpts or customized print-
ings can also be created to fit specific needs. For details, write
or phone the office of the Kensington special sales manager:
Kensington Publishing Corp., 119 West 40th Street, New
York, NY 10018, attn: Special Sales Department, Phone:
1-800-221-2647.

Pinnacle and the P logo Reg. U.S. Pat. & TM Off.

ISBN-13: 978-0-7860-3255-6
ISBN-10: 0-7860-3255-3
First Pinnacle Mass Market Edition: January 2014

eISBN-13: 978-0-7860-3256-3
eISBN-10: 0-7860-3256-1
First Kensington Electronic Edition: January 2014

10 9 8 7 6 5 4 3 2 1

Printed in the United States of America

# AUTHOR'S NOTE

I learned about this case in May 2009 while I was on the phone with Sergeant Dave Byington, of the Newport Beach Police Department (NBPD), for *Dead Reckoning*, my book about the murder of Tom and Jackie Hawks by Skylar and Jennifer Deleon.

Byington's team of detectives did such a thorough job with the Hawks case—a complex investigation of murder for financial gain, resulting in five defendants and three trials—that I decided to follow some of the same players as they went after the killers of multimillionaire entrepreneur William "Bill" McLaughlin. This case turned out to be just as intriguing, with two defendants and two trials. It also featured the same prosecutor, Senior Deputy District Attorney Matt Murphy, and one of the same defense attorneys, Gary Pohlson.

But this case is somewhat different from others I've written about. First, it's a cold case, which started with a two-pronged fraud-and-homicide investigation in the mid-1990s, the homicide portion of which was resurrected in 2008.

Even though Bill's murder occurred nearly two decades ago, this case is a sign of the times even more today—not just in Southern California, but across the United States, where the pressures to appear unnaturally wealthy, to beautify ourselves with cosmetic surgery, and to win success at any cost only seem to be growing stronger.

Nanette Anne Maneckshaw Johnston Packard, the woman who stars in this true-crime reality—which reminds me of an episode of *The Real Housewives of Orange County–Gone Bad*—should be the spokesmodel for the greed and epidemic of materialism that have plagued our nation for years and have put so many into the throes of crippling debt.

Because of the passage of time, the sheer volume of legal and financial information at my disposal was really quite extensive. Bill was an accomplished businessman who had a complicated asset portfolio and was also fighting a pro-tracted legal battle; his killers had fifteen years after his death to live their lives—spending money, getting remarried and divorced, and having more children, before they were arrested.

To help me flesh out the story, I went through the NBPD's early investigative reports and every court exhibit from both trials. In addition to incorporating police witness interviews, I also did many of my own interviews with key players as I explored Nanette's psyche and her family his-tory. By honing in on the dynamic between her and her series of men, my goal was to pinpoint and illustrate what made this woman so attractive and so successful in conning Bill and the others. (Someone joked to me, "What, does she have gold [genitals] down there?") I also wanted to get to the bottom of why this case didn't get prosecuted back in the 1990s, a major issue raised by the defense in both trials.

I used official sources wherever possible to re-create the scenes in this book. I also drew from people's memories to write approximated dialogue, cross-checking sources wher-ever possible. Some dialogue was edited for storytelling purposes, but no text was created, embellished, or exagger-ated. Any errors are unintentional.

I wasn't able to talk with Nanette, but I was able to paint a telling portrait of this mercurial femme fatale, partly *because* of the lies she told to the men she seduced, manipulated, and victimized, frequently painting herself as a victim and her past boyfriends and husbands as monsters. I am includ-ing these allegations only to show how she operated, not for their truth. Based on the fact that she is a convicted killer and has admitted to theft, forgery, and fraud, I assume that most, if not all, of her accusations are false, because she is a proven and vindictive liar.

Her first husband, Kevin "K. Ross" Johnston, whom she repeatedly characterized as a sexual deviant and accused of all kinds of illicit behavior, categorically denied that he'd done any of the bad acts she'd claimed.

"I am not those things. They are all false," he told me. "I'm just an additional victim to her manipulation."

I tried but could not reach her second husband, John Packard. K. Ross said he's been told by someone close to John that John no longer believed any of the negative things Nanette had said about K. Ross because she'd accused John of many bad acts as well, and John knew they weren't true. It was just her MO.

I investigated the contents of Nanette's résumé, cross-checked many of her stories, and gathered the firsthand observations of her lovers, including her third husband, Billy McNeal, and ex-boyfriend Tom Reynolds, to track the evolution of her motivations, sexual prowess, and crafty deception.

Eric Naposki was far more accessible than Nanette. I sat down with him twice in an Orange County jail for nearly seven hours. He is an incredible storyteller, so I wanted to include the colorful tales he told me about his life before, during, and after Nanette. However, because his stories involving the crime changed so many times during the investigation, I wanted to tell readers up front that I cross-checked his other tales with news reports or public documents wherever possible. But, obviously, I couldn't confirm them all. His college and the National Football League gave me only limited information, so many of his experiences from those years and during his two marriages came directly from him (other than what I took from his divorce files).

Where I felt it was important to flag quotes he gave me directly, I marked them with a double asterisk**.

I used pseudonyms for two characters in this story to protect their privacy: Bill's former HemaScience business partner, whom I called Jacob Horowitz, and Eric's partner in Midnight Moon Productions, whom I called Juan Gonzales.

I live in San Diego, so researching this book required quite a bit of out-of-town travel. I repeatedly drove to Santa Ana to attend the trials and sentencing hearings, did numerous interviews, took photos of relevant landmarks, and went through many court records. I also flew to Oakland, California, and to the East Coast to do court research, driving all over Connecticut to read Eric's divorce files and to see where he was living when he was finally arrested.

All in all, I found this to be a fascinating case, even more compelling because the NBPD and Orange County District Attorney's Office never gave up on it. I hope my readers agree.

# PROLOGUE

Everyone in the McLaughlin household thought Kevin was going to be at his regular Alcoholics Anonymous (AA) meeting that Thursday night, but for some reason he decided not to go. Instead, over a dinner of leftovers at their house in the affluent enclave of Newport Beach, California, Kevin and his father discussed how he was doing in the brain injury program at Orange Coast College.

Bill McLaughlin, a fifty-five-year-old entrepreneurial multimillionaire, had just flown his Piper Malibu back from Las Vegas, where he routinely spent a couple of days a week. Claiming residence at one of his two houses there, rather than in Newport Beach, saved him $500,000 in taxes each year.

Bill's twenty-nine-year-old fiancée, Nanette Johnston, was out that night. Knowing that Bill and Kevin would get home before she did, she'd left them a Post-it note on a lamp in the den, saying that she was at her son's championship soccer game: *Bill and Kev, we won our game, so we are playing again tonight. See you later, Nanette.*

After dinner, Kevin went upstairs to his room to listen to his Walkman—probably some Bad Religion or Megadeth, his two favorite bands—while Bill settled down with a nightcap and some paperwork in his usual perch at the dining-room table.

Just after 9:00 P.M., Kevin was startled by a series of gunshots downstairs.

*Pop pop, pause . . . Pop pop, pause . . . Pop pop, pause.*

Hearing Goldie barking like crazy, Kevin jumped off his bed and hobbled out of his room as quickly as his slow, awkward gait would allow. Their golden retriever wasn't an aggressive or protective guard dog. She was more of a licker that Nanette had fallen in love with at the pound, so all that barking was unusual.

Three years earlier, Kevin had suffered a severe brain trauma, which had put him into a coma for four months during which he was dependent on a ventilator. After he came out of it, he had difficulty walking, so it took him almost a full minute to travel from the second-floor balcony, down two flights of stairs, and into the kitchen to see what was going on.

To his horror, he found his father lying on his side in his blue robe and slippers, his right arm tucked under his stomach, surrounded by a handful of bullet casings and a few dark red splotches of blood across the white tiles. Bill had a fresh cut on his brow and his wire-framed glasses lay twisted and askew beside him. But there was no sign of a gun, let alone the shooter.

Kevin grabbed the phone and frantically dialed 911.

It was 9:11 P.M. on December 15, 1994.

# CHAPTER 1

Bill McLaughlin, who had enlisted in the U.S. Marines at seventeen, right out of high school, was a health-conscious fitness fanatic who insisted on being the master of his domain.

He loved his three children unconditionally and was very affectionate with them, completely indifferent to what people might think when he exhibited his love for his son. He and Kevin made a habit of kissing, hugging, and exchanging "I love you, son," and "I love you, Dad" endearments in public. They also acted wacky together, karate-chopping at each other like Bruce Lee as they stood in line at the movies, embarrassing the rest of the family.

Bill believed in a tough-love approach to drugs, but when he ordered Kevin to go to AA meetings, he wasn't just some hard-ass overreacting to his son's recreational use of marijuana, Pacifico beer, and the occasional vodka binge. Kevin's pot-smoking habit had hurt and upset Bill even before a drunk driver going sixty-five miles per hour had struck the twenty-one-year-old as he was skateboarding home from a bar.

After Kevin was seriously injured and almost died in October 1991, Bill was understandably even more concerned.

His son had spent eighteen months progressing through several rehab facilities, finally coming home to live in the quiet, gated community of Balboa Coves.

Now twenty-four, Kevin was finally able to walk on his own again, so the last thing Bill wanted was for Kevin to derail his recovery by smoking and drinking out of frustration with his disabled body and lagging communication skills. Bill was also worried that Kevin's addictive behaviors could result in a fall, triggering new injuries.

As a result, Bill forced his son to sign a contract to stop using drugs and alcohol. He also kept the refrigerator stocked with drug-testing kits. If Kevin broke the contract, Bill said, he would put him in a board-and-care home. Kevin didn't like the restrictions, which caused tensions between them, but the pact seemed to be working.

Kevin's two-pronged recovery was challenging for him and his family, who were still very close, even though time and circumstances had sent them in different directions around the globe. Bill's oldest child—his sunny and warm daughter Kim—was living in Tokyo, where she taught second grade at an international school. Jenny, the more reserved daughter, a high-school science and physics teacher, lived in nearby Laguna Niguel. And his ex-wife, Sue, had moved to their house in Hanalei, Hawaii, not long after she filed for divorce in 1990, leaving twenty-four years of marriage behind her.

Now that Bill was "retired" and had plenty of money to pay for his son's therapy, he insisted on taking care of Kevin full-time. But their home in Balboa Coves was anything but a bachelor pad.

By December 1994, Bill's fiancée, a fellow divorcee named Nanette, had been living in their two-story home for three and a half years. Most friends and family believed the couple had met "through friends," but Bill and Nanette knew the truth.

On a shelf in the master bedroom's closet, Bill kept a small chest containing several dozen greeting cards. All but one of the envelopes had no address, indicating that they'd been hand-delivered. The one at the bottom of the stack, which was kept in Bill's usual meticulous chronological order, was a handwritten card that Nanette had mailed to him at the very beginning to introduce herself, apparently after he'd answered her personal ad. She was blondish, thin, had advanced degrees, wrote business plans for a living, and worked out to stay fit, just like he did.

They were a good match. Or so he thought.

Even though his family couldn't or, perhaps, didn't want to believe that Bill would have responded to such an ad, they later learned that Nanette had placed one titled, "For Wealthy Men Only" in the February 1991 issue of *Singles Connection,* right around the time that she and Bill had started dating: *SWF, 25, 5'5" 100#, classy, well-educated, adventurous, fun and knows how to take care of her man. Looking for an older man, 30+, who knows how to treat a woman. You take care of me and I'll take care of you.*

If that was, in fact, the deal they'd struck, Bill certainly had held up his end of the bargain. He and Nanette hadn't been dating long before she moved in that August. They made a second home in Kim and Jenny's old rooms for Nanette's kids—four-year-old Lishele and six-year-old Kristofer—who often stayed over. Nanette agreed to quit her sales position, and with their new arrangement came the promise that her only job would be to take care of Bill, pay the household bills, and help him run his affairs.

Nanette, with her ambitions and entrepreneurial spirit, reminded Bill of himself. As he took the young woman under his wing, she tried to bring them even closer, asking him to reverse his vasectomy so they could have a child together and get married. Recently divorced, however, Bill wasn't eager to tie the knot again anytime soon. Instead, he gave her a ring with a sizable diamond, hoping to satisfy her for the time being, and breast implants, to boot. He told a friend that this was a "companion's" ring, which might explain why he and Nanette never had an engagement party, set a wedding date, or made any plans for a ceremony.

"He told me she was pressuring him to get married and have a child and he got her the ring to keep her [happy]," Jenny recalled.

Nanette, on the other hand, proudly told Bill's friends and family about the engagement and showed off her big rock. But what Bill didn't know was that she never wore it to the exclusive Sporting Club gym in Irvine, where she kept her slender figure in shape, met and secretly dated a series of athletic men, who were quite a bit younger than her wealthy fiancé.

Although she later contended that she and Bill had an "unspoken agreement," which allowed her to see other men as long as she didn't embarrass him, his family and friends never heard anything about it, nor did they believe it had ever existed. They all thought Bill and Nanette were happily seeing each other exclusively.

Bill's daughters never volunteered their feelings of distrust and dislike for his girlfriend, but they were honest when he questioned them directly.

"Do you think she's with me for my money?" he asked.

"Yes," they replied.


Bill had been exploring various business ventures since he'd sold the Plasmacell-C, a groundbreaking medical filtration device that separated plasma from blood, in a deal that paid him a small fortune in royalties every year. Counting his property assets, including two homes in Newport

Beach, two in Las Vegas, and a condo development project with an airstrip in the desert, he was worth about $55 million. In addition to investing in real estate, he was also researching new uses for his blood filter and searching for a cancer cure, no less.

"He just loved the challenge and learning new things," Kim recalled.

Over time, Bill shared more and more with Nanette. He discussed his projects with her, and he bought her a new red Infiniti convertible. But after she rolled that car and was arrested for a DIU in 1992, she insisted on driving Bill's green Cadillac.

Bill set up a joint checking account, in which he generally kept a balance of $10,000 to $20,000, and authorized her to sign checks on it to pay the bills. He also provided for her in his living will, made her a trustee of his estate if he should die, and listed her as the beneficiary of a $1 million life insurance policy. The will gave her a year rent-free in the beachfront house he owned on Seashore Drive, as well as $150,000 in cash and the Infiniti.

Bill seemed content in his life with Nanette, whom he took on ski trips and exotic vacations—always bringing her children with them. He was just as affectionate with them as if they were his own, and his fondness for them was mutual. Nanette was constantly taking snapshots of them together as he let them steer his speedboat, cuddled with them on the couch as they watched TV, and hugged them in front of his plane, where he let them take the controls during flights to Las Vegas, to ski in Utah, or to other vacation spots.

Usually, though, Bill went alone to Vegas to conduct business, which lately had involved a protracted legal battle against a former business partner, and also buying firearms at gun shows.

Since Congress had passed the "Brady Bill" in 1993,

making it more difficult to buy guns, Bill had stockpiled about one hundred of them, mostly as an investment, but also for protection. He kept a Jennings .380 under the seat of his white Mercedes, the car he drove between Balboa Coves and the airport, and a nine-millimeter Taurus in a lockbox next to his bed.

On the days Bill was out of town, Nanette usually went shopping and did as she pleased back in Newport, staying the night with the men she met at the gym when she wasn't with her kids. She also helped take care of Bill's son, Kevin, who had come a long way since he came out of the coma.


Kevin McLaughlin was extremely proud that his AA buddies had appointed him secretary of their weekly meeting, because it came with the important duty of taking notes. Because he still suffered from tremors, it took him half an hour to write a one-page letter. He'd also had to learn how to talk all over again, and speaking was a challenge he had yet to master again. His slurred speech could make him sound drunk, especially when he was tired, upset, or under stress. And although his family and his girlfriend could understand him most of the time, it was harder for strangers, especially under these circumstances.

Imagine his frustration that December night as his father lay bleeding on the kitchen floor and Kevin struggled to convey the most important message he'd ever tried to deliver.

"My father's been shot," he said to the 911 dispatcher at the Newport Beach Police Department.

"What do you need the police for, sir?" she asked, unable to make out his garbled moans. "I can't understand what you're saying."

"My dad was shot."

"Say it to me again, sir."

As he tried to convey the nature of his emergency, he felt

helpless as he saw his father's life slipping away, right in front of him. However, Kevin's words were jumbled together, and because he was so upset, he was also yelling, which made it even more difficult for the dispatcher to make out his urgent, guttural tones.

"Are you hurt?" she asked. "Is there anybody out there that can talk to me? . . . Is it your father or your dog? . . . What's the matter with your mother?"

Although the dispatcher was able to pick out the word "gun" and realized that she needed to send paramedics, she still couldn't discern what else Kevin was trying to say.

"Do you think he shot himself?" she asked.

A second dispatcher came on the line to see if she could calm the distraught young man so they could understand him better.

"Is—is your dad breathing?"

"No," Kevin said.

But try as she might, she, too, misunderstood many of his responses. "Did he just fall over? . . . Do you know what happened to him? . . . Heart attack? . . . Did you say 'a gun'?"

"Yeah."

"Where is the gun?"

"I don't know."

"But you think he shot himself?"

These details would all be sorted out later, but there was still the matter of the locked main gate leading into the community, which the police and paramedics couldn't open without some assistance.

"Do you know how to open the gate?" the dispatcher asked.

Although it took nearly five minutes for the dispatchers to decipher Kevin's cry for help, they were able to alert some bike patrol officers in the area, who were the first to gain entrance through the main gate and pedal over to the

McLaughlin house. But by the time paramedics arrived and rolled Bill onto his back, they realized there was no point in trying to revive him. He was gone.

It was maddening for Kevin not to be able to communicate better with the dispatchers. He told his sisters that he was angry he hadn't been able to do more to help his father. However, the minutes that ticked by while he was on the phone didn't make much difference to his father's chances of survival.

The autopsy showed that any one of the six 9mm Federal Hydra-Shok bullets fired into Bill's chest could have been the fatal shot, killing him almost immediately. The hollow-point bullets, designed to tear through tissue as the tips mushroomed upon impact, had torn right through Bill's heart and upper torso. Based on the "stippling" marks on his skin—a circular pattern of dots created by firing a gun at close range—the coroner said that at least two of the bullets, presumably the last two, were fired from about two feet away. All the shots were fired from front to back, downward and to the left. Because Bill stood at nearly five feet ten inches, this indicated that the killer was probably taller than he was.

The 911 tape was tragic to hear in 1994, and even though seventeen years had passed by the time Kevin's mostly incomprehensible statements reverberated throughout a Santa Ana courtroom, they still ripped open the emotional scars in Bill's family and close friends.

After climbing over the wall into the McLaughlins' front yard, the bike patrol officers saw that the front door was wide open, and a silver key was stuck in the lock. A gold key also lay on the doormat, apparently dropped by the shooter in his haste to flee. Both keys looked new—they were shiny and had the small temporary rings that some hardware stores attach to freshly ground copies.

The police soon learned that the gold key opened a pedestrian-access gate across the cul-de-sac, which led to an asphalt path for biking, jogging, and walking. The gate was kept locked, but the spring wasn't so tight that it couldn't be accidentally left ajar or finessed to keep it propped open. On either side of the gate was a chain-link fence, topped with barbed wire, that surrounded the community. Today, that fence has been replaced by a higher and more substantial plaster wall, which is covered with a thick, prickly layer of bougainvillea.

In 1994, the jogging path wound around to a flight of stairs up to a sidewalk that took pedestrians across the four-lane Newport Boulevard Bridge and over the Newport Channel to Lido Marina Village. At the time, the Lido area had a bustling Mediterranean plaza, with a cluster of popular restaurants and nightclubs, including the Thunderbird.

The homeowners' association for Balboa Coves, which consisted of sixty-eight bayfront homes, limited the distribution of keys to residents. And even then only a few were given to each family. For security reasons, copies of the keys were supposed to be stamped "do not duplicate," and each recipient was to be recorded on a master list.


Officer Glen Garrity found an agitated Kevin McLaughlin in the kitchen. Garrity led the young man, a Brad Pitt look-alike who was wearing nothing but blue jeans, into the living room, took a preliminary statement and bagged Kevin's hands to preserve any traces of gunshot residue. While the other officers cordoned off the crime scene, Kevin got out of his chair several times in a panic, wanting to check the doors for a break-in, but Garrity kept him in that room until the detectives arrived to formally interview him.

Kevin said he heard three shots fired, although neighbors reported hearing five or six. It wasn't just his speech that was impaired by the brain injury, but his short-term memory as well.

"Is there anyone who might want to harm your father?" the police asked him.

Kevin suggested Jacob Horowitz (pseudonym), referring to the combative former business partner who had cost his father millions in delayed royalty payments and mounting legal fees as the lawsuit made its way through the courts.

Asked if there were guns in the house, Kevin directed them to the locked metal box his father kept in the master bedroom, as well as the fourteen guns and several boxes of bullets that Bill stored in the guest bedroom's closet upstairs. Because small children lived in the house, Bill stored the rest of his gun collection in Las Vegas. Kevin said that he'd fired some guns in Vegas himself about three weeks earlier, but none that day.

With no key to open the lockbox, the detectives had to pick it. Inside, they found a fully loaded nine-millimeter Taurus PT92 AFS, but it didn't smell or look as if it had been fired recently.

Kevin said he didn't know the origin of the keys in the front door and on the mat, noting that his own key ring was in a pair of pants in his bedroom.

As the detectives went from room to room, they could see that Bill slept upstairs, down the hall from Kevin. Nanette's bedroom was downstairs, next to her kids', and smelled like her Calvin Klein Obsession perfume, billed as having "a powerful sensuality." An apt scent for her, as they soon found out.

Detective Tom Voth found Kevin's clothes thrown haphazardly over a chair in his room. His keys, attached to a ring with a bottle opener, were on the floor next to his gray pants, right where he said they would be. Voth saw no blood in the room, nor any trace of a gun or ammunition, and Kevin's hands tested negative for gun residue.

Including housekeeper Mary Berg, who had scrubbed the white kitchen tiles until they shone earlier that day, only a half-dozen people in the McLaughlin domain had keys to the pedestrian-access gate. The others were Nanette, Bill's three kids, and a neighbor who looked after the dog while they were on vacation.

When Nanette rolled up in the Cadillac around ten o'clock, she identified herself as Bill's fiancée and said she'd just come from Christmas shopping at the mall. But even Detective Voth, who was working his first and only murder case with no homicide training, couldn't help but notice that the athletic young woman's key ring was missing a key to open that gate.

# CHAPTER 2

Because the house was a crime scene the police wouldn't let Nanette come inside. But even after chatting with the responding officers, she didn't call anyone else in the McLaughlin family to inform them of Bill's death.

Once the detectives arrived, Sergeant Steven Van Horn and Detective Bill Hartford asked her to get into the police cruiser to answer some questions. Asked to outline her activities that day, Nanette said she'd gone shopping at noon, returned to write the housekeeper a check, then grabbed her son's soccer uniform out of the dryer and drove him to his championship game in Diamond Bar.

The game was supposed to start at 6:00 P.M., but had been delayed until 6:30. Then it went into double overtime, which lasted until sometime after eight o'clock. Originally, she'd planned to bring her kids home to Balboa Coves that night, but they'd stayed with their father because it was so late and they had school near his house in the morning.

After that, she said, she headed to South Coast Plaza in Newport Beach. Showing them several shopping bags on the passenger side of the Cadillac, she also produced receipts from Crate & Barrel and Bullock's, time-stamped

9:29 and 9:45 P.M. She said she'd bought a vase, which she'd shipped to her parents, and purchased about $138 worth of other items before the mall started to close.

Asked who had keys to the house, she cited most of the same people as Kevin had, and said there could be one in the hide-a-key box on the dock behind the house. She, too, noted that Bill's former partner, Jacob Horowitz, had sued Bill over the blood device, but she said she didn't know who would want to harm her fiancé.

"Do you have any idea why this would happen to him?" Detective Hartford asked.

"I have no idea," she said. "I have no . . . never heard of threats, never heard, you know, anything. I had no clue."

The detectives asked Nanette if she would object to a search of the house or to having her hands swabbed for gun-shot residue.

"I understand it's probably upsetting," Van Horn said. "It's just procedure we have to go through."

"I have no objection," she replied.

Nanette told police she oversaw the day-to-day aspects of Bill's various business activities, which included several investment projects. Bill had a number of insurance policies he kept in the home safe, she said, and he was being audited by the IRS concerning his Nevada residency claim. She led detectives to the safe and gave them the combination so they could look inside.

She told them about Bill's gun collection in Vegas, but she said she purposely stayed in the dark about all of that "gun stuff."

"Personally, I don't like guns, so I stay out. I have kids in the house. I asked him if he would move the guns to the other place for that reason. So most of them are over there, but I'm not sure how many."

On the other hand, she said, she knew everything about his "business stuff."

"I write all the checks and I pay all the bills," she said.

Voth tried to offer some helpful information about changing the locks on the house, but Nanette said she wasn't going to stay there. She was going to move her things to Bill's second beachfront house on Seashore Drive, which was about four minutes away.

"I cannot go back in there, where he . . . ," she said, trailing off.

And yet, four days later, she was back at Balboa Coves with her kids—and several times after that, meeting with various people. No one lived at the Seashore house fulltime, she said, adding that it had been broken into two Thanksgivings ago, when they'd filed a police report.

"When I went over there one day, all the lights were on. I opened the garage, and . . . I didn't want to go in, so I called the police. And the police went in and found—and it was like a robbery, you know. . . . Somebody was, like, staying in there and they kind of messed stuff up and, like, vandalized it."

Everyone grieves differently, but this attractive young woman didn't seem particularly distraught over her fiancé's murder. And although she said the incident was "too much to comprehend," her voice seemed rather monotone and her general affect seemed rather flat.

She also never mentioned how lucky it was that she and her children weren't home that night, as originally planned, or that she was thankful that they were all safe, thanks to her decision to leave them with her ex-husband and go shopping. Nor did she seem to be scared that the killer might hunt her down at the beach house.

Escorting her to the house on Seashore, the police assured that she got safely inside around one in the morning.

\* \* \*

Back in 1994, the city of Newport Beach, also known simply as Newport, had about 66,000 residents. Today, its population has grown to about 87,000 people, who are fortunate enough to live in one of the nation's wealthiest communities.

Located about fifty miles south of Los Angeles, and about eighty-five miles north of downtown San Diego, Newport spans fifty square miles of land surrounded by water, which flows around seven islands and is home to more than ten thousand recreational vessels. The clean white, beige, and pastel facades of the waterfront homes— many of which have pristine landscaping and private docks—convey the unspoken language of money.

Some folks here are so affluent they can afford to keep a helicopter on the deck of their yacht, where they enjoy cocktails and watch the sun set, or sail over to Catalina Island for the day. In the ritzier parts of town, attire can range from yacht club or business casual to upscale designer wear, with sparkling multi-carat diamonds or trendy boutique jewelry.

And then there are the wannabes, the gold diggers who want some of that money but don't want or know how to work for it themselves. So they hang around the swanky restaurants and nightclubs, perch themselves seductively along the boardwalk, and hope to snag a sugar daddy or mama.

Newport's natural beauty, juxtaposed with the ostentatious materialism of some of its residents, made this area the perfect setting for the television show *The O.C.*, as well as frequent episodes of the hit reality show *The Real Housewives of Orange County*. In addition to the nouveau riche women who keep their hair perfectly coiffed, their nails manicured, and their clothing just so, Newport Beach has drawn celebrity athletes such as basketball's bad boy Dennis Rodman and superstar Kobe Bryant. Eccentric actor Nicolas Cage made news here when he expanded his boat dock to 156 feet to accommodate his personal flotilla and later sold his home for a record $35 million.

Every December, Newport has its renowned "Christmas Boat Parade," an event that dates back to 1907 and features more than one hundred boats of all sizes, lit up with bright holiday lights, cruising around the harbor like beacons of the good life.

In 1977, Bill and his then-wife, Sue, purchased their home in Balboa Coves, to which they eventually added a second floor. Tucked into the southernmost corner of the community, just south of Coast Highway and east of the Newport Boulevard Bridge, the McLaughlin house abutted the Newport Channel, which feeds into Newport Bay and pours into the Pacific Ocean.

In 2012, homes in Balboa Coves were selling in the $3 million range, and this particular 2,932-square-foot house was valued at $2.3 million.

In 1992, after Sue left, Bill purchased the 2,376-square-foot beach house on Seashore Drive as a teardown, intending to fix it up and sell it later. He had good instincts, because the home sold in late 2004 for $3.54 million.

Farther to the south and west of Balboa Coves, a finger-like stretch of land called the Balboa Peninsula juts out into the ocean. Locals simply call it "the peninsula."

As of 2012, the murder of Bill McLaughlin was only the second—and the last—murder to occur in this community. As many as nine murders have occurred in one year in all of Newport Beach, but often there is only one or even none.

* * *

On the night of the murder, Detective Tom Voth, a tall, mellow father of three, was relaxing at home when his lieutenant called around nine-forty.

Lieutenant Doug Fletcher told Voth that Sergeant Steven Van Horn and Detective Bill Hartford were already headed into the station. Fletcher told Voth to do the same. From there, the investigators caravanned over to Balboa Coves, where they arrived just before eleven o'clock.

Voth was respected by his colleagues as a quiet, earnest, reserved, and "country strong" man. A good man. With a big, strapping frame and a gentle smile, he was seen as a powerhouse after playing football in the early 1970s at California State University, Fresno.

"But he's got a big heart," said Dave Byington, a retired homicide detective sergeant who worked in narcotics with Voth during the late 1980s.

The NBPD, the small agency responsible for keeping order in this town of mostly white, wealthy, and well-educated folks, has routinely moved its officers and detectives between specialty areas so they can gain experience solving all types of crimes. The department has traditionally thrown most of its available officers into the rare murder case, which meant that at least a couple dozen took some part in this investigation.

After working three years as an officer in the city of Seal Beach, and thirteen more for the NBPD, forty-two-year-old Voth was soon appointed the lead detective on this case. But, as he pointed out later, this mostly meant that he was in charge of taking copious notes and keeping the records organized. He said his more experienced superiors made the decisions on how to proceed.

"People were not coming to me and asking me what to do," he recalled recently.

The product of a modest upbringing, Voth grew up with

two sisters in Norwalk in Los Angeles County, a long way from his parents' native state of Kansas. His father, who was in the army, had been making his way from a training camp in the Philippines to Okinawa, Japan, when World War Two ended, and he decided to move the family to California.

A star jock in his teen years, Voth was voted "Athlete of the Year" for his performance on the baseball, basketball, and football teams at Excelsior High School. After graduation, he played football at Cerritos College, then transferred to Fresno State to study criminology. While he was on a two-year football scholarship, the scouts came out to watch him play.

As Voth got older, he switched from tight end to wide receiver and punter. He took some pretty good hits from behind, feeling lucky to have gotten through high school and college without a serious injury.

"Like everybody," he recalled, "you dream you're going to go to the NFL."

But he never got a shot at the big time. Little did he know that his athletic experiences would play into a murder investigation.

# CHAPTER 3

The morning after Bill McLaughlin was murdered, Nanette took his son, Kevin, out for breakfast at Denny's. Kevin found this unusual because she'd never offered to do that before. Despite his speech difficulties, she told him that he was the one who needed to call his sister Jenny to tell her what had happened.

Doing as he was told, Kevin tracked down Jenny at work.

"Are you sitting down?" he asked.

"Yes, what's going on?"

"Dad's been shot."

"Is he okay?"

"No, he's dead."

"How did this happen?"

"I don't know. Somebody shot him."

"Okay, where are you?" Jenny asked. "I'm going to come get you. We're going to figure out what's going on."

"I'm at the beach house with Nanette."

With that, Jenny immediately left the high school where she was teaching and called Nanette for more details on her way to the Seashore house, where she planned to pick up her brother and take him back to Balboa Coves.

Jenny thought the ensuing call was very awkward and oddly short.

"Is it true?" she asked Nanette. "Kevin called me and said our dad's been shot."

But Nanette had very little to say other than to confirm what Kevin had said.

"Yeah, it's true," she said. "It sucks. It really sucks."

Worried this might be a trap, and that the shooter might be lurking around and would try to shoot them, Jenny asked Nanette to have Kevin meet her outside the beach house. Then Jenny called her mother, who, in turn, called Jenny's sister, Kim.

It was late in Tokyo when Kim got the call, just in from a night out with a friend. By that point, their mother was already making arrangements to fly to Newport Beach, where she ended up staying for several months, sleeping in the room she'd once shared with Bill, so she could take care of her disabled son and try to hold her grieving family together.

As Jenny pulled up to the house in her gold Mercedes, Kevin was just coming out the front gate. Jenny was stymied why Nanette only peeked out the front door and then shut it quickly without coming outside to speak to her, console her, or try to share in their grief.

After striking out with Nanette and Kevin for more details, Jenny decided to go straight to the police. She arrived at Balboa Coves with her brother just after 9:00 A.M. Finding no detectives, she headed over to the station, where she found Van Horn and Voth, who had been trying to reach her too.

Like Kevin, the only person Jenny could offer as a possible suspect was Jacob Horowitz.

Asked about her father's relationship with Nanette Johnston, Jenny said she knew of no problems, even given the difference in their ages. As far as she knew, her father wasn't seeing anyone romantically besides Nanette.

Anyone with access to keys was a suspect at that point, so the detectives asked Jenny where she'd been around nine o'clock the night before. She said she was horseback riding with a couple people at the Nellie Gail Ranch in Laguna Niguel. Afterward, she headed home to visit with some friends, until nearly 11:00 P.M. After confirming her alibi, the police had Jenny take a lie detector test. She passed, as did her sister, Kim. Detectives crossed them both off the list of possible suspects.

Meanwhile, Nanette called her ex-husband, K. Ross Johnston, to tell him what had happened.

"Bill has been shot," she said.

"I'm sorry to hear that," K. Ross said. "Is he going to be okay?"

"He's no longer with us."

"Oh, I'm sorry. I didn't know."

Nanette explained that Bill had been killed at the house after Kristofer's soccer game, while she was out shopping, and she had receipts to prove it. But she said the police would probably be calling him to confirm her "alibi" all the same.

"When they do, you don't need to tell them anything about Eric, because he's not involved," she said, referring to Eric Naposki, the professional linebacker and nightclub bouncer whom she'd been bringing to Kristofer's games for the past eighteen months.

\* \* \*

Kevin McLaughlin didn't have anywhere to go that Friday. Because the police were still processing the house for evidence, they didn't want him wandering around, so he rode his three-wheeled bike around the community, presumably looking for Goldie, the family's golden retriever, who had run off after the murder. Nanette had to call Animal Control to see if they could find her. The dog turned up a couple of days later.

Told for the second consecutive night that he couldn't stay at the Balboa Coves house, Kevin called his girlfriend, Sandy Baumgardner, who worked in pharmaceutical sales, around four o'clock to come get him.

"Someone came in last night and shot my dad," Kevin said.

Sandy heard someone in the background telling him not to say anything more. "Who is that talking to you?" she asked, confused.

"That's Bill," he said.

Now she was even more confused. *I thought he just said Bill was dead,* she thought.

"Put me on with Bill," she ordered.

Sandy could hear Kevin explaining who she was to a man who then took the phone and identified himself as Detective Bill Hartford.

"What happened?" she asked.

But Hartford didn't say much. Sandy wasn't sure that Bill McLaughlin was dead, but she suspected as much because the detective was being so cagey. She immediately called her father, a college buddy of Bill's, who split his time between Newport and Colorado Springs.

"I think Bill McLaughlin was murdered last night," she said. "I'm going down there and I'll call you back when I know more."

As soon as she arrived at Balboa Coves and saw the yellow police tape around the house, her suspicions were confirmed. Hartford met her out front, lifting the tape so she could get under it.

"Whoever did this had intimate knowledge of his schedule," Sandy said.

Hartford seemed irritated that Jenny had dropped off Kevin and left him there all day, because he couldn't be left alone while the detectives were trying to work.

After talking briefly with the police, Sandy took Kevin to the house of a family friend who had done business with Bill and was a surfing buddy of Kevin's.

"There's only one person who stood to gain from this," the friend said. "Nanette."

# CHAPTER 4

After interviewing Jenny McLaughlin, Detectives Voth and Van Horn headed back to Balboa Coves to continue their search for evidence at the house.

Voth looked for the spare keys in the dock box on the rear patio, but the box was empty. He hadn't expected the shiny keys left by the killer to be from there anyway, because they showed no signs of rust or salt corrosion.

In an interview that afternoon at the station, Nanette told detectives that she'd met Bill in early 1991 while in-line skating on the boardwalk, where they were introduced by some mutual friends. Only she couldn't remember their names.

As they reviewed her activities the night of the murder once more, she mentioned that "we" left the soccer game around 8:00 P.M. However, the detectives apparently didn't catch her slip of the tongue, perhaps because she didn't mention *with whom* she had left.

Pressed for more details about her role in Bill's finances, she said that since they'd been together, Bill had given her increasing control over his money, including making her a trustee of one of his accounts.

Jacob Horowitz, she said, was one of Bill's former scientist employees who had helped Bill develop his blood-plasma separator. After an internal dispute with Horowitz, Bill and his partners bought out Horowitz, then sold the company. Bill had been receiving royalties from that sale, but several "nuisance" suits by Horowitz had blocked the flow of money, she said. Just recently, however, Bill finally heard he'd won the legal battle.

His Swiss bank account was the only one she didn't know much about, but she thought it had been established because of concerns about the recent IRS audit. Elaborating on most of his five life insurance policies, she said one was for the trust, one was for the family, one was for the business, and one named her as the beneficiary. But she claimed not to know the value of the payouts, which detectives later learned came to a total of $9 million.

They also learned that Bill had taken Kevin out of his will, apparently because Kevin's government-funded medical costs would no longer be covered if he came into an influx of money. With this in mind, Bill had set up a special-needs trust to take care of Kevin's medical costs and monthly bills. This would also continue his eligibility for public-assistance programs, such as Dial-a-ride and speech therapy programs, which were important because Kevin had already capped out his insurance after the accident. The trust was designed to kick in if and when Bill died.

Nanette told detectives that she'd been concerned about Bill's recent dealings in the gun market, and she gave them the name of his gun dealer.

Asked about Bill's usual habits, she gave them a general rundown: He usually left for Vegas on Tuesday or Wednesday and returned Thursday or Friday, almost always during daylight hours. He never filed a flight plan. He normally wore the blue robe he'd been wearing that night. He typically drank four to five beers around dinnertime and maybe some wine with dinner. (Curiously, the glass where he'd been sitting at the dining table contained hard liquor.) They rarely used the alarm system in the house, unless they were on vacation. When he was in Las Vegas, he didn't gamble. And she didn't know anyone else with whom he had regular contact there other than his Realtor, David Mitchell.

She also said that a number of keys to the Balboa Coves house hadn't been returned by workmen, such as window cleaners, gardeners, and painters, but she hadn't copied any keys herself. Nor did she know where Bill would have had any made.

"You can call me anytime," Nanette said. "I want to help in any way that I can."

When her gunshot residue test came back, her hands were clean.

# CHAPTER 5

That Saturday morning, December 17, the first news story hit the local paper, stripped across the front page. Few details were released and no suspects were cited in the *Daily Pilot* story, which said, *Police were tight-lipped about William Francis McLaughlin's death, citing a need to protect their investigation.*

The NBPD wouldn't even acknowledge that the divers seen combing the waters behind the house were part of the homicide investigation. But, in fact, two sets of divers scoured the channel for a day and a half, looking for the murder weapon. One was a team of Newport Beach lifeguards and the other was a U.S. Navy dive team, stationed in San Diego, that used metal detectors to search through the thick marine grass covering the channel floor.

In the article, Bill was described by neighbors as *a physically fit man who would jog through the complex, and when a homeowners' association fund fell short of the kitty needed to install the community security gate in 1990, McLaughlin was among the residents who made an additional donation.*

Although neighbors said Bill had been affectionate with Kevin at a homeowners' association party, they also said they found Bill and his family to be "standoffish," because they hadn't socialized much with neighbors over the two decades they'd lived in Balboa Coves.

The regional paper, the *Orange County Register,* also played the story on its front page, with the headline NEWPORT MILLIONAIRE SLAIN IN GATED HOME.

"He was a really nice guy," twenty-six-year-old Jenny McLaughlin told the reporter. "This has always been a really quiet neighborhood, but who knows."

Citing court records, the article characterized Bill and Sue's divorce as "bitter," noting that she'd gotten a restraining order to stop him from transferring any holdings and from calling her early in the morning to bully her into taking a payout of $1 million of his "hard-earned money." If she didn't, he'd threatened to take "unpleasant tactics."

*He's very controlling and domineering,* Sue's filings stated.

In Bill's filings from May 1990, he explained that Sue *should not be given any direct control over any of the property.* He needed full control over all of it, he said, as leverage for business purposes or his investments would fail. He offered to pay his wife $5,000 a month for living expenses.

Bill also explained that the two 8:00 A.M. calls he'd made to her were never intended to harass her, only to save money on long-distance rates. He said he'd been threatened with legal action since 1989 by a former business partner, presumably Jacob Horowitz. Someone had been trying to serve him with papers, and he was simply trying to find out if it was Sue's representative or someone else. He said he also wanted to question her about whether the $11,000 in charges on that month's MasterCard bill were real or "unsubstantiated," as they'd been the previous month, when he'd had to cancel the credit card.

He said he'd started setting up a number of trusts to protect their assets from this litigation, including a Cook

Islands Asset Protection Trust, as well as a living trust and an asset protection trust for his separate property after Sue had left the "family home."

Just as he later did with Nanette, it had been his practice with Sue to give her a certain amount to pay the household bills.

*Since I handled all the business of the community, all she would have to do was tell me how much she needed to run the household each month and I would give it to her,* he stated in court papers. *In this manner, I have provided substantial payments to my wife each month over the past several years. I never asked on what these moneys were spent even though I felt they were rather excessive.*

These filings indicate that Bill watched his money quite closely when Sue was managing the household. This begs the question whether Bill trusted Nanette so much that he blindly let her manage the bills and appointed her as a trustee to his estate, or whether he was still keeping an eye on things and could have figured out what she was doing just before he was killed, as his brother Patrick suggested.

Although Nanette may have thought Bill had trusted her completely, it's possible that she didn't understand how these trusts and his estate worked as well as she'd thought. She also may not have known that Bill had designated a close friend to be the "protector" of his estate, which meant that the friend had the power to correct or change any of Nanette's actions relating to the living trust.

In his divorce declaration, Bill estimated the value of his estate at only $8.15 million, including $3.9 million cash in the bank. He listed $9.43 million in "liabilities," including money that he figured he would have to pay Jacob Horowitz, who later cited these documents as proof that Bill knew he owed him money when the two were fighting in civil court.

In the end, Sue got to keep the Hawaii home, valued at

$2.5 million, as part of a $4.5 million package that included a 1986 Isuzu Trooper and annual payments of $300,000. Bill kept a twenty-one-acre avocado ranch in Fallbrook (valued in 1990 at $690,000) in neighboring San Diego County, the Balboa Coves house (valued at $600,000), and his two homes in Las Vegas. He also kept his airplane, two boats, two Mercedes cars, and a 1986 Chevrolet station wagon. In addition, he held on to all future earnings and royalties from the Plasmacell-C device.

Because Bill's character flaws and his total worth were cited in public divorce papers, they ended up in the newspaper and being batted around by neighbors and former business associates, which further upset his children and close friends.

Reporters were also using the divorce file to track down Sue and question her, so she had the records sealed. However, some of the documents still remain today in the archives of an Alameda County courthouse, where they were filed as part of Horowitz's several lawsuits against Bill and Baxter Healthcare, which were still pending when he was murdered.


Bill McLaughlin's slaying rocked the tiny bedroom community of Balboa Coves, where residents were rattled that such an incident could happen within the perceived safety of the gates. This was the kind of place where the well-off moved to get away from the dangers of urban life and the riffraff that went with it.

"People came there to avoid getting their front door kicked down and shot," Dave Byington, the retired homicide sergeant, recalled recently.

But this case also had an air of intrigue and mystery. The shots were fired at close range, and the shooter left behind the bullet casings, which the police saw as a clue because the killer must have known that he (or she) had left no fingerprints on the shells. Early on, however, the police kept these details secret, which left the neighbors frustrated by the lack of cold, hard facts.

"No information is available, so everybody is guessing," Stan Love, a leader of the homeowners' association, told the *Los Angeles Times*. "It sounds like somebody was mad at [Bill]."

The impact of the incident wasn't contained by the chain-link fence surrounding Balboa Coves—the entire city of Newport Beach was buzzing about it.

"It was big news in Newport," Byington said. "He's a millionaire. Initially they were truly shocked because this just doesn't happen in Newport. . . . It was fodder for the local papers' front page forever."

Bill's neighbors were, in fact, living under a false sense of security. The police figured that the killer used the shiny pedestrian-access key to get in. Then, after dropping it, he must have escaped via the abutting Newport Channel, in a car driven by an accomplice, by jumping the fence and running away, or through the pedestrian gate, left purposely ajar. In those days, all you had to do to get through the main entrance gate was punch in a simple code and drive in.

It didn't take detectives long to determine this was no random killing. Because so few people had copies of the keys the killer had left behind, detectives were pretty confident within a day or so of the murder that this was an inside job. So they promptly started surveilling both of Bill McLaughlin's homes in Newport Beach, where they watched Nanette come and go—and they kept an eye out for any suspicious characters to show up.

# CHAPTER 6

Sandy Baumgardner met Kevin McLaughlin at a Memorial Day party in 1989. She met Nanette about five weeks after Kevin's accident in 1991. And after Thanksgiving dinner with the McLaughlins in 1993, Sandy dropped a note to Kevin, saying, *If you want to get fish tacos, let me know.* They began dating on and off after that, and she'd since become very close with the family.

Sandy recalled recently that Kevin was good-looking, with a cute personality, noting that his brain injury had affected his time perception and speech, but not his overall ability to think.

By the Saturday night after the murder, the police had cleared the Balboa Coves house for the family to return, so the McLaughlin clan gathered in the den with Nanette and a couple of Bill's best friends from college to process what had happened. Nanette sat at the bottom of the staircase. Sandy and Denis Townsend stood next to Nanette, while Don Kalal and Kevin sat on a couch.

"We were so shocked," Sandy said. "Our wheels were all turning."

Thinking Nanette needed consoling, the group tried to comfort her with small talk, but she didn't seem to want or need it. Nanette said she was going to continue to sleep at the beach house.

"She didn't seem very emotional," Sandy said, and "for whatever reason, she seemed to be clingy with me." Sandy couldn't put her finger on what Nanette was feeling that night, but she kept catching Nanette staring at her in "kind of a needy way. She always struck me as very insecure. . . . If I were to speculate, she was trying to lure in a supporter, someone on her side."

Sandy called her father back to give him an update. As she was describing Nanette's odd behavior, he said, "Let me give you some sage advice. You stay away from that woman."

Her father's comment put her off a bit, because now that she was approaching thirty, she didn't feel she needed his advice, even though he was a former special agent criminal investigator in the U.S. Air Force. But Ken Baumgardner didn't need to see Nanette's odd demeanor for himself. He'd had suspicions about her already.

"He'd always told me that she was a little too aloof," Sandy said.

Bill had apparently complained to Ken about Nanette's lack of involvement in his kids' lives and in McLaughlin family get-togethers that past year.

"My dad's impression of her from the get-go was that her background didn't add up—the whole story about the basketball scholarship and [being a] child prodigy," Sandy said. "His impression was that she was a gold digger with two little kids, trying to find a rich guy to latch onto."

Sandy's father told her that he'd never discussed his impressions with Bill because he felt it wasn't his place. Sandy hadn't said anything to Bill about her perceptions either. However, she, Kim, and Jenny often joked among themselves about Nanette's antics and malapropisms, mocking her boasts that she'd scored a very high score on the Law

School Admission Test (LSAT), for which the best possible score was only a fraction of the number she cited.

Nanette also told them she'd graduated early from high school in Phoenix after playing on the basketball team, then got a basketball scholarship to attend Arizona State University (ASU). There was some photo floating around of her playing basketball, Sandy said, but the girls didn't believe much of that talk either.

"The tongues would wag behind the scenes when Bill wasn't in earshot," she said. "Kim and Jenny just couldn't stand sitting at the table with her. It was eye-rolling time, because Nanette would try to hijack the conversations and it was usually to talk about her kids or that she could bench-press four hundred pounds." If everyone else started talking, "she would just sort of pout."

To Kim, Jenny, and Sandy, Nanette never seemed very cerebral, which was a marked and rather disturbing contrast to Bill.

"Nanette didn't have much intelligent to say at the dinner table or anything, and my dad was a real smart, bright man, and he would love to philosophize and pontificate," Kim McLaughlin Bayless recalled recently. "People would come to our dinner table to discuss business with him because he was very well-respected in our community and with our friends, and he liked to take risks. . . . I thought it was odd that Nanette didn't take part in many of those conversations. She didn't really say much at all. Maybe she was intimated by us kids, I'm not sure."

Other than the obvious physical attraction, Bill's adult children just didn't get what he saw in Nanette. But he'd never said a harsh or critical word about her, and he spoke just as highly of her kids as he did of his own.

* * *

Nanette wanted to go grocery shopping that Saturday evening to buy some food for the beach house, so Sandy went with her to Lucky's, still trying to support the woman she assumed was grieving and eventually would need some comfort. She figured Nanette's flat affect was just a mask to cover deeper emotions.

*The poor thing, she's going to explode.*

Looking back later, Sandy said that Nanette seemed "kind of glazed over. It was almost an act." But at the time, Sandy was simply puzzled by it.

"At the very least I expected her to be, by that time, upset that her kids had been so close to that kind of danger."

Sandy just nodded as she listened to Nanette engage in what seemed like "pointless banter." Nanette said nothing about Bill's death, and made "robotic-like" conversation about her own situation as she threw a box of cereal into the shopping cart for the kids, who were still staying with her ex-husband.

"What am I going to do?" Nanette asked rhetorically. "I just don't know what to do next."

But there was no needy hug, and no emotional explosion.

*Well, that was a goddamn waste of time,* Sandy thought as she left the store. *There is something wrong with her.*

The next morning, Sue McLaughlin went to pick up her oldest daughter, Kim, from the airport. When Kim arrived at the house after her ridiculously long flight from Japan, she met Kevin halfway into the foyer, dropped her duffel bag, and embraced him. Then she grabbed him by the arms and looked him in the eye.

"Oh, my God, Kevin, what happened?" she asked. "What do you know about these keys?"

But Kevin just shook his head. He had no idea who had left them in the door and on the mat.

# CHAPTER 7

As soon as they cleared the crime scene, Detectives Bill Hartford and David Szkaradek drove to Santa Barbara that Saturday to interview Jacob Horowitz.

Horowitz gave them an alibi for the night of the murder, saying he'd gone to the barber, then to Vons, and returned home to spend the evening with his wife.

The detectives explained that they'd found documentation of the complex legal battle between the two former partners, and they'd traveled up the coast to question him. The litigation, they said, seemed like a pretty good motive to kill Bill.

Asked if Bill had ever threatened him, Horowitz said, "Way back in '82, he said, 'If you don't do this . . . I'll sue you,' which he did."

Horowitz confirmed that he knew of others who had also been involved in litigation with Bill, but he declined to elaborate or speculate, noting that it was a matter of public record. He also declined to discuss his personal relationship with Bill or whether he felt bitter toward Bill. Even though he had no attorney present, he said, he believed he'd already answered the detectives' questions about his business relationship with Bill as truthfully and fully as he could.

As for any character discussions, he said, "I wouldn't have anything complimentary to say," so he preferred to say nothing.

He acknowledged that Bill's death did surprise him initially. "It's a shocking thing. And I'm sorry to hear it." But upon reflection, he said, he wasn't all that surprised.

"The way he conducted himself or his business activities, do you think he would cause someone to go to that extreme?" one of the detectives asked.

"I'm no expert in that kind of thing," Horowitz said coyly.

Still hoping Horowitz would open up, the detectives said they'd interviewed others who volunteered that they didn't care for Bill and who also weren't surprised by the way he died "due to the way he treated other people."

"If other people have told you that, that does not surprise me," Horowitz said. "I would not dispute their opinion."

In contrast, Horowitz described Bill's ex-wife as a "marvelous, dignified person" and a "nice lady."

After the detectives confirmed Horowitz's whereabouts the night of the murder, he was no longer a prime suspect, unless they found some incriminating evidence, such as proof that he'd hired a hit man.

Meanwhile, Detectives Tom Voth and Steven Van Horn drove to Las Vegas to search Bill's house and to talk with his Realtor, David Mitchell, one of the few people Bill interacted with there.

Mitchell said he'd met Bill several years earlier when he was looking to buy property. He'd sold Bill one home on Harbor Cove to live in and one more as an investment. Since then, he said, they'd become friends.

During a search of Bill's house, Voth found a safe in the bedroom closet, where Bill kept paperwork for a trust fund that showed a balance of $488,000, as of October 1990. He also found a promissory note, signed by Nanette and dated July 20, 1991, that showed he'd loaned her $35,000. (Detectives later learned that about a month after she'd moved in with Bill, she'd paid her ex-husband, K. Ross Johnston, $28,000 of the $38,000 they'd borrowed from his parents while they were still married.)

The detectives learned that Bill didn't gamble when he was in Las Vegas, that he belonged to a shooting range where he shot guns as a hobby, and that the phone number of a woman, found on a piece of paper next to the phone, belonged to a friend he'd met through flying.

"It just eliminated the whole potential of [the theory that] he owed way too much money to someone in Las Vegas or he had nefarious activities there," Voth said.

Back in Newport, Detective Hartford interviewed Bill's ex-wife, Sue, who said they'd divorced in 1991 after he'd had several affairs, but no more than she could count on one hand. He also had never hit her.

She later told police that when they used to make new house keys, they always had to be reground before they worked smoothly in the front door's lock. Being so close to the ocean corroded the door locks with salt.

Housekeeper Mary Berg told detectives that Bill had had girls over to the house when Sue was out of town, but she'd never seen him do that since he'd been with Nanette, and she figured she would've found indications if he had. Berg described Nanette as incredibly loving and accepting of everyone in Bill's family, and she had no sense that Nanette was seeing other men.

Berg backed up Nanette's story that she'd come home to wash Kristofer's soccer uniform while Berg cleaned the house the day of the murder, and that Nanette had left the house around noon after writing Berg a check. Bill didn't like to be around while Berg was cleaning, she said, so she tried to stay out of his way.

Hartford also interviewed a neighbor, Rosemary Luxton, who lived across the channel from the McLaughlins. Luxton said she'd heard shots the night of the murder, had looked across the channel for several minutes, but hadn't seen anyone getting into a boat. Based on this and other neighbors' observations, the detectives narrowed the killer's means of escape to be on foot or by car.

# CHAPTER 8

There were two camps of opinion when it came to Bill McLaughlin. Some people loved and admired him and thought he was a good, generous man. Others had issues with Bill because of the way he interacted with some of his business associates.

"We heard from some businesspeople that he was a little bit eccentric," Detective Tom Voth said, explaining that sometimes Bill showed up to meetings wearing loafers with no socks, when everyone else was wearing a suit. "I call it eccentric, or is it a power play?"

Born on October 12, 1939, William Francis McLaughlin was raised by working-class parents on the South Side of Chicago. His father, John "Mac" McLaughlin, worked for the city water department, and his mother, Mae, designed and sold women's hats at a friend's store.

Bill had two brothers: Patrick, who was seven and a half years his senior, and John Jr., who was thirteen months older than Patrick. Raised during the Great Depression, the family never had much money, but Bill and his brothers thought it was normal not to have everything they wanted.

One day riding in the backseat of the family car, nine-year-old Patrick said to his parents, "I just love turkey.

When we get rich, can we have a turkey for dinner?" And so the next Sunday, Mae cooked a bird, even though it wasn't Thanksgiving, which was a rare treat.

"[My father] knew what poverty was. He grew up in poverty," said Kim McLaughlin Bayless. "Once he'd made his fortune, he told us, 'We've got to pass this [wealth] on to those who are less fortunate.'

Bill's extended family always got together for holidays. As a result, Bill became close with his cousin Barbara, who was about three years older. Barbara said Bill had a strong personality, but he was always personable.

"He would make you laugh. He had a good sense of humor. He wasn't inward at all. He was fun to be around," she said. "He was just, to me, a smart, above-average kid."

Barbara, whose last name is now LaSpesa, also remembered Bill as a good son who loved to tease his mother. "She was crazy about him, being [he was] the youngest."

She said Bill was always a health nut. "He just watched his intake and what he was eating at all times," she said. "He always was fit and trim. What he devoured in food was strictly healthy food."

Bill attended St. Philip High School, a private Catholic school for boys, while Patrick attended public school.

"My brother was much brighter than me," Patrick recalled fondly.

From early on, Bill's extended family could see that he was ambitious. "He told me when we were kids that by the time he was thirty, he would be a millionaire," Barbara recalled. "And here he came from nothing."

After high-school graduation, Bill enlisted in the U.S. Marine Corps, with the tearful permission of his parents. The teenager, a chronic asthmatic who felt he had something to prove to himself and to his family, went through basic training at Camp Pendleton, in San Diego County.

By the time he came back from training, he'd matured significantly. "I didn't even recognize my brother," Patrick recalled. "He was a kid before he left. He looked different, and so was his conduct—he even called me 'sir.'"

Patrick had been drafted by the army into the Korean War and completed his training program, but to Patrick, that was nothing like what Bill had gone through. "He was truly a marine and always a marine," he said. "He was truly disciplined, he gained a great deal of respect for life itself, and, I would say, was the utmost gentleman."

After spending several years in the military, Bill enrolled at what is now known as Loyola Marymount University in Los Angeles, becoming the first person in his immediate family to attend college, and a private one at that.

There, in the Student Worker Program, he met his lifelong friends Denis Townsend and Ken Baumgardner. He met another lifelong buddy, Don Kalal, through the Pep Band, for which he played the clarinet and saxophone. Bill loved jazz.

The discipline he'd learned in the military carried over into his studies. "Bill is screaming smart," Sandy Baumgardner said. "My dad said in college he was so disciplined. . . . If he had his nose in books over the weekend, you didn't want to bother him and throw him off. My dad, Denis, and Bill definitely worked hard for their education."

Bill had a benefactor, "Mrs. B," who helped pay his tuition, a favor that he later returned by doing the same for some other students.

Because his asthma had improved so much in college, he stayed in California after graduating in 1964, with a bachelor's in biology.

"He said his health was always better out there," said Barbara, who moved to the Bay Area when she got married in 1963.

As the two cousins grew older, they chatted by phone and visited each other occasionally. During this period, she said, Bill dated quite a bit.

"He had a lot of 'dollies,'" Barbara said, quoting the word Bill used to describe his dates or girlfriends. She also noted that he often brought different women to stay with her and her husband in San Francisco.

"He liked women," she recalled, and he had a particular "fetish" for blondes. "I remember when we were teenagers, he loved Doris Day."

All that dating stopped after he met his future wife, Sue, who was a flight attendant and later became a substitute teacher. The whole family approved of her when Bill brought her back home to Chicago.

"[Sue] was a nice, wonderful girl and very pretty," a kind and all-American–looking blonde, Barbara said.

When Bill married Sue in 1966, Don Kalal was his best man, and he, in turn, was Kalal's.


Setting his sights on the pharmaceutical industry, Bill first moved the family to Blue Bell, Pennsylvania, in the late 1960s, where he worked his way up to national sales manager for Extracorporeal Medical Specialties, Inc., in a small town called King of Prussia. Extracorporeal made hemodialysis products, such as artificial kidneys and blood-infusion pumps.

But he wanted to get back to California, so he made sure that his next job was on the West Coast. The McLaughlins moved to Huntington Beach when Bill landed a gig as director of marketing in Irvine for Shiley, which, at the time, was producing small endotracheal tubes for children whose airways had been blocked through pneumonia or surgery. The company went on to develop the Bjork-Shiley heart valve.

"I think it ran in the McLaughlin family . . . that we wanted to be in a business where we could help people," said Patrick, who also went to work for Extracorporeal, but in sales.

Kim was Bill and Sue's firstborn child. Jenny came two years later, and Kevin two years after that. By the time Kim was ten years old and in the fourth grade, the McLaughlins had settled into the house in Balboa Coves.

In the early 1970s, Bill entered a weekend MBA program at Pepperdine University for CEOs, which he completed in 1974. He went on to become an entrepreneur, developing a dialysis catheter he dubbed the "McLaughlin Duocath," created for Medical Device Laboratories, Inc., a firm he founded and later sold to C.R. Bard, Inc., in New Jersey in 1977.

The patented device was designed to halve the damage to a dialysis patient's veins through a technology that put a hollow tube within a hollow tube to take the blood out of the artery, clean it, and return it to the vein using only one needle, rather than two. Bill also invented a single-roller pump to replace one with a double roller, thereby reducing the damage to the red blood cells squeezed into the needle during dialysis.

"This is how my brother was," Patrick said. "He was always thinking of the patient."

Bill first met Jacob Horowitz around 1973 at Rohé Scientific Corporation, where Horowitz was working as a consultant to develop kidney dialysis machines. While Bill was visiting Rohé, and a director was showing him around, Bill was introduced to Horowitz.

The two men met again in 1978, by which time Horowitz was working as a senior scientist at Hughes Aircraft. Bill proposed that they form a business partnership: Horowitz would develop the technology for a blood-plasma separator, and Bill would handle the business and licensing end of things. They entered into a five-year agreement in November 1978 to split any proceeds fifty-fifty after expenses.

Horowitz said he continued to work at Hughes while he developed the device, which he finished in March 1982. The device extracted a donor's blood, separated the plasma, then returned the remaining blood fluid to the donor in a continuous flow. This was safer than the previous practice, which kept the extraction and return of blood as two separate processes and was therefore vulnerable to the human error of sending the wrong person's blood back to a donor.

The business, which operated out of the garage of another partner in Santa Ana, obtained a patent that December. By May, Bill had brought in some investors, including the Hillman family's venture capital firm in Pittsburgh, which put in at least $1 million. Bill incorporated various businesses to invest in this technology, which he ended up licensing to HemaScience Laboratories, Inc., a company that he and Horowitz formed in 1981, with Bill as its president.

Horowitz came up with the initial concept for the device, "but when he built it, it didn't work," Michael "Mick" Hill, Nanette's attorney, said later. Hill explained that the workings of the device involved a film that spun around a centrifuge, but the film was too flimsy so it wobbled and malfunctioned. A younger engineer came in and fixed the problem.

Summing up the falling-out he had with Bill, Horowitz told police, "I was frozen out of the company. . . . He sued me. I sued him. That suit was settled in December 30, 1983. . . . I didn't get what I had coming, but I got some."

Bill ran the company, then sold it to Baxter Healthcare Corporation in 1986 for tens of millions of dollars in anticipated royalties, which would come in quarterly payouts. Horowitz believed he should have been cut in on the deal, so he filed a lawsuit against Bill and Baxter in June 1990. He cited a dozen causes of action, including the failure to pay royalties, interfering with Horowitz's business activities, unfair competition, and antitrust violations. After that, the only contact Horowitz had with Bill, he said, was through their attorneys.

Bill and Baxter countersued, and Horowitz followed up with two more lawsuits, in 1992 and 1993, with claims of fraudulent misappropriation and deception. Bill responded by saying that Horowitz "has engaged in conduct that constitutes a waiver of his rights," that he had "unclean hands," and that he was simply trying to circumvent the pending arbitration process by filing more lawsuits.

This extensive legal battle became very expensive, complicated, and time-consuming. Bill had received tens of millions in royalties from the blood-plasma device since 1986. However, since the 1990 lawsuit, the disputed half of the quarterly payments had been going into a holding fund Bill couldn't touch, known as an interpleader account, until the courts could decide whether to grant Horowitz's claim.

Between October 24, 1991, and December 9, 1993, a three-person arbitration panel conducted 126 days of hearings, involving twenty-three witnesses and 1,500 exhibits. More than seventeen thousand pages of court transcripts were generated, and more than 850 pages' worth of final briefs were submitted. Final arguments were heard in May 1994.

Horowitz claimed to have lost an estimated $25 million in royalties over a fourteen-year period, and he wanted to be compensated. Accusing Bill and Baxter of secretly conspiring to amend the patent and use the technology to develop products, he tried to block the use of the patent, which, in turn, Bill and Baxter said cost them money.

This highly technical, scientific, and legal morass ended up incurring hundreds of thousands of dollars just to pay the arbitrators, not to mention the millions in legal fees for all the parties involved.

On the personal side, Bill was described as loving, extremely affectionate with his children, and also very giving to Nanette and her children. But it caused concern for Kim to see him being so affectionate toward Nanette, when his girlfrield didn't seem to return that affection.

"I felt like it was just a little strange and not very romantic," Kim said.

Patrick said his brother was very generous, pointing to the time when Bill and Sue took in Patrick's young adopted Korean daughter while she worked out some personal issues. Bill was also a very giving donor to other causes, both on foreign land and at home.

Patrick said Bill always taught his family that because they were more fortunate than most, he wanted his children "to be pilgrims, if you will, and go to some of these places in Mexico or Central America and give back, help them by bringing gifts and wheelchairs and stuff like that down there."

The message sunk in. Kim not only went to work in orphanages in Mexico during college, she also tried to live her entire life by the credo Bill taught them.

"My dad never took his successes to heart," she said.

But according to Bill's cousin Barbara, he was not so generous with his money and goodwill when it came to his wife, Sue. Early on, as he was trying to get ahead in the business world, Barbara said Bill "would dictate to [Sue] what to wear, where she had to go with him. To me, he treated her somewhat like she had to do what he said."

"Bill was a very controlling individual," Barbara said. "And when they started out, they didn't have any money, like the rest of us. . . . They had a child right away. He couldn't get any help from his family because they weren't in any position to help him."

Later, after he and his businesses started earning money, she said, "[Bill] would make it a point that it was *his* money . . . and he would make a point of saying that it wasn't [Sue's], because she didn't work for it."

Sue "went along for many years, and privately I said to myself, 'I don't know how she's doing this. . . .' It was unacceptable to me, because she was a lovely, lovely person. She would go out of her way for anyone, and he turned into a person that I didn't even know anymore."

Barbara said she saw Bill change over time—changes that she blamed largely on his escalating alcohol consumption.

"He had a good heart. There was no doubt about that," she said. "He really was good, but I think alcohol interfered with his life."

Patrick agreed that his brother "drank more than he should have, but there were times where we all [did that]." He noted that he and Bill always walked home from the bar when they imbibed, and he said he never witnessed any abusive behavior.

"I don't know that he was an out-and-outright alcoholic," he said. "I do know that he was always of sound mind, because he would be up the next morning—no matter how late we were—and we'd be running down the beach."

Kim viewed the failure of her parents' marriage differently, saying they had not spent enough time connecting with each other over the years, so it went bad after Bill "retired" and started working at home.

"They were at home all the time, driving each other crazy," she said. "They had lost communication skills."


A few months after meeting Bill, Nanette moved into Balboa Coves, and Bill called his cousin to tell her about the pretty new woman in his life.

"I am dating this lady, with two small children," he said. "She's wonderful. She's very bright, and I enjoy talking to her. She has a couple degrees."

"Good for you," Barbara said. "I'm glad you found someone."

To Barbara, Bill sounded sure that the relationship was going to work. "He was very confident that this was meant to happen, how well they gelled together," she recalled. "He was very happy—very happy with her."

Patrick didn't see it quite that way. To him, it seemed that Bill was happy to have met Nanette, whom Bill described as "a sweetheart and a dolly," but he never mentioned anything to his brother about her being intelligent. It was more along the lines of "she's a good piece," as in piece of ass.

"I think what Bill wanted . . . he wanted a good-looking chick on the arm," Patrick said. "I don't know if he thought she wasn't worthy to be called his wife," but that was the kind of thing that would have come out of Bill's mouth. "He was a very proud guy."

Patrick wasn't all that impressed with Nanette. During one visit, Bill asked Nanette to cook his brother some fried eggs, and "she looked at him like he was stupid," Patrick recalled. Once she made the eggs, he said, "they were terrible. They were runny. She wasn't a housewife. She was someone who could show a man a lot of fun if he was interested in her."

Bill's brother also didn't care for the large nude photo of

Nanette displayed at the Seashore Drive house for everyone to see as they walked in. For Patrick, it was a disgusting show of narcissism.

"There it was in your face, and that's the way she showed her interest in men," he said. "She's proud of herself. She's a nice-looking woman. She had a great-looking body, apparently."

When Barbara learned about the age difference between Bill and Nanette, she thought his new girlfriend was too young for him—and truly too young to have advanced degrees—but Barbara didn't say anything.

"With Bill, he was going to do what he was going to do. . . . You don't tell Bill what to do."

What was the attraction between him and Nanette? "I think he loved blondes, number one," she said. "He was always talking sexual innuendos and the guy stuff about sex, and here was this young chickiepoo . . . and she's telling him what he wants to hear."

Patrick also thought that Bill liked having Nanette on his arm because it brought cache to his business image.

"I think he just figured she was an attractive woman and she was worth something because of that to the business, and whatever dealings she needed to know, Bill would tell her," Patrick said. Nonetheless, Bill "may have given her a little too much rope and maybe that's when he found out she was taking him to the cleaners and he was pissed about it. But no, he never said she was a sweetie pie and she'd make a good wife. That would make me throw up."

Bill's divorce filings offer some insight into why he likely enjoyed having Nanette around to discuss his entrepreneurial ventures and to accompany him on business dinners.

*My wife has never been interested in the business of the community [property] or how the money was made,* he wrote. *Indeed, she was only interested in being there to spend it. I* *made not only <u>one</u> million dollar investment, but many such investments without ever having my wife complain, let alone comment. I would always inform her in conversation as to what was going on, but her interest was always only of a conversational nature. She did occasionally accompany me for social engagements done for purposes of conducting business. But she was interested, if at all, only in the social part, never the business.*

Obviously different from Sue, Nanette was *very* interested in soaking up everything he could teach her about his business affairs. If only Bill had known *why* she'd been so interested.

# CHAPTER 9

Just as Nanette had predicted, the Newport Beach police did want to interview her ex-husband, K. Ross Johnston.

K. Ross told Detective Bill Hartford that he and Nanette had met in Arizona in the early 1980s, were married in 1983, and had two children. Five years later, he said, Nanette told him she'd fallen out of love and wanted a divorce. She didn't contest his move for sole custody of the kids, and the divorce became final in 1989. He moved with the children to Mission Viejo, California, in March 1990.

In 1991, Nanette told him she was living with Bill McLaughlin, whom he'd met once when he picked up the kids, but Nanette claimed it was a purely professional relationship.

When K. Ross talked about Nanette, it was obvious that he was still hurt from all the lying and cheating Nanette had done while they were married. Thinking it odd that Nanette made a point of saying, "Eric has nothing to do with this," K. Ross made sure to relay her comment to the detective and to describe Nanette's twentysomething boyfriend.

K. Ross said Eric Naposki had helped coach Kristofer's teams in soccer, baseball, and basketball, and he'd thought it was odd that Eric had worn shorts to the soccer game the chilly night before Bill's murder, but Eric "was like a rock" and did not complain.

Despite Nanette's claims that it was "strictly business" with Bill and that he was just her "mentor," K. Ross was pretty confident that she was seeing Eric *and* Bill romantically. After all, K. Ross was only too familiar with her expertise at juggling men.

Recounting the evening's events to Detective Hartford, K. Ross said the final championship game started later than its scheduled six o'clock kickoff, and then the two teams tied. They were still tied after two overtime periods, so the winner had to be decided in a shoot-out, with five shots per team. It was a formal and dramatic procedure: The goalie came out each time an opposing player lined up the ball and took his shot. The parents screamed whether a point was scored or missed.

Kristofer's team ultimately came in second place, but there was still reason to celebrate because his team had made it into the championships. That said, Nanette and Eric seemed to be in a real hurry to leave before the end-of-season commemorative medal ceremony, saying that Eric had to get to an eight o'clock appointment. Even though it was her turn to take the kids, Nanette said she would leave them with K. Ross and take them another night.

K. Ross looked at his watch. Noticing it was already 8:20 P.M., he wondered why Nanette, who had come to every one of her son's games, would purposely miss watching him get his championship medal.

"Well, it's eight-twenty right now," he told her. "There's no way [Eric] can make it to an eight o'clock appointment. Just stay and watch the ceremony."

But Nanette and Eric were already rushing off toward the parking lot, which was at least a soccer field away.

"No, that's okay. We've got to go. We'll see you later,"

Nanette called over her shoulder as they took off in a manner that K. Ross described as "skedaddling," or "hoofing it."

Detective Dave Byington, who was pulled from patrol to do surveillance on this case, posed as a scruffy beach bum as he assumed his position on the sand behind the Seashore house on December 20, the night before Bill's funeral.

He watched Nanette park out front, carry her shopping bags down the side of the house, and go inside. Nanette had told police that she was worried the same killer might be looking for her, and yet, Byington saw no fear on her face or in her body language. She didn't look over her shoulder, or draw the blinds across the big picture window in the living room. From his spot on the beach, Byington watched Nanette and the kids through a big picture window, decorating the tree together as if they didn't have a care in the world.

On Wednesday, December 21, Bill's memorial service was held at Our Lady of Mount Carmel Church, complete with a mass, Communion, and about seven priests in attendance. Bill was a good Catholic, who said grace before dinner, even when the family went out to eat at Chart House.

In fact, all the McLaughlins were good Catholics. After Bill was gone, Monsignor Bill Barry, his neighbor at Balboa Coves, used to hold mass for Kim, Kevin, and Sandy at his kitchen table.

Because Bill had made good after enjoying the benefits of the Student Worker Program at Loyola Marymount, he endowed a scholarship to his alma mater, a Catholic university from which Kim and Jenny also graduated, and Kevin attended for two years before dropping out.

K. Ross Johnston and his girlfriend, Julia, had wanted to attend the funeral to pay their respects to the man who had been so kind to Lishele and Kristofer, but Nanette told them it was just for close family. She said they could attend the wake afterward, but then she called to tell them it had been canceled.

Sandy drove Jenny, Kevin, Sue, and Kim to the church for the 9:00 A.M. service. Kim, who was sitting in the front seat, burst into tears when she recognized some of the priests from Loyola.

"Kim was just destroyed by this," Sandy recalled. "I'm not saying Jenny wasn't, but she didn't show it."

As they pulled into the church parking lot, they could see the priests wearing their elaborate ceremonial garb—the white robes with ties and tall hats. Unbeknownst to them, they were all being filmed by Newport Beach cops, who were watching for suspicious behavior as they searched for Bill's killer.

Nanette came with her two children in tow: nine-year-old Kristofer wearing a little-boy suit and necktie, and seven-year-old Lishele in a dark dress with a floral print. Nanette wore a businesslike black skirt suit, with the jacket buttoned up. Sandy was admiring it so much that Nanette later asked Sue what size Sandy was, saying she wanted to buy one for Sandy as a gift.

Nanette's face was blank. She never showed much emotion anyway, but on that day, she seemed especially aloof and hard to read, while everyone else was in shock. But more than that, Sandy couldn't believe that Nanette had brought such young children to the service.

"I thought it was inappropriate," she said. "I didn't even know what she had told them. Did she tell them he had a heart attack? To this day, I still think she used those kids as props to draw sympathy in her direction."

Nanette sat with the McLaughlin family in the front pews on the left side of the church. The room wasn't full, but a healthy crowd of about one hundred people had filed in, including some of Bill's business associates, his brother Patrick and his kids, and Bill's extended family, who had flown in from Chicago.

With a blowup photo of Bill on an easel in the foreground, his friend Denis Townsend gave the eulogy, trying to offer some words of compassion for Nanette, who he assumed was in mourning like the rest of them.

"That kind of raised the hairs on my neck a little bit, because I'd had five or six days actually of looking at Nanette from a different vantage point," Sandy recalled later. "I was feeling very funny about her at this point. As aloof as she was to Bill, I didn't think she deserved that callout. . . . [Denis] was kind of showing her sympathy, because we were all starting to act strange around her. I think Denis picked up on something."

Kevin was so upset that it was even more difficult for him to speak, but he still got up to say a few words. He was more uncoordinated than usual and so angry about his father's murder that his nose crinkled up. Jenny and Kim sniffled to themselves, but they were keeping it together until they heard a wail erupt from nearby.

As they turned to look, they saw the sound was coming from Lishele, who was shaking and sobbing loudly as she stood up and turned away from the poster of Bill. Nanette didn't shed a tear, at least not that anyone could see, and she also didn't take her traumatized daughter into her arms and cradle her, as some mothers would have. Nanette just sat there, stonelike.

After the service, the McLaughlin family and friends congregated in the rectory. Patrick and his sons were trying to make chitchat with Kristofer when he let a bomb drop.

"My mom's boyfriend plays football," he said.

Patrick and his sons didn't mention this comment to

Bill's children, but they quickly realized that the police needed to hear this—immediately. The information came as quite a shock to those who thought Bill and Nanette had been in an exclusive relationship.

Afterward, Nanette, her kids, and the McLaughlin family headed over to have lunch at Bill's favorite Italian haunt on Balboa Island, where he'd often ordered the gnocchi. On the way there, they talked about the service.

"Oh, my God," Jenny said, "I was holding up okay during the service, but Lishele was making me cry."

From there, Nanette said she had some things to do. Undercover detectives, who had been monitoring the funeral, followed her to the Champion Yamaha shop in Newport, where she used Bill's credit card to pay off the balance on three motorcycles for which she'd already made a deposit. Including an earlier purchase for a trailer, helmets, and other equipment, the total came to nearly $8,000. She signed the bills, *Nanette McLaughlin*. Then she went to the bank and got a $3,100 cash advance on one of Bill's credit cards.

# CHAPTER 10

Following up on Kristofer's comment at the memorial service, the Newport Beach police kept an eye out for a strapping guy who looked like he played football.

The next afternoon, around four-twenty, they were watching Nanette and the Seashore Drive house when a man pulled up in a black Nissan Pathfinder, with New York license plates. Nanette's kids ran outside to greet the athletic-looking guy, and they all went inside together.

*Who is New York boy?* Detective Dave Byington wondered from his post near the house. *The way those kids are hugging him, he must be a relative.*

The undercover officers, who watched the man leave about ten minutes later, hopped into an unmarked car to follow him, alerting dispatch to have a marked car do a "cold stop," once they found some kind of probable cause. That wasn't too hard, the vehicle code book was full of potential violations.

An officer in a patrol car subsequently stopped him, took his name and address, and ran a background check. The man said he was Eric Naposki, and that he lived in an apartment in Tustin. But after the police let him go, they followed him to a Ramada Inn, where they learned he was registered. Why had he lied to the detectives?

When they discovered he had an outstanding warrant for "failure to appear" on a $343 traffic violation, they had a legal excuse to bring him in for questioning.

Later that night, uniformed officers followed him to the Thunderbird nightclub, where he worked. After he got off at 2:00 A.M., they arrested him on the warrant, brought him to the city jail, and searched his car.

In his Pathfinder, they found a notebook that served as a journal and datebook planner.

*Once you get your ass out of this financial disaster, do not overextend yourself anymore,* he wrote.

Two other notations read: *Look into work positions in Lido* and *Get Nanette Ring $2,500 so far—Why?* And a calendar showed that he was planning to propose on New Year's Day.

Sergeant Van Horn and Detective Voth arrived a couple of hours later. After being briefed about the items found in Eric's car, they read him his rights.

"Am I in trouble for something?" he asked.

"I hope not," Voth replied.

"I hope not too, because I don't understand."

Voth told him he would understand things better soon.

Eric said he'd recently started working at the Thunderbird, which had only just opened in Lido Village two or three weeks earlier. He ran through all the football teams with which he'd played briefly, as well as the local jobs he'd had in between, including physical trainer at the Sporting Club and head of security at the Metropolis sushi bar and nightclub, both in Irvine. He was in between apartments, he said, was carting his belongings around in his truck, and had been living at the Ramada Inn for the past day or so.

"What other kind of security work do you do?" Van Horn asked.

Eric said he worked as a bodyguard for private clients, such as a clothing manufacturer in Glendale, whom he occasionally accompanied to Mexico. He said he also worked security at some apartment complexes with another guy.

"I'm just now getting kind of into it, because football for me just really ended this year, because I was in Canada to play in the Canadian League, but I've had so many injuries," he explained.

"Do you do any armed work?" Van Horn asked, meaning that he carried a gun.

"No, I don't do any armed," Eric said.

"Not even in uniform?"

"No, even in uniform. I don't even have a sidearm. That takes at least six months to get."

Asked about his relationship with Nanette, Eric described her as a "pretty good friend," whom he'd met two and a half years earlier when he was running a kids' program at a gym in Irvine. He said he had two kids of his own, and that's why he and Nanette got along. They started working out together, and he also liked doing things with her kids. In fact, he'd just taken them Christmas shopping, he said, because Nanette had to move.

"She's going through some hard times this week," he said, "so I told her I'd take the kids."

"How about Bill McLaughlin?" Van Horn asked.

"I never met Bill."

"Do you know who he is?"

"I just know of him . . . and his, you know, his partnership with Nanette, as far as business goes and stuff like that."

Eric said he didn't know anything more about Nanette's relationship with Bill and didn't believe it was his place to ask. "It wasn't like that. She didn't ask me about my ex-wife, and I didn't ask her about her ex-husband."

Asked how he viewed Nanette's relationship with Bill, Eric said, "From what I gathered, it was kind of a mentor—almost like a father-daughter—type thing. . . . Nanette is a pretty smart girl. She's aggressive businesswise, and I think she learned a lot of that from Bill, you know, kind of like a . . . I don't know what you call it, apprentice, or someone, you know, like that or higher stature."

"You didn't see it as a romantic relationship or a boyfriend-girlfriend?"

"No, I didn't," Eric said.

Eric said she'd had boyfriends before she got romantically involved with Eric. As a matter of fact, even since they'd been dating, and he still didn't see them as being exclusive. "I wouldn't say [it's] a solo, total [relationship], like, I have girlfriends, you know, and people that I date also." Rather, he said, he saw it as a "dating relationship that has potential, you know, to get better."

"Do you think this is headed toward a serious relationship? A marriage or engagement or—" Van Horn asked.

"I hope it is, yeah."

During the search of Eric's car, detectives also found a green towel with reddish brown marks, and a floor mat with brown stains.

"When the officer looked in your car, there's a towel there he says looks like [it] has blood on it," Van Horn said. "Do you know what that is?"

Eric pointed to his chin. "Yeah, right here. See a little, it's a shaving nick. . . . I think I still have the scar."

"I can't see a scar there," Voth said.

"I got it the other day."

"How long ago?"

"I'd say two days ago, when I shaved."

"Okay, you said there's also some brown stains on the floor. Do you know what that is?"

"I have no idea."

"Any blood or anything that's been in there?" Voth asked.

"No."

Eric said he didn't know why they needed to search his car.

"We're investigating a murder," Van Horn said.

"I want to be totally helpful to you guys, not play good guy/bad guy," Eric said, "because I know I'm a good guy and I'm on the outside of this thing. I mean, I'm on your side."

"Have you ever been to the house on Balboa Coves?" Van Horn asked.

"No," Eric said, adding that he'd only been to the house on Seashore Drive, "like, one time, you know, and that was probably way back closer to when I first met her. I saw her down on the beach when she was out there."

Asked where he was the night of December 15, he said he was with Nanette at the soccer game. Afterward, she dropped him off at his apartment in Tustin, where his truck was, "somewhere in the vicinity of nine, nine-fifteen. . . . [Then] I got dressed and went to work later on, probably around nine-thirty, quarter to ten."

He said Nanette didn't come inside while he changed for work. "I was in a rush because I had to get to work and she was in a rush . . . to get to the mall."

Asked for his typical work schedule, Eric said he might get to the Thunderbird at 8:00 P.M. if he had a meeting, but not till 9:00 or 10:00 P.M. if he didn't. But he said he didn't have a meeting that night. "No, we have a meeting tonight."

"You said you don't own any firearms at all?" Van Horn asked.

"No, I bought one, [but] I haven't seen it in so long. I bought one in Dallas that I gave my dad. It was a .380, a little . . . I forgot what kind it was called. But my dad was mugged in New York, dropping asbestos off in the Bronx."

Later in the interview, completely unsolicited—and before the murder weapon had even been analyzed by the crime lab—Eric brought up the fact that he'd bought a nine-millimeter Beretta about four or five months earlier. But he said the gun was stolen in June after he'd loaned it to a coworker, Joe David Jimenez.

"Had the gun three weeks, never fired it, never taken out," Eric said. "He was supposed to get ammo."

Eric said he'd never reported the gun stolen because he was hoping it would show up. "He could have sold the fuckin' thing, for all I know."

Asked where he kept his belongings, Eric said they were in his car and hotel room at the moment.

He never inquired why the detectives had pulled him over on a traffic warrant in the middle of the night to question him about a murder, which Voth saw as a natural query from an innocent man.

The detectives gained Eric's consent to search his hotel room at the Ramada in Costa Mesa, where they found muddy shoes and a receipt for a $599 Movado watch, paid for in cash, at Bullock's in South Coast Plaza the morning of December 22. They also found his Wells Fargo bank statement for December showing a balance of only $956.

After one of Eric's friends posted bail for him, the police let him go, released his car to him, and continued their surveillance. They subsequently followed him to a storage facility in Tustin, which he'd never mentioned. They also got a call from a confidential informant who said Eric had rented a storage unit in Huntington Beach on December 20, and had requested that no one give out information about it.

By placing a tracking device on Eric's car, the detectives

were able to find the storage unit in Huntington Beach. During a search there on January 19, police found the three motorcycles Nanette had paid for after Bill's funeral on December 21.

Working in private security, Eric clearly knew he was being tailed and began to use countersurveillance techniques—making abrupt U-turns, turning off his lights, or suddenly pulling over to the curb—which indicated to police that he had a guilty conscience.

A closer examination of Eric's notebook pages, which involved cross-checking Eric's statements with notations he'd entered in the journal chronologically, revealed that a series of letters and numbers—*2WWL034*—was written in early December, before the murder. Checking DMV records, they matched that entry to the license plate number for Bill McLaughlin's white Mercedes, which was parked in the garage in Balboa Coves when Bill was in town.

Why would Eric have Bill's plate number, they wondered, and how would he get it if he'd never been to the house? To Detective Voth, it meant that Eric was involved in the murder, and the detective's suspicions only increased as Eric continued to change his story.


The Orange County District Attorney's homicide division works as a "vertical unit" with law enforcement agencies. That means prosecutors and DA investigators are supposed to work closely with detectives, starting at the crime scene if possible.

For example, a prosecutor—and sometimes a DA investigator—might sit in on police interviews with witnesses or suspects, observing and passing notes with suggested questions. In some cases, a veteran DA investigator might even conduct the interview.

The night of the murder, Detective Bill Hartford called

Deputy District Attorney Debora "Debbie" Lloyd, who was relatively new to the Homicide Unit, having transferred about a year earlier from the Sexual Assault Unit, and she signed off on the consent search of the house.

Within a week, Lloyd came down to the NBPD for a roundtable discussion with about eight of the police officials working the case. Lloyd was the only woman at the table. In her view, Nanette was the prime suspect.

"The evidence looked pretty strong that she was involved," Lloyd, who has since retired, recalled recently. "They, on the other hand, were more interested in Naposki."

At that point, she said, the detectives didn't "have a whole lot of information, but there was enough. I suspected that she did it, and maybe she had him help her, so that's kind of what I went away with."

Lloyd received some updates from detectives in the beginning, she said, but because homicides were so rare in Newport Beach, she didn't know the detectives well and hadn't had much chance to work with them. She also got the sense that they didn't want her help—a belief she felt was confirmed when she asked a veteran DA investigator to offer his help in putting the case together.

"He came back and said they weren't interested in us getting involved," she said. "I said, 'Oh, man,' and there was nothing I could do because it wasn't our case. We can't take a case away from a police department."

As the NBPD continued to check into the background of Eric Naposki, Detective Craig Frizzell talked with folks at the Sporting Club, an exclusive gym in Irvine, where Eric had worked as a fitness instructor for about three months in 1993 and where Nanette had also been a member. Eric had been fired for having a bad attitude and for threatening the staff after they had his motorcycle, which he'd knowingly parked illegally, towed away. Nonetheless, Eric returned to the gym to work out with Nanette, who paid for his $200 membership.

Frizzell interviewed two valets at the Thunderbird, who said that Eric routinely gave them his keys to park his car in a loading area rather than paying the $4 parking-garage fee. But neither of them could remember what time he came to work the night of the murder, or whether they'd parked his car.

The Thunderbird was one of about twenty nightclubs scattered around the peninsula, where the young, affluent, and attractive twentysomething patrons paid enormous cover charges to gain entrance.

"They were the pretty people. Everyone went there to be seen," said Dave Byington, the retired homicide sergeant. "Always had a line out the door."

Eric worked security at the front door. In those days, the NBPD's vice squad was busy monitoring these nightclubs and chasing down narcotics crimes: "Coke was huge, high-end prostitutes, escorts," Byington recalled.


Frizzell followed up on Eric's gun story by trying to interview Joe David Jimenez, who had reportedly lost Eric's nine-millimeter gun. But Jimenez was in Texas visiting his parents for the holidays, so Frizzell talked to Jimenez's roommate, Robert Trednic, instead. Trednic, who had worked with Eric at Metropolis, described him as a sneak and a liar.

According to Trednic, Eric had said, "If there is a shooting going on, don't worry, I'm holding," although Trednic said he'd never actually seen any gun. Trednic also said he'd never known Jimenez to carry one either.

Reached by phone the next day, Jimenez confirmed that Eric had loaned him a gun as protection for a few nights on a security job in August 1994, but it wasn't a nine-millimeter. It was a Jennings-Bryco .380, he said, and it was never stolen. That's just what he'd told Eric the day he'd pulled up on a motorcycle that Eric said his girlfriend had bought for him and asked Jimenez for the gun.

Jimenez told Detective Frizzell that he'd sold the gun to his boss, Art Menaldi, for $240—fully loaded, not empty of bullets, as Eric had claimed—after Eric failed to pay him that same amount for the security job. When Eric finally paid Jimenez his $240, Jimenez offered to repay Eric the $100 that Eric said the gun was worth. Records showed that Eric had bought the .380 from a pawnshop in Dallas, Texas, in January 1994.

Jimenez said Eric called him at one point and said he'd lost his nine-millimeter gun *and* his .380, so he was unsure which one he'd actually loaned to Jimenez—apparently trying to solicit a statement that other weapons could have been stolen out of his car at the same time. That's when Jimenez confessed to Eric that he'd actually sold the .380 to Menaldi.

Eric called Jimenez in Texas the same day Frizzell did. But before Eric could say anything, Jimenez asked him what was going on.

"The police are calling me, asking me questions about you and a murder or something."

Eric got quiet for a moment and said, "Someone's trying to frame me."

"Oh," Jimenez said.

Then Eric hung up abruptly.

The NBPD tracked down the .380 and got it back from Art Menaldi's brother, Dominic, who told police that Eric had asked for it some weeks earlier, saying he needed it because of some problem. Describing the gun to Dominic as "a small, snub-nosed, little piece-of-crap gun that fits in your hand and looks like a nine-millimeter," Eric apparently wanted to prove to police that it hadn't been fired recently.

A few months later, Jimenez passed a lie detector test and also turned over six Hydra-Shok bullets that he'd removed from Eric's .380 before Dominic Menaldi had returned it to police. This was the same type of bullet that had killed Bill McLaughlin, who had no such ammunition in his arsenal.

When the detectives learned that Eric had paid $540 for the Beretta 92F, nearly twice the value of the .380, they knew that Eric wouldn't have confused the two guns. Why would Eric lie and say he'd loaned the 9mm to Jimenez?

"There's no reason in the world [for Eric] to lie about that, unless that gun was used in the crime," Detective Voth said.

Voth wondered what role Eric might have played in the crime. Was he the shooter? Or was Nanette the shooter and he simply helped her? Under the law, Eric was just as guilty either way.

At the end of December 1994, Detectives Frizzell and Hartford located Kevin McDaniel in Los Angeles. McDaniel had sold the nine-millimeter Beretta to Eric in June or July 1994, about six years after they'd met on a bodyguard job in Mexico through Art Menaldi's company, MPP Bodyguards.

McDaniel told detectives that he'd only just spoken to Eric, who still owed him $1,400 of the $2,000 he'd loaned him. Eric had written some checks that bounced and said he was going through some "stuff right now," but he would try to repay McDaniel as soon as he got some cash.

Before Thanksgiving, Eric had told him that he'd loaned the Beretta to Jimenez, but it had been stolen from Jimenez's car, a similar story to what he'd told police.

"You need to report my gun stolen," Eric said.

But McDaniel told Eric no, that *he* should be the one to report the gun stolen, because it was no longer McDaniel's weapon. The detectives thought it was looking more and more like this Beretta was the gun that had killed Bill McLaughlin—and that Eric was the shooter. Now if they could just find it.

# CHAPTER 11

Kim and Jenny McLaughlin soon discovered that their concerns and dislike for Nanette had fallen tragically short of reality.

Kim didn't know where her father had really met Nanette, but Kim didn't appreciate the fact that Nanette was only one year older than she was, or that Nanette's kids had moved into Bill's daughters' bedrooms within a few months of meeting Nanette.

In Kim's view, Nanette was a mooch, quitting her sales job as soon as she moved in. She also sucked up to Bill for his money, persuading him to send her kids to soccer camp and to take them all on exotic vacations. Kim told police that the only people she could see wanting Bill dead were Jacob Horowitz and Nanette Johnston.

Kevin McLaughlin, who lived with the couple, saw things a little differently. Although Nanette had her own bedroom, he often saw her go into Bill's room at night.

"They didn't think I knew what was going on, but I knew," he told police.

Then again, he also didn't know that Nanette was seeing anyone on the side.

* * *

After Bill's murder, Kim and Jenny told Nanette that they were taking Kevin for a weeklong trip for Christmas to their mother's house, their childhood vacation home on Hanalei Bay, Hawaii. They planned to mourn their father's death together, clear their heads, and scatter their father's ashes on the bay he'd loved. Nanette, they said, could take that time to move her things out of Balboa Coves and transfer them to the Seashore house, per Bill's will.

When the four of them returned from Hawaii, however, they were shocked to see that half of Bill's home office had been cleared out: his desktop computer, fax and copy machines, as well as various boxes of corporate documents and files. Nanette also had taken the Cadillac, even though Bill's will had specifically provided her with the Infiniti. To top it off, even his favorite baseball, signed by Babe Ruth, was gone.

As they went through Bill's walk-in closet to pack up his things, they found a pair of red high-heeled pumps, the size of Nanette's feet, next to his Armani suits, as well as a matching red teddy and a vibrator.

"So she took care of him in that respect," Sandy Baumgardner said.

They noticed that she'd left behind photos of her and Bill together. However, she'd taken the portraits of herself, which Bill had kept on his desk at Balboa Coves, including those of her wearing a lacey bra while posed on a motorcycle.

When the McLaughlins went to the Las Vegas house to go through his things, they were repulsed to find a poster-size photo from the same motorcycle shoot. Knowing that there were no small children around in Las Vegas, Bill had apparently felt free to display a much racier shot of

Nanette—leaning back, topless, showing off the fake breasts that he, as her benefactor, had bought for her.

"Kim hated her so much," Sandy said. "She just wanted to stomp on it and tear it apart."

The McLaughlins tried once more to explain to Nanette that they would give her the Infiniti, which was in Las Vegas, if she would please return the Cadillac, per Bill's living will. Yet, she still continued to ignore their pleas.


After evading police for weeks, Nanette finally agreed to take a polygraph test on January 5, 1995. Although she tested as truthful when she answered "no" to the question "Did you shoot Bill McLaughlin?" she came up as deceptive when she responded with "no" to these three questions:

"Do you know for sure who shot Bill McLaughlin?"

"Do you know for sure where the gun is that was used to shoot Bill McLaughlin?"

"Did you participate in any way in shooting Bill McLaughlin?"

She said she'd never said anything to Eric that would have made him want to kill Bill, but she thought that Kevin and some of his buddies could have committed the murder.

She made an excuse that she had to pick up her kids and couldn't stay for the follow-up interview after the polygraph. When she came back the next day, she was told that her initial test came up as deceptive and said she didn't want to complete the process. Eric refused to take the test from the start.

In an interview on January 6, Nanette said she felt guilty for giving out so many keys to workers around the house, including gardeners, painters, housecleaners, and such. The detectives asked if she stood to gain anything from Bill's death, and she said no. She stood to gain more if he'd lived, because that way they could carry out the business deals they'd been working on together. She noted that although the life insurance policy would give her $1 million, she would have gained $10 million in royalties if she'd married him.

Bill was everything to her, she said, contending that he'd known about Eric being a friend who did things with her that Bill didn't like to do. She said she knew Eric wasn't involved in the murder, because he didn't even know where Bill lived. She started out saying they were just friends who hung out during the day, and besides, Eric had a girlfriend. But later in the interview, she admitted that Eric was a lover—just not someone she could settle down with, and certainly not a marriage partner. She didn't love him that way, she said, and she assumed the feeling was mutual.

She said Eric came to the Seashore house after the break-in to install an alarm, and was planning to put in a better one soon. Police later learned that there was never an alarm in that house.

The detectives asked if Eric had ever shown Nanette any paperwork where he'd handwritten the license plate number for Bill's Mercedes, and she said no. Asked why he would have the number if she'd never shown him the car, her response was "I don't know." She claimed that she never told him exactly where she lived, and that all she'd bought him for Christmas was a pair of sweats.

Detective Voth told Nanette that they had more incriminating information showing that Eric had killed Bill, but they couldn't tell her about it, because Eric might run if he found out. Voth said he hoped Eric hadn't asked her for any money.

Nanette said he hadn't. "I don't have any anyway. Well, some, but . . . ," she said, trailing off.

This revealing statement was only a hint of what the McLaughlin family and the NBPD were about to uncover.

Around this same time, Kevin McLaughlin confronted Nanette directly at Balboa Coves one day when she was gathering some of her belongings. Later he recounted the scene to his girlfriend, Sandy.

"Did you have my dad killed?" he asked.

"Nooooooo," Nanette replied, acting shocked.

This was no laughing matter, but Sandy got a kick out of the story. Kevin's speech difficulties could cause a lack of normal inflection, so he really had to put a lot of effort into doing voices and imitations. She was also proud of him for confronting Nanette.

The police were still interested in what Kevin had to say about the murder, given that he was a witness and had been in the house when Bill was shot. However, he had little substantive information to offer. He told them that although Bill had talked about marrying Nanette, he shared a private joke with Kevin that he was going to "dump" her when she turned thirty.

On January 13, Kim McLaughlin called Detective Voth to let him know that the family had decided to put up a $40,000 reward for information leading to the arrest and conviction of suspects in Bill's murder.

Five days later, Kim told Voth that she and Jenny had been going over her father's accounts, trying to get a handle on what bills and taxes needed to be paid, and had discovered some disturbing irregularities.

"We were trying to get things to Brian [Ringler], our accountant, and we couldn't get things paid and we couldn't get things done, and things weren't clear," Kim said.

But when Kim and Jenny tried to question Nanette about these issues, she'd been strangely uncooperative and evasive.

"As things would come up, we would ask her questions about 'Do you know this person?' or 'Do you know about this situation? Can you enlighten us?'" Jenny recalled, but Nanette didn't return calls or follow through when she said she would get back to them.

Nanette simply didn't seem to understand—or refused to—that although she was a trustee of Bill's estate, she wasn't in complete control of or entitled to all his money. Jenny and Kim were very suspicious.

The bank statements from November 1994 showed a balance of $650,303 in Bill's U.S. Funds W.F.M. Holdings account, which was titled with his initials, as were several other accounts and properties. This was his biggest account, which received about $550,000 in Plasmacell-C royalties each quarter.

The McLaughlin trust was set up for asset protection and estate-planning purposes, with a PriMerit Bank account as the operating fund. For asset protection purposes, Bill couldn't sign on that account, so he made Nanette a managing trustee in November 1991. Ringler was a cotrustee, but only Nanette was authorized to sign and issue checks to pay the household bills and take care of small-scale financial matters. Kim was the successor managing trustee in line, who would take over if Bill should die.

The royalties went into the trust account, and then were transferred by the bank to the W.F.M. Holdings account, on which only Bill had signing power. But once he died, Nanette, as his estate trustee, could go down to the bank and stop that transfer of funds.

"We were extremely concerned," Kim said.

The family asked Nanette for three months of bank statements, but she said she couldn't find the one from December, so they had to ask U.S. Funds for it, while Ringler did cash flow projections to keep the estate going and pay outstanding bills. They were worried to see a check for $30,000 had already cleared in January.

When the missing statement finally came in the mail, Kim made an even more disturbing discovery: Line items for a $250,000 check that had cleared four days after Bill's death and for a $75,000 check written in early December.

She immediately called Jenny. "I found it," Kim said. "I found some evidence that she's stealing from us."

Brian Ringler asked to see a copy of the actual $250,000 check so he could try to figure out what was going on. Once he received it, he saw that check #1158, paid to the Nanette Johnston Trust, appeared to have been signed by William F. McLaughlin on December 14, the day before his murder, when he had been in Las Vegas. Endorsed by Nanette, the check cleared on December 19, two days after the police allowed her and the McLaughlin family back into the house. The money was deposited into Nanette's First Interstate Bank account.

Why would Bill have paid his girlfriend such a large sum, especially when he'd been complaining of an increasing inability to pay his bills of late? The simple answer, Ringler thought, was that he wouldn't have.

"He was always very methodical, had great credit," Ringler said. "He never would have [spent] a quarter million dollars while he was having all these problems."

The next questions: Were there more checks like this one? And was there money moving between Bill's other accounts as well?

From there, Ringler and the family asked for statements from a half-dozen accounts, going back to 1993. When they couldn't get them by simple request from Nanette or the bank, they asked for the police department's help, which was subpoenaing records as well.

As soon as Detective Hartford heard about the $250,000 check, he asked Ringler to forward copies of all Bill's canceled checks from the past three months.

Ringler soon calculated that Nanette had written $125,000 in checks from another one of Bill's accounts shortly after his death, placed that money into the PriMerit trust account, then proceeded to spend at least $80,000 of it. (This was the household account that generally had a balance of $10,000 to $20,000.)

Upon closer inspection of the checks, they also found multiple credit card payments that went to Bill's various accounts, but to Nanette's credit cards as well. Nanette had chalked up at least $24,000 in charges to Bill's credit cards by signing as *Nanette McLaughlin*—both before and after his death.

Ringler went back through the handwritten ledger to 1992, where he saw that Bill had been paying Nanette $1,000 each month as an allowance. Once Ringler had the checks in hand, he compared the amounts on the documents with the amounts Nanette had entered into the ledger, and also with the amounts she'd entered into a computer Quicken register, which served as the official accounting record for the year.

He saw nothing of note in 1992 and 1993. However, starting in February 1994, he began to find discrepancies. Checks written for $3,000 and $5,000 were entered into the computer register for only $1,000, or sums were voided out entirely, meaning that she was taking thousands more dollars each month than her allowance. By October 1994, those amounts jumped significantly on multiple checks totaling $47,000.

A fax from U.S. Funds showed that between November 17 and December 14, 1994, six checks totaling $611,096 and signed by William F. McLaughlin had cleared. Two of those checks, totaling $105,000, were made payable to Bill's PriMerit trust account.

As Ringler tracked the money, he could see that sums were flying between accounts, with Bill appearing to have signed off on the transfers. However, these transfers continued after his death between accounts Nanette was allowed to access, but also between those she was not. Subsequent statements showed that the balance of the W.F.M. Holdings account had dropped from the $650,303 to only $40,000 by January, then to a pitiful $10,788.

Other discrepancies turned up as well. Checks were written out to Nanette, and yet the official register listed another entity, such as contributions to World View. There were also what appeared to be some legitimate payouts for Bill's property investments, such as three checks totaling about $256,000, which went to Rancho Mirage Associates, Salomon International Investment, Co., and W.F.M. Hacienda, L.P.

One questionable check for $11,000, written on the W.F.M. Hacienda account, dated December 12, 1994, was cashed on January 5, 1995, by Nanette. It was made out to her, and allegedly signed by Bill. Nanette was not authorized to sign checks on that account.

Ringler turned over all of these documents and his analysis to the NBPD, which then forwarded the stack of canceled checks to its documents expert, Detective Charles Beswick. Comparing the signatures to those found on other documents, Beswick determined that Nanette had forged Bill's signature on the $250,000 check, as well as on checks from the W.F.M. Holdings and W.F.M. Hacienda accounts. Everything else was taken out of his trust account once he died, as she wrote checks to herself and paid her credit card bills.

By the time Ringler finished his calculations, he'd identified $341,000 worth of checks that Nanette appeared to have stolen from Bill's various accounts. He and the McLaughlin family decided they should remove Nanette as trustee before she could do any more harm. In addition to the amount she stole, Ringler suspected that Nanette may also have been counting on getting paid $5,000 a month for her work as an estate trustee.

By this point, Captain James Jacobs, of the NBPD, had decided to separate the McLaughlin investigation into two parts, assigning Detective Hartford to lead the financial-fraud aspect and having Detective Voth continue as lead investigator on the homicide.

After serving a number of search warrants for Nanette's bank records, computers, and other financial documents, Hartford's team found more discrepancies and raised the amount stolen to nearly $500,000, figuring they probably hadn't even found all of the illegal transactions.

Meanwhile, Nanette, who continued to claim that Bill's Cadillac was hers, had Barry Bernstein, her attorney, fax Kim's attorney a DMV certificate of title. The title showed that Bill had signed the car over to Nanette on July 3, 1994. However, upon closer examination, Detective Beswick determined that Nanette had forged this signature as well.

Apparently, the diamond promise of being married to Bill someday had not satisfied Nanette's need for short-term gratification. She'd been spending this stolen cash on luxury items for herself, dinners out, and gifts for her boyfriends. And she continued to spend Bill's money after his death.

On January 9, 1995, Nanette paid for her and Eric Naposki to join Club Met-Rx for three months. After that, she told the manager, they would be leaving the area.

# CHAPTER 12

As the detectives began looking into Nanette's background, a pattern began to emerge: Eric was the latest in a series of men younger than Bill, whom she'd met at the gym and slept with behind Bill's back.

On December 17, 1994, while looking through police reports associated with the victim and his friends and family, the detectives found a report that listed Glenn Sharp as Nanette's "boyfriend" and a witness to a traffic collision involving Nanette two and a half years earlier in Costa Mesa.

In an interview with Detective Hartford at Sharp's home in Mission Viejo on December 28, 1994, Sharp said he'd met Nanette at the Sports Connection juice bar in April 1992. They struck up a conversation and started dating a week later, in between a week-long ski trip she took to Mammoth with her boss, Bill McLaughlin.

Nanette said she and her kids were living full-time with Bill, but her relationship with him was all business. Bill was often away, she said, traveling to Palm Springs and Palm Desert to work on his development projects.

"I was under the impression that she was working for him, doing his books or whatever," Sharp said.

Before meeting Bill on the bike path with some friends,

she said, she'd been living on the peninsula, making good money working for a medical-supply company. Sharp never understood how she came to live and work at Bill's house, but she made it sound like she needed to be at his beck and call. It was just easier for them this way.

Sharp worked as a firefighter, and she called him at the station when Bill was out of town. He got the idea pretty quickly about their no-strings arrangement, which suited him just fine as a single man in his late twenties going through a divorce and seeing a number of women.

Still, Nanette had some strange rules: She could call him, but he was not allowed to call her. They had sex in the Balboa Coves house, but he was not to go upstairs. She took Sharp to the house on Seashore Drive as well, but their rendezvous had to be prearranged—and only when Bill was out of town.

"It was really a shaky deal," he said.

There was also a more serious problem. "She had a hot temper. She could be violent at times," he said. "That was one of the reasons why I finally had to break it off with her. . . . She tried to run me over twice with her automobile."

A couple of months after they met, they had an evening that raised some concerns. It was a Monday night, May 19, when Bill was away, so she and Sharp went out to dinner and listened to some jazz. They drank their fill of alcohol, he said, then started driving south to Newport on the 55 freeway. Sharp was in his car and Nanette was in her brand-new 1991 red convertible Infiniti M30.

"She decided that she wanted to race me," he recalled. She took off, and Sharp tried to catch up and get her to slow down, but driving faster than one hundred miles per hour got to be too much for him. He slowed down at Victoria, near where the highway ended. That's when Nanette lost control of her car, spun out, and crashed, taking out a gas pump at a Union 76 station and totaling the Infiniti.

"I thought, for sure, it killed her," he said.

A bystander called 911, which brought out the police and fire departments, and an ambulance took her to the emergency room.

When a police officer told her to pee in a cup and warned that she might have to go to jail, "she pitched a fit," Sharp said. After being arrested on suspicion of driving under the influence, she was released to Sharp.

"That accident was never reported to Bill the way it really happened," he said. "She swept it under the rug, kept him in the dark about her activities." Bill was simply told that Nanette got into an accident and broke her nose.

"Would you call her a player?" Hartford asked.

"Definitely a player, yeah," Sharp said. "She liked the life in the fast lane. She liked the money and she liked to spend it."

Nanette told Sharp that Bill was paying her six figures. Based upon her incredible wardrobe and collection of accessories, Sharp believed it. She had to be "bringing in money from somewhere."

Nanette was quite a talker, aiming to impress, and it worked on Sharp. She boasted that she had a potential deal going with hair care mogul Paul Mitchell, with whom she said she was meeting in Beverly Hills. She had "something to do with some fandangled brush and comb" that had just come out in Europe, which she was trying to peddle to Mitchell. On top of that, she had an idea for a pet-grooming supply business. She bragged that she had some Hollywood connections as well, saying that when she and Bill went out to the desert, they had dinner at Frank Sinatra's house.

The beach house on Seashore Drive was also going to be hers, she told Sharp. It was just a matter of time. "Glenn, be patient," she said. "Within six months, I'm going to own this beach house outright."

At first, Sharp was sucked in by Nanette's spiel. "It was

five months of living on the edge. She had a lot of money. I guess Bill McLaughlin was very wealthy. She took me to a lot of places, told me about a lot of things that she was doing. For me, I got kind of caught up in living in the fast lane in Newport Beach."

Asked how she would deal with a sudden loss of income, Sharp replied, "She couldn't handle it. I don't think I could have ever seen Nanette working a nine-to-five job."

Sexually, she could get wild, he said, and be rather, well, "extroverted." To a virile young man like him, that was pretty exciting.

"Would you call her deviant?" Hartford asked.

"Yeah, she had some kinky ways about her," he said. "Anytime, anywhere, anyplace. I think that certain things represented a challenge to her. She liked to play with fire, in other words—see how far she could push it to the end of the envelope."

Although she claimed Bill was just her boss, Sharp said, "it always seemed to me that she appeared to be more to him than just a business associate." She and Bill went on a two- or three-week cruise-and-dive trip to the South Pacific, for example, and took numerous excursions in Bill's private plane.

After a while, Sharp questioned her claim that she was just renting a room in Bill's house—but not too closely, because he was enjoying himself.

"For me, she was just fun to date," he said. "She wasn't putting any kind of pressure on me." But he eventually realized that "she was just jerking my chain."

He also began to take note of some rather troubling and puzzling stories she told him. For instance, she described a rocky relationship with her ex-husband, whom Sharp met at a Little League game. Nanette alleged that K. Ross "would expose himself to her when she would drop the kids off over at his residence—things of that nature. Always trying to make him out to be a little bit of a deviant."

To Sharp, it seemed as if "things were going on in her head that maybe had happened in her past, maybe things she was dealing with, as far as her childhood or her growing up. She just seemed like, at times, that she was very angry about things. Very angry."

Nanette also lied to Sharp about being pregnant with his child.

"I know that she was a very, very disturbed young woman," he told Hartford. "It was all just one big lie."

She regaled Sharp with stories about Bill as well, saying that he'd spent time in Vietnam in the early 1960s in a clandestine unit, and had had a hard time dealing with that. "He was basically an alcoholic," she told Sharp. "She said he could be violent when he drank. He could get very upset."

Having never met Bill, Sharp didn't know what to believe, but he never saw anything in the well-kept house that supported her claims or indicated that Bill was a destructive person.

After five months, Sharp decided he'd had enough. He and Nanette had gone out for dinner and dancing at Peter's Landing, a collection of restaurants on the marina in Huntington Beach, which is between Newport Beach and Long Beach. Sharp had to work the next morning in Long Beach, so they left his car at the gym and drove to the restaurant in her car.

During dinner, Nanette got irritated with the way he'd called over the waitress to bring them drinks.

"I don't know exactly what was on her mind that night," he recalled. "You never knew what Nanette was thinking at times. And she just went off [and] left me. Literally, left me there."

He went outside to wait by her car to get a ride back to his vehicle, and she kept him waiting there for quite some time. She closed the club at two or two-thirty in the morning before meeting him at the car, where they "got into it."

"She tried to back over me with the car, with the car door open, then proceeded to leave the scene and then came back," he recalled.

After some persuasion, she agreed to drive him back to get his car at the gym, but it started all over again, once they got there. She stopped, got out of the car, and he had to "fend her off. I knocked her down, basically, getting her away from me," he said.

As he jumped into his car, she grabbed his door and got her hand caught as he was closing it. "It was everything I could do to get the door back open, and get her away from me so I could get out of that parking lot."

When Nanette threatened to call the police, Sharp challenged her to follow through.

"Well, why don't you?" he demanded.

But she didn't carry out her threat, nor did they see each other again, which was fine with him.

"I think she stopped seeing me or didn't really ever push anything because she didn't want Bill to find out," he recalled.

That said, she continued to call him at the fire station. After the second call, he warned her that he would contact Bill if her harassment continued, and the calls stopped.

He saw her at the gym sometime later, when she made a point of flaunting herself in a flirtation with a construction worker named Bart, for whom she'd always had a thing. But by that point, Sharp didn't care.

"Her bubble just didn't go to the top, so to speak," he said.

Pausing, Sharp posed a question to Hartford that he'd been wanting to ask about all these queries concerning him and Nanette and the late Bill McLaughlin.

"Is it okay to ask how he passed on?" Sharp asked.

"He was murdered."

"I'm really sorry to hear about that, because from what I knew about Bill, he was a good family man."


A couple of months later, the Newport Beach police got a call from Richard Baker, a forty-two-year-old businessman who had seen the news stories and wanted to help.

Baker told Detectives Voth and Byington that he'd met Nanette in February 1992 (shortly before Sharp) while inline skating on the boardwalk near 14th and Oceanfront in Newport. Nanette was there with her son, Kristofer, when she and Baker started talking. He gave her his phone number and she called him.

"I don't think I should be doing this," Nanette said mysteriously.

She told Baker the same story, that she lived with a wealthy man named Bill McLaughlin, with whom she had a purely platonic business relationship.

"He's a mentor. We have everything in writing," she said, adding that she got a certain percentage of the business deals they did together.

She seemed very intelligent, so he didn't question her story that she'd graduated from ASU with a 4.0 grade point average. At the time, Baker recalled, he had no reason to disbelieve her.

By the sound of it, Nanette had big plans and was already off to a good start. She said she'd made her money through a business deal involving a company that made plastic hairbrushes, which absorbed water from hair, and showed him some samples. She'd bought the company for $250,000 of her own money, she said, then sold it for more than $1.1 million within four months.

Bill, she said, received about $4 million in royalties each year, of which she was interested in "draining off" about $1 million. She also said she'd kicked in $400,000 toward Bill's second house, a $1.2 million property on Seashore Drive, and she intended to buy out Bill's majority share.

Given that Baker's job involved working with big corporations, he saw Bill as a potential source of funding and wanted to meet him. He asked at least five times, but Nanette never made it happen.

At some point, Baker started noticing that some of her claims were inconsistent. Why, if Bill was paying her so much and they were dealing with such big-dollar amounts, did she buy a computer and start learning how to use Quicken accounting software, which was geared toward households and small businesses?

It also seemed odd to him that when she gave him photos of herself, she always asked for them back, saying she wanted to give them to her father.

But she really seemed to like Baker, spending hundreds of dollars each month on daily cell phone calls to him. And after they'd been dating for about six weeks, she took him to Arizona to attend a high-school friend's wedding.

Of course, there was also plenty of sex. They slept together in her downstairs bedroom at Balboa Coves, but she never took him upstairs. They had sex about ten times there, and additional times at the beach house, but only at night, when the house was empty, and Bill was out of town.

Baker got into Balboa Coves by driving through the main gate off Pacific Highway, using the code Nanette gave him to get in, and entering the house through the garage door. He rang the doorbell or knocked on the front door, and Nanette let him in through the garage by hitting the remote opener from the inside.

"She had the power of a man, which she has developed well," he told detectives. "Makes you drop your defenses very easily. She'd use her kids a lot to help her do that. Her kids are part of her arsenal."

But things apparently backfired with Baker. "Her son started calling me 'Daddy' a couple of times," he recalled, and "all of a sudden, things changed. . . . The kids were getting too attached to me."

Nanette also didn't like Baker chatting with her ex-husband at Kristofer's baseball games.

"She always wanted to keep us away from each other," he said. "She got really upset and tried to stop that from happening, as though he would find out what she was doing."

By May 1992, Nanette was acting strange and distant. Then she sent Baker a letter, saying a friend had come to town and she no longer had feelings for Baker. He didn't get it, so when she called and later sent him a Christmas card, he didn't respond.

"I just avoided her," Baker said. "I turned and I never came back."

Sometime after they stopped seeing each other, he saw Nanette "all kissy-face" with a big guy, right in front of Baker, at a gym called Club Met-Rx. Baker was quite surprised when he saw the news stories about Bill's murder.

Nanette had a purpose for the men with whom she chose to be involved, Detective Byington told Baker. "She uses some people for fun, some people for finances," he said.

But her interaction with Baker, he said, was one of the closest to a relationship they'd seen.

Other than Eric Naposki, that is, who was likely the big guy Baker had seen kissing Nanette at Club Met-Rx.


Once detectives obtained Nanette's various records—from her car phone, for example—they took note of a few telling calls from the night of the murder, as well as some other curious activity. Back in those days, mobile-phone bills were nowhere as detailed as they are today. For one thing, they did not list originating numbers for incoming calls, only the time and duration.

On December 8, 1994, a call was made to the Jewelry Exchange in Tustin. When police went through Eric's notebook, they found a notation in the journal for December 23 that stated *the diamond store* on the same page as *Insurance New York.* He also had the store's business card in his wallet, which indicated they were ring shopping—together.

From that, they extrapolated that some of those entries were made before they flew back east over Thanksgiving. (After minimizing their relationship to the police in 1994 as "not solo, total," he confirmed** in 2011 that he and Nanette had been talking about getting married and were ring shopping around December 1994.)

On the day of the murder, the detectives learned, Nanette had purchased a $364 pair of horned alligator boots and a matching belt, exchanging a cheaper pair of black lizard boots she'd bought two weeks earlier for the nicest boots in the store.

"These are for my boyfriend, who plays in the NFL," she told the clerk.

Later that night, at eight twenty-four, a call was made from Nanette's car to pick up voice mail messages, followed by a call a minute later to a number that was one digit off Eric's business phone.

At 9:52 P.M., Nanette's car phone received a two-minute call, just minutes after she was done shopping and before she pulled up to the house. This could have been an "all-clear" or "done-deal" message, signaling that it was okay to return to Balboa Coves.

Police believed that Nanette checked her voice mail at 8:24 P.M. as she and Eric were driving toward Newport Beach. She dropped Naposki off somewhere—it's unclear where, although they both claimed that she took him to his apartment—but police believed she probably dropped him at the bridge next to Balboa Coves before she sped off to the mall.

The detectives found it curious that shortly after they interviewed her and escorted her back to the Seashore house at 12:51 A.M., she went outside to retrieve her messages from her car phone at 1:36 A.M. Nanette then called Eric's pager at 1:37 A.M. rather than using the landline inside. Was this so the call wouldn't show up on the bill, or was she driving while talking? The detectives believed it was the latter, because she got a four-minute incoming call two minutes later.

The detectives timed the drive, and it took four minutes to get from the Seashore house to the Thunderbird, which was about 450 feet—a little longer than a football field, or a two-and-a-half-minute walk—from the McLaughlin house. Eric had just started working at the nightclub on December 1. Coincidence?

Police believed it was Eric who called Nanette back at 1:39 A.M., and that she picked him up at the Thunderbird. They don't know whether she took him home to his apartment in Tustin, or back to the house rented by his friend and on-and-off-roommate, Leonard Jomsky, where Eric may have parked his truck, as he later claimed.

Either way, the records showed she called him at his apartment at 9:09 A.M. later that day.

# CHAPTER 13

It wasn't all that easy to piece together the intimate details of Nanette Anne Maneckshaw Johnston Packard's life, especially her childhood and formative years. The few close friends and family who were still standing by her formed a pact not to talk to anyone, apparently to keep her background private and her secrets from being revealed.

"They're a close family, but they don't like to address issues," said Billy McNeal, her third husband, whose last name she never took.

Keeping secrets has always had an underlying purpose for Nanette. As she progressed from one stage of her life and one con to the next, it's evident that she tried to keep her various groups of friends and associates away from each other, to prevent them from comparing stories. This enabled her to perpetually reinvent herself and to tell different stories in different situations to her benefit, so much so that it was difficult for the people who knew her—or thought they knew her—to determine what was fact and what was fiction.

"It's crazy the lengths she went to to create these stories

and compartmentalize everything," Billy said. "It was the perfect puzzle no one could ever put together."

Despite Nanette's efforts to keep the truth hidden, however, in the end she couldn't hide who she really was: a person who spun a web of deceit, told tall tales of the person she truly wanted to be, and adopted the accomplishments of the people she most admired.

In the final analysis, it seems that what she really wanted was to be someone successful and respected—and, most of all, someone other than herself.

On July 3, 1965, in Chicago, Nanette was the first child born to Adi and Margaret "Marge" Ann Maneckshaw.

Now in his early seventies, Adi immigrated to the United States from Bombay, India, on a thirty-day voyage aboard the *Queen Mary,* during which he had to eat so much spaghetti that he vowed never to eat it again.

From photos, Marge, whose maiden name was Johnson, appears to have had reddish brown hair and freckles. She graduated in the class of 1961 from the now-defunct Alvernia High School, an all-girls Catholic school run by the School Sisters of St. Francis, on the Northwest Side of Chicago.

Adi's dark complexion and Indian features were passed on to Nanette's brother and two sisters. Nanette has her father's dark eyes, but her skin tone and hair seem lighter than her siblings'. Nanette also appears to have inherited her mother's nose, chin, and facial shape, features that she wanted to alter through cosmetic surgery.

Nanette's oldest daughter, Lishele, whose married name is Wigand, is a brunette with an even lighter complexion than Nanette. A trace of her Indian heritage is still visible in her features, but she seems more proud of and open about them than her mother was.

In Lishele's cooking blog, "Nutrish by Lish," she took note of her family's ethnic ancestry, sharing recipes such as curry crusted chicken. The dish's caption read: *Since I am Indian, I have to master the curry dishes!* (She also noted that *I met my husband in church and married him quickly.*)

Adi and Marge had four children: Nanette, Michele, Jimmy, and Stephanie, in that order. They apparently moved to Maryland at some point, and the couple ultimately got divorced. Nanette later told Billy McNeal that while she was growing up, she and her brother fought with her father.

"Lots of drama," said Billy, who described Nanette, Michele, and Jimmy as "kind of aggressive," compared to Stephanie, who was a "meek, little peacemaker."

Adi, an engineer who worked at the Pentagon, subsequently married a mother of three named Carol, with whom he's been ever since. Adi and Carol now live in Rehoboth Beach, Delaware, where their grown children and extended family come together for a reunion every summer.

After her parents split, Nanette and her siblings moved to Arizona with their mother. Over time, Nanette apparently healed any old wounds from fights with her father, because she had a number of photos featuring the two of them together in family reunion portraits. Nanette, whom Billy characterized as the "mother hen" of her siblings, was still talking by phone with Michele and Jimmy every other week in 2009. That closeness did not exist with her mother, however, from whom Nanette, Michele, and Jimmy had long been estranged.

Billy said Marge Johnson worked as a teacher and later as a probation officer for juvenile offenders in the Phoenix area. At some point, Marge hooked up with a man who Nanette later claimed had inflicted extreme physical abuse on her and her brother. Nanette told Billy that her stepfather had also abused alcohol and drugs, sexually abused one of her siblings, and went to prison for a while on drug-related charges.

"Nanette went as far as to tell me that he broke her arm or leg, and he used to beat her up pretty bad," Billy said.

None of this could be confirmed through official sources, because Nanette never mentioned her stepfather's name, but Billy said he believed her story.

"I'm imagining there's something to it," he said, because to his knowledge Stephanie was the only one of Nanette's siblings who still talked to their mother. The others did not, apparently blaming their mother for allowing the alleged abuse.

Jimmy was in pharmaceutical sales, Billy said, and Stephanie taught grade school in Scottsdale, Arizona, where in the mid-1990s she got married. Michele lived in the Baltimore area. Before Michele had a baby in 2009, Billy said she'd worked in marketing at the National Zoo in Washington, D.C.

Unlike Nanette, who was obsessed with materialism and appearances, Billy said Nanette's siblings "could[n't] care less about money. They live humbly," he said. Even Jimmy, who had done well in his sales career, "doesn't live beyond his means."


Nanette claimed to have graduated early from Greenway High School in Phoenix, leaving at sixteen *and* as the class valedictorian. Nanette purported to K. Ross—whom she met when she was seventeen and he was five years her senior—"that she had ROTC scholarships . . . and that her father wanted her to do that instead of marrying me," he said.

According to Classmates.com, of which Nanette has been a member since 2001, she was in the class of 1983 at Greenway, where her classmates remembered her as "ambitious." Because she didn't come up in an online search of the 1982 or 1983 yearbooks, it looks like she dropped out sometime after 1981, the last year her photo appeared. She later went on to earn a GED, an unnecessary step for a valedictorian.

Nanette also claimed that she'd played on the basketball team (it's unclear if she was referring to high school or college or both), noting that she and her teammates would get really hungry, then go out for hamburgers. But anyone who saw her try to dribble or shoot baskets as an adult could see that she lacked the skills to be a starter, and that she was better suited for the bench or helping out the team manager. That said, she did seem to know quite a bit about the game.

Nanette and Billy McNeal had been together less than a year when she took him to her twentieth high school reunion in 2003. Her former classmates seemed to recognize her, even though she looked quite different since they'd last seen her.

Once they were no longer together, Billy searched through Nanette's personal belongings, looking for answers about the woman he'd thought he'd known. He found a checklist dating back to 1998, noting that she wanted her cheeks, chin, breasts, and nose done. Based on a comparison of recent photos with those taken during her late teens and early twenties, she seemed to have fulfilled her wish list.

Oddly, though, she vehemently insisted to Billy that her ample breasts were real. He said he didn't know any better because he didn't see any of the usual scarring he'd seen with previous girlfriends who'd admitted to having enhancement surgery.

"From day one, she said, 'They're real. They're real. They're real,'" he recalled in 2012.

But she went even further: She also posted a multicolored sparkly sticker with the message *Yes, they're real* in her closet, and that sticker came with her whenever she moved to a new house.

Later he realized that she'd never shown him any photo older than 1999. "Obviously, that was intentional on her part," he said.

Billy recalled a summer around 2007 when they made the annual pilgrimage to Delaware for the Maneckshaw reunion. About twenty relatives were hanging around the house, including Nanette's three siblings, who were gathered together on the couch, paging through photo albums.

"Billy, you've got to see this picture," they said, beckoning him over.

As he examined the snapshots of the girl with the short, curly dark brown hair, he sort of recognized Nanette as a teenager, then a little older, cradling a baby or two.

"Who do you think this is?" they asked.

"Oh, don't show him those pictures," Nanette said, laughing.

He couldn't believe he was looking at the same woman. Nanette had apparently started coloring her hair blond early on, and later, while she was with Billy, she also had it chemically straightened every five months or so. But the girl in the photos looked *really* different.

"That's crazy," he said.

At the time, it didn't register that the young Nanette was flat-chested in those photos, because he was focusing on her face. But she was dead set on keeping her secret.

Early in their relationship, Billy had expressed concern that Nanette's left breast felt stiff and hard to the touch.

"You've got to get that checked out," he told her.

Right before their son was born, he urged her more forcefully to talk to a doctor, because he wanted to see whether she could, in fact, breast-feed their baby. But Nanette dismissed his concerns, telling him that she'd already talked to a physician and there was no problem. Her breast had been this way at least since she'd had her third child, Jaycie.

"A breast can get hard from breast-feeding," she said. Given that she was a mother, three times over, and he was about to have his first child, he didn't question her further.

After Cruz was born, Billy saw her breast-feeding their son, so he didn't worry any more about it. He didn't put two and two together until later, when he found a letter showing that she'd sued the manufacturer of her silicone implants, which had gone bad, and had won a $10,000 settlement.

All of this to hide her breast implants showed just "how far she would go to perpetuate her stories, lies, whatever," Bill said, adding that she also seemed to believe her own lies, which made them harder to detect.

Graduating high school early wasn't a grand enough lie for Nanette. She also bragged that she'd graduated at nineteen from ASU. Her résumé from the early- to mid-1990s, which spelled her name with two *n*'s—as *Nannette A. Johnston*—stated that she'd earned a business administration degree there in 1984.

According to a university spokesperson, Nanette did apply to the college as an undergraduate, but she never enrolled in or attended any classes. Nanette apparently did visit the campus while she and K. Ross were married, but she may have just been walking around, trying to meet men.

Nanette also claimed that she'd earned advanced degrees, including an MBA from ASU. Her marriage license to John Packard stated that she had nineteen years of education.

Under the education section on her résumé, she listed the Bobby Ball Academy, which K. Ross paid for her to attend. According to the *Arizona Republic,* the academy offered training in acting, modeling and stunts to both children and adults. The talent school/agency was run by the late Roberta Helen Ball, who died at eighty-one in April 2009. Those skills must have come in handy when Nanette pretended to be someone she wasn't.

Her résumé also listed Ford Schools, but it didn't specify whether she meant the modeling school or the one that offered continuing education in health and insurance licensing and securities in Phoenix and Tucson.

Finally the résumé stated that she held a life, health, and disability license, which she did, in fact, obtain in 1986, when she lived in Mesa, Arizona. It expired in 1991.


K. Ross Johnston met Nanette Maneckshaw while they were both working at a Nautilus health spa in Arizona. She started there as an aerobics instructor, joined him in sales, and soon became a manager.

In a photo from that period, the short-haired Nanette wore a big grin as she held a game box labeled *The SEX Education Game,* which covered all but two words on the front of her orange-sleeved baseball shirt: *I'm Kevin's.*

Other photos featured the young girl, with soft eyes and a quiet smile, looking almost shy and optimistic. Her unadorned, unrevealing, and almost tomboyish way of dressing as a teenager marked a stark contrast to her later style, which included pricey designer gowns and short strappy dresses, with plunging necklines that revealed cleavage and dipped down in the back.

K. Ross said neither of them made much money back then, noting that Nanette had about $2,000 when they got married in Mesa on November 11, 1983.

In their wedding photos, she looked wide-eyed and virginal in her simple, modest white veil and conservative white dress, which covered her arms with sheer fine netting, showed no cleavage, and was topped with lace that crept up her neck. The happy groom, who had brown hair and a thin, dark moustache, wore a white tuxedo with tails, a dark red bow tie, and a white ruffled shirt, with red edging. As they cut the four-tiered white cake, adorned with decorative wedding bells on the top layer, Nanette appeared to be quite content with her new husband.

As the years progressed, Nanette posed for photos in which her belly was pregnant and swollen, in a high-necked white church dress, with three-quarter sleeves and big ruffles down the front. These shots provided another dramatic contrast to the revealing boudoir photo she later used in her notorious singles ad, in which she wore a white teddy and a feather boa.

K. Ross delivered their first child, Kristofer, at home in the summer of 1985, feeling "beyond ecstasy" to be a parent. Lishele was born two summers later.

"We were very much in love, very much happy to be parents," K. Ross recalled.

Meanwhile, on the professional front, the Johnstons both worked in sales at the Federated Group electronics store. Later they sold time-shares as K. Ross moved into real estate financing.

Nanette's résumé listed the Bud Crawley Real Estate School, although owner Bud Crawley couldn't confirm that she'd attended, and the Arizona Department of Real Estate doesn't have licensing records that old. However, California records show that she did obtain a real estate license in 2006 under the name of Nanette Anne Packard while she was working in Ladera Ranch, an affluent community in Orange County. That license expired in 2010.

When she and K. Ross were first together, he saw Nanette's desire for more money and nice things as a healthy desire and a sign of ambition.

"I didn't think it was out of the ordinary," he said. "I couldn't afford any of the things that she would like."

As Nanette's ambitions evolved, so did her sexuality, evidenced by the changes in her figure and the fashion choices featured in photos that were found on her computer years later. She grew her hair into long, bushy curls, which she either chemically lightened or were bleached by the sun. Her shorts and skirts got shorter, and she went from modest one-piece bathing suits to more skimpy bikinis.

Her loving behavior changed too. "She was dating men before we were separated," K. Ross said, explaining that he discovered she'd been lying to him about going to business meetings at night.

His first clue came when he found one of her business cards on the windshield of an expensive car with this nota-tion: *You caught my eye while driving down Scottsdale Road. If you are unmarried, I'd love to meet you. I will be at "What's Your Beef?" tonight looking for you. Nanette.*

She grew increasingly reckless about hiding her indiscre-tions. On Thanksgiving Day, she showed up in a new BMW, which she said a man named Ted had bought for her. K. Ross ultimately learned that Ted, who lived in Tempe, found out that she'd been cheating on him with a man named Doug, so Ted had the car repossessed about a month later. She owed Ted $1,000, but after writing him a check, she put a stop payment on it. Ted talked to K. Ross by phone and sent him the stop-check notice as proof.

K. Ross's heart was broken. Being a religious man, he also couldn't take the unfaithfulness. Nanette moved out ten days short of their five-year anniversary, and he filed for divorce in February 1989.

"It was five hundred dollars to get a divorce and I had to make payments," he testified, saying that the attorney took half up front and the rest in installments. "There were no assets of any significance."

In family court, K. Ross won sole custody of their two small children. Nanette was ordered to pay $538 a month for child support, and she was allowed time with them every other weekend. The couple was ordered to split the $38,000 debt they owed to K. Ross's parents—but only if Nanette's monthly income grossed more than $2,500.

He moved to California in September 1989. That same year, Nanette got caught writing bad checks—seven of which were bundled into two misdemeanor cases, for which arrest warrants were issued. Two were deemed "not sufficient funds," and the others were written on closed bank accounts, according to the Maricopa County Attorney's Office.

Detective Tom Voth called Maricopa County officials in January 1995, requesting faxed copies of the backup materials on those warrants.

Both charges were ultimately dismissed in paperwork filed as late as 2000, a spokesperson said recently, adding that the two warrants had been "quashed" by the judge and deemed inactive. No additional details were available.

K. Ross Johnston wrote in a 1998 court filing that he moved Nanette to California, paid all her expenses, packed her belongings into a U-Haul truck, and drove it out himself, because he was hoping for a reconciliation.

*But she did not follow through,* he wrote. *She quickly obtained a post office box and within thirty days, she was gone again, leaving the children with me.*

K. Ross recalled this story differently when he testified in 2012, saying that Nanette came out to visit him in California, and surprised him by saying she wanted to get back together. He wanted to forgive her, to feel the bliss they'd once felt together.

"I was ecstatic," he recalled. "An answer to prayer. Many prayers."

The day she moved in, he got a call from her father asking where she was.

"She's right here," K. Ross told him.

He handed the phone to Nanette, who told her dad that she and her ex-husband were getting back together. K. Ross didn't quite know what to make of this. Why hadn't she told her family that they were reuniting?

"It was a shocker," K. Ross recalled.

They'd been together for four days when one of Nanette's ex-boyfriends showed up at the home of K. Ross's nephew in Arizona. The boyfriend, also unaware of her whereabouts, asked where she was.

"She's at Kevin's," the nephew said, referring to K. Ross.

"No way," the boyfriend said.

By this point, K. Ross recalled, he could see that she wasn't serious about giving him another chance. And the renewed possibility of a future together quickly faded to black, once he learned that she was placing singles ads in magazines. Within a month, she was gone, looking for the next big thing.

# CHAPTER 14

That next big thing, as it turned out, was a six-foot-tall twenty-eight-year-old named Tom Reynolds, who had literally been a choirboy.

One night in September 1990, Nanette showed up at the Red Onion in Santa Ana and stood by the front door, talking to Reynolds, who was working security. He offered to "buy" her a drink, a perk of his job, and followed up with another.

As they were sipping Long Island Iced Teas, she said she'd just left Arizona and was still getting situated in Orange County, trying to get away from her ex-husband, who was attempting to win primary custody of her two young children. Although she didn't mention where they were that night—and Reynolds didn't ask—she said she was scared that her ex would take them away from her.

Alluding to an arrangement with a landlord, Nanette said she was going to live in a house on the peninsula in Newport Beach, but because the place was undergoing renovations, she didn't really know where she was going to sleep that night. Not one to ignore an obvious opportunity to take an attractive and willing woman home, Reynolds brought her back to the three-bedroom house he shared with two female roommates in Huntington Beach.

Months later, he learned that Nanette had nowhere else to go that night because she'd been evicted from her apartment for not paying rent. In contrast, Reynolds said, he had perfect credit and had been working two jobs since he'd moved to Orange County from upstate New York recently.

There was no courtship, and no dating; Nanette just never left. What started as a one-night stand sped straight into a hot and heavy sexual tryst, followed by a relatively quick decision to move in together at her new place—a two-bedroom duplex that had just been remodeled out of a two-story home. Because it was unfurnished and she had no job, Nanette expected Reynolds to pay the move-in expenses and buy all new furniture.

Within the next several months, Reynolds's life and his relationship with Nanette would take a short trip to hell, putting him $91,000 in debt, with a domestic violence arrest on his record and a bankruptcy filing, to boot.


In the first few weeks of meeting Nanette, Reynolds went to his two jobs, but he had no idea what she did during the day except go to the beach and supposedly look for a sales job.

She showed up at the Red Onion at night, but after Reynolds told her she couldn't keep hanging around the door with him, she didn't seem to mind mingling with other patrons. And when they got home, she was always sexually available, which was a good trade-off for a guy who had been happily uncommitted before this woman started laying a claim to his bed every night.

Nanette never said much about her upbringing. She

didn't talk about her father and virtually dismissed the subject of her mother, whom she painted as a pathetic woman with substance abuse and emotional problems. Reynolds pictured an older woman sitting alone in a cluttered apartment in Arizona, with a bottle of gin in hand, a lifestyle that Nanette seemed determined to rise above.

Characterizing herself as a victim, Nanette made it sound like "she was going to end up being someone much better, and she was going to succeed at what she did," Reynolds recalled in 2012, now a businessman with his own company, a husband of thirteen years and a father of four.

Once, after sex, they were examining each other's scars and telling the stories behind them. After showing Nanette the gash on his knee from the swimming hole in New York, he asked about the small, round scar on one of her butt cheeks. Nanette replied vaguely that it was from a cigarette burn. Reynolds didn't push for more details, because it was the appropriate size and shape to fit that story.

Nanette indicated she'd been born and raised in Arizona, or at least let Reynolds believe that's where she was from, and said she'd put herself through college there. She mentioned a sister somewhere back east, but no other siblings.

From how she talked about her family—or didn't— Reynolds got the idea they wouldn't be attending any intimate family dinners together at Thanksgiving or Christmas. Other than her two kids, Nanette made it sound like she was doing it alone and depended on Reynolds to take care of her needs, especially given her ongoing custody battle with her ex-husband.

She said she'd "gotten weighed down by her ex, who had pretty much forced her to flee Arizona with her kids to California." When she'd first mentioned K. Ross, she gave the impression that she was hiding from him. And then it was "Oh, my God, he's found me."

* * *

When Reynolds had driven across the country to California in a U-Haul van some months earlier, he hadn't wasted any time before taking off for his first-ever trip to Las Vegas, which coincided with the grand opening of the upscale Mirage hotel and casino.

During his stay there, he scored a surprising win of $28,000 while playing blackjack at a $5 table, and left town before he could lose it. He was subsequently courted by the hotel, which treated him like a "whale," meaning that he was assigned a personal casino host to persuade him to continue betting and spending money. When he took Nanette with him, they were treated with extra special personal service.

"Oh, this is your beautiful companion," the host said. "Is there anything I can get you?"

Given this royal treatment, Nanette most likely believed that Reynolds either had money to spend, or that he was willing to burn through whatever cash he had so they could live in style. She proceeded to help him do so, not only racking up charges on his several credit cards, but taking advantage of their cash-advance features as well.

"I need something for Kristofer," she told him.


They'd been together about six weeks, when Reynolds saw the first red flag, right after another winning trip to Vegas. This time it was $8,000.

In those days of computer-network infancy, he wasn't able to deposit his out-of-state profits directly into his Bank of America account, so he wired the money back to Nanette and asked her to deposit it in two chunks for tax purposes: $3,000 one day, and $5,000 the next. But when he got home and looked at his account balance, he saw that it was $2,500 short. He asked the bank to check, but the money was just, well, gone.

This was his first relationship since he'd been in California. When Reynolds asked Nanette about the money, she came up with some excuse he didn't really believe, but the seed was planted. Something wasn't quite right.

"I confronted her," he recalled, but "it didn't escalate to anything."

The fact that they were about to move in together had something to do with it. Two days after he returned from Las Vegas, they used most of his remaining winnings to buy $4,800 worth of furniture for the duplex on Balboa Boulevard, which rented for something like $1,800—no small sum in 1990.

"I wasn't used to having money," he said. "It was like winning the lotto."

It was Nanette's idea that they move into the beach house together. There was plenty of room, she told him, and they would have more privacy than they did in his bohemian apartment life, with roommates roaming around all the time.

"We're better than this," she said. "We're a couple. They've got friends coming and going."

Besides, he was pretty taken with Nanette by this point. He quit his job at the Red Onion so he could spend more time with her, and he also traded in his job selling audiovisual equipment in Lakeview for a more prestigious gig selling luxury cars in Newport. It was a step up the career ladder, he thought, and a more fitting job for this new chapter in his life. To top it off, he got to drive a new Jaguar instead of his ratty old Supra.

He and Nanette took more trips to Vegas, spending as much as $7,000 for room service at the Mirage. On one trip in October 1990, they got ringside seats for the Evander Holyfield versus Buster Douglas boxing match. And because they were spending good money at the hotel, they were comped with Dom Pérignon and shrimp in their room before the fight.

But mostly, he and Nanette spent too much of Reynolds's money trying to keep up with their new image and lifestyle at the beach house.

"Here I was, living it up," he said. "It was something I was not accustomed to."

Some of his friends tried to warn him when they saw him living on the edge of financial responsibility.

"What, are you an idiot?" one buddy asked. "Are you following your [penis] now?"

Still, Reynolds wanted to trust her. Wasn't that what you were supposed to do when you lived with someone? Plus, she'd started contributing some money toward the rent.

Reynolds felt a little better once Nanette finally got a job—as a sales rep for an industrial cleaning-materials company. She worked out of the house, and the firm supplied a Dodge Caravan for her to meet with clients and to carry samples. Her frequent "business trips" however, soon became a source of conflict.

One time, when she was supposedly out of town, he tried to call her at 10:30 P.M. and she spoke to him as if he were a stranger. Claiming she was in a meeting, she acted cold and distant, and didn't call him back until the next morning.

Then, around Christmas, Nanette began playing psychological games with him. Chatting with her sister on the phone, he overheard her say, "Tom is probably going to get me a ring for Christmas, but it will just be a 'this-woman-is-taken' ring. It definitely won't be an engagement ring."

"Well, that's a nice thing to say," he said, feeling hurt. "What if I did want to get you an engagement ring?"

* * *

The next red flag was a guy named Bob, whom Reynolds found pacing outside the duplex one evening. Bob, one of Nanette's ex-boyfriends, said he was looking for her because she'd racked up a bunch of charges on his credit card.

"You'd better watch out," Bob cautioned. "Don't trust her."

When Bob said Nanette liked to keep a "jackhammer" next to the bed, Reynolds figured he had to know something, because Nanette definitely liked her vibrator.

But when he mentioned Bob to Nanette, she dismissed him as "some crazy stalker." Yes, she'd known him, she said, but "he was infatuated" with her and "couldn't get enough."

Reynolds came home another evening to find a phone message for Nanette from a guy named Dan. After that, he started hitting redial on the phone as soon as he walked in the door.

"I was watching my back all the time," Reynolds recalled.

After he'd caught her lying again, in January 1991— saying she was out of town when friends had seen her around Newport Beach—he decided to investigate more closely. Although his mother had taught him never to go searching through a woman's purse, he thought dire measures were in order. He climbed into her van for a looksee, and what he discovered only confirmed his suspicions.

In a small lockbox, which he pried open with a screwdriver, he found a collection of letters addressed to a post office box, photos from men introducing themselves with platitudes about how they liked taking walks on the beach, and a canceled $25 check for a personal ad in *Singles Connection*.

He immediately went out and bought a copy of the magazine, a sort of "*AutoTrader* for sex." He was horrified to see a softly lit glamour shot of Nanette, wearing a skimpy "come-hither" top in the ad, titled, "For Wealthy Men Only."

When Nanette showed up, he confronted her. "What the fuck is this?" he asked.

Her response completely surprised him. "Well, what do you expect?" she said coldly. "You're a loser. You're going nowhere. You drove me to this."

After being so angry, Reynolds somehow found himself on the defensive, trying to stick up for his manhood and deny that he was pathetic. But he quickly returned to feeling angry.

"I'm paying the bills. I treat you nice. With respect," he said. "You're a whore. Why would you be looking elsewhere?"

"Because I have to," she said. "You've made me do that."

"We're over," he said.

He had no idea what would happen next. This was her house, after all. But before he had a chance to say that he was leaving her, she surprised him again.

"So what," she said, "I'm leaving you. I've already got a place. You're so stupid, you didn't even know what's going on. Why would I stay with someone who can't even tell I'm cheating on them?"

Things escalated from there. In 2012, as he recounted the following events, he said some of the memories may have blended together from two separate incidents when the Newport Beach police were called in January 1991. However, this was his best recollection of what happened.

Nanette started packing and loading up her van, starting with his little TV.

"No, you don't," he said. "That's mine. I paid for that."

Nanette took the TV out of the van and purposely dropped it on the ground. The glass screen shattered—a warning of sorts. Then she turned around and walked into the house to get more stuff. He followed her up the stairs, hoping to get an explanation of what was happening.

She turned to him with a callous, snide expression and said, "I've got you by the cojones."

Then she slapped the inside of her arm hard enough to leave a red mark. "You just did that," she said.

"You fucking liar," he said.

But he was taken aback even more when she flew at him in a flurry of fists, knees, and feet. It was all he could do to fend her off. He threw her down on the couch to get her off him.

*Oh, my God*, s*he's setting me up,* he thought.

He ran upstairs to the master bedroom to get away from her and try to process what was going on. In the meantime, she called the police.

When the cops arrived, Nanette told them that Reynolds had attacked her.

"He assaulted me for no reason," she said.

Reynolds tried to explain to the police what had happened, just as he did several years later when they questioned him during the McLaughlin murder investigation.

"She was actually assaulting me," he said. "I actually pushed her away. She went down on the couch."

Police didn't immediately arrest Reynolds that first time in 1991. They tried to tell him to leave the house and cool off somewhere, but Reynolds was insistent that they understand his side of the story.

"Wait a minute," he said, "*she* did this."

"Don't make me tell you again," the officer said. "Hit it. Walk on down the sidewalk. Go to a friend's."

Reynolds tried again. "But wait a minute. You don't understand."

When he wouldn't leave, as instructed, the police arrested him on charges of domestic violence and kept him overnight in the lockup.

"All of a sudden, there's this just vicious, hating person,

lying or saying you're a loser, and I'm trying to explain things to police," he recalled recently.

He came home the next morning, but because he didn't have his keys, he had to climb through the window. Nanette didn't return for a couple of days, and he later learned that she'd claimed she'd been in the hospital with an injury to her spleen.

In 1994, Reynolds acknowledged to Newport Beach police that after they'd arrested him in 1991, someone from the DA's office said they had to file charges against him. But he also said he'd watched Nanette sign paperwork at the DA's office, admitting that the fight was mutual and that her injuries were unintentional. However, he still had to attend a diversion program, and the charges were expunged after six months.

In 2012, the NBPD had no record of the 1991 arrest, because it shreds records after a certain period of time, unless they pertain to a homicide. Reynolds said he didn't keep any of his paperwork, because this was not an incident he wanted to remember, and no criminal court records of this incident exist today.

According to family court records filed by K. Ross Johnston in 1998, Nanette called him after Reynolds was arrested, asking K. Ross to pick up the kids because she was going to the hospital after fighting with Reynolds, and he was going to jail. Those records also quote K. Ross as saying that Nanette filed charges against Reynolds, but then dropped them. This wasn't technically accurate, but it did support Reynolds's story.

While Nanette was purportedly in the hospital, Reynolds said he met with K. Ross, who brought a six-inch-thick file of incriminating evidence against Nanette. "He came over to my house and he wanted copies of everything I had," Reynolds recalled.

K. Ross told him he was interested in getting something

on Nanette in case they had custody issues and she tried to stop him from seeing the kids. The two men shared some of the same stories about hearing unfamiliar male voices on the answering machine and her lies about going to business meetings at night when she was really out on dates with other men. Reynolds now knew where his missing $2,500 in Las Vegas winnings had gone.

Soon after that, Reynolds came home from work to find Nanette loading the new furniture he'd recently purchased into her van.

"You try and stop me," she said, "and I'll have you arrested again."

Accepting the dare, Reynolds called the police himself this time. When the officers arrived, Nanette tried to enlist them in helping her take his furniture.

"He's on probation. He's assaulting me," she said. "Get him away from me."

Reynolds told police to wait, because he had receipts for these items. Once he brought them proof, the officers told Nanette she needed to leave everything in the house, except her clothing and personal belongings. She'd have to fight Reynolds in civil court for the rest.

Even so, Nanette managed to get away with another television set. "That's my TV," she told police.

Days later, Reynolds demanded that she bring back his TV. She did as he asked, then seduced him on the living-room floor. Reynolds chalked this up to irrational and lustful breakup sex, thinking to himself, *Why not?*

"She just had her way," he recalled recently. "She was very good at the things that she did."

Not long afterward, Reynolds looked out his kitchen window to see Nanette making out with Dan, the contractor who had remodeled the duplex and had left that message on their answering machine.

"Do you think that [make-out session] was for your benefit?" Detective Voth asked Reynolds in 1994.

"I think so," he said.

By this point, Reynolds was $91,000 in debt, part of which came from a $10,000 "marker" that his Mirage casino host told him about after the breakup. Apparently, Nanette had charged that amount to his account without his knowledge. Reynolds had to file for bankruptcy.

After Bill McLaughlin's murder in 1994, K. Ross's girlfriend, Julia, suggested that Detectives Voth and Hartford contact Reynolds, which they did.

During the interview, they told Reynolds that Nanette had, in fact, found her wealthy man—one worth about $55 million.

"He's now dead," Hartford said. "Died at the hand of somebody else."

"I'm not surprised," Reynolds said, adding that he'd had his suspicions as soon as he heard about the murder on the news. He'd even called the Orange County jail to see if they had an inmate named Nanette Johnston.

"She was extremely manipulative," he said.

# CHAPTER 15

To Detective Tom Voth, the two keys left in the McLaughlins' front door and on their doormat seemed "key" to solving this case, because so few people had access to them. One of the keys was embossed with an Ace Hardware logo; the other key was simply stamped *Ace*.

"You're boiling down to family, and friends of family, and Nanette," he recalled in 2011. Although the housekeeper, Mary Berg, kept a house key pinned to the inside of her shirt, Voth saw no benefit to her killing Bill. Besides, she was never given a key to the pedestrian-access gate.

"It put the suspects into a little package, a percentage of less than one percent in the world," he said, which got even smaller once the McLaughlin sisters passed their polygraphs.

Voth suggested to one of his supervisors that he take the keys to area hardware stores and show them a photo lineup featuring Eric, but he was told he would be wasting his time.

"Who's going to remember who's getting a key made?" the supervisor asked.

But Voth was determined to figure out the keys' origin. Searching through the phone book, he found an Ace Hardware store on West Main Street in Tustin, called Tustin Hardware, right down the street from Eric's apartment.

He went there and showed the keys to manager David Vandaveer, who said they used the same type of "blanks" as the one Voth showed him, embossed with the national chain's Ace logo. Although he said they usually stamped the store name and phone number on the back of their key copies, he said, they'd recently sold some without the stamp, like this one. Vandaveer later testified that he thought the key had been made in his store because of the way it was cut: he had a higher-quality key-cutting machine that cost three times more than machines used by other stores.

When Voth showed him the photo lineup, Vandaveer recognized Eric right away.

"Yeah, I know this guy right here," he said, which surprised Voth as much as it did his supervisor. "This guy is from New York. He works for me."

Vandaveer went on to say that he'd headed the committee that had chosen Eric to head up security for Tiller Days, a three-day annual agricultural festival in Tustin.

Voth couldn't believe it. "Did he have any keys made?" he asked hopefully.

"Yeah, he had a couple keys made," on a couple of different occasions, sometime after Tiller Days, which was in October, Vandaveer said. "You might want to talk to one of my guys. He made something else for him."

Vandaveer's employee Michael Rivers told Voth that he'd responded to an unusual request from Eric. "I made a fake silencer for him," he said.

Rivers explained that Eric had come in to get a key copied around the time of Tiller Days, and asked if they could make a silencer for his nine-millimeter Beretta to use as a movie prop. Rivers said yes, he could rig something up. He went in the back to put a contraption together, using a piece of plumbing pipe with an adapter at the end. Eric said he was worried about scratching his gun, so they discussed taping the device to the weapon.

If Eric's gun was stolen in the summer, as he'd told police, then why did he ask for a fake silencer to fit it in October or November? For Voth, this wasn't a question of whether the silencer would work. Rather, it was more important in the context of Eric's conflicting statements about when he still had possession of the nine-millimeter. The detectives also never found any evidence that Eric had been involved in a movie in which he needed such a prop.

In another key-related incident, Detective Hartford interviewed Bill's college buddy Don Kalal, who said he was going to stay at Balboa Coves for a couple of days two months before the murder. Nanette was supposed to mail him the house keys, but he never received them.

Bill said that he'd sent the keys in an envelope, with a return address in Las Vegas, and assumed they'd gotten lost in the mail, because the envelope never came back. When a week went by and the keys still hadn't shown up, Bill confirmed with Kalal that he had sent it to the correct address.

On January 26, 1995, the same day as this interview with Kalal, Nanette's attorney called the detectives and told them not to speak to his client any further.

Roy Rauschklob, who had been the head of security at Metropolis and hired Eric to work there in August or September 1992, told police he saw Eric and Nanette at the movies at Triangle Square on February 20, 1995. Nanette looked stressed-out.

When Rauschklob asked them how they were doing, Nanette replied, "Ninety percent of what is in the news is made-up, and only ten percent is true."

On February 23, 1995, police booked into evidence a "change of address" form authorizing Bill's mail to be forwarded from Balboa Coves to the house on Seashore Drive. It was dated December 28, 1994, with the alleged signature of William McLaughlin, who had been dead for two weeks. Detectives saw this as Nanette's attempt to divert incoming mail and hide her covert activities from Bill's family.

During this time, detectives conducted a multitude of timed driving tests on various routes from the soccer field in Diamond Bar to Eric's apartment in Tustin and then to possible drop-off areas near the McLaughlin house. They also drove directly from the field to Balboa Coves, which took thirty-five minutes to drive the 35.7 miles.

In every scenario they tried, they determined that the trips—the longest of which took forty-one minutes—still left enough time for Eric to shoot Bill before the 911 call, then walk or run across the bridge to the Thunderbird, where coworkers remembered seeing him between 9:30 and 10:00 P.M.

In addition, the detectives tested Nanette's story by timing the trips from Eric's apartment to South Coast Plaza, where they parked and went inside Crate & Barrel. The earliest arrival time got them inside the store by 9:19 P.M., leaving her ten minutes to buy what she needed before the nine twenty-nine time-stamped on her receipt. The maximum drive time of fourteen minutes still got her inside by 9:26 P.M.

On March 2 at 4:30 P.M., the detectives carried out a search warrant at the Seashore house. After Nanette had made such a fuss about not wanting any guns around her kids, the police found two of them: a nine-millimeter Astra, dating back to the World War Two era, and a .380 Davis. Neither was on the ballistics test list of possible murder weapons, but Voth found it curious that Nanette would have them at the house.

"They're Bill's guns," she said. "I brought them here for protection."

Because the guns weren't listed on the warrant, the police couldn't seize them. Detective Dave Byington told Nanette's attorney that she needed to bring them down to the station because they didn't belong to her.

The next day, James Box, the investigator working for Eric's attorney, Julian Bailey, brought in the guns as requested.

"Nanette was paying for everyone's attorneys . . . with Bill's money," Voth said. "Where else would she get any money to pay for it?"

# CHAPTER 16

After Nanette and K. Ross Johnston divorced, they agreed that she would introduce him to anyone she was dating, because he wanted to meet the men spending time with his children. Even so, she never told him that she was romantically involved with Bill McLaughlin, let alone that they were engaged. Instead, she concocted a story that she was paying $800 a month to rent a room at a house with Bill, whom she described as an "old man" who was hardly ever home.

"I just knew he was gone a lot, traveling, business," K. Ross said later.

K. Ross met Bill just once, in the spring of 1994, when K. Ross came to pick up the kids. Nanette had said that Bill hated him, so K. Ross was quite surprised when Bill ran over to shake his hand and appeared very pleased to meet him. Nanette, on the other hand, did not look happy.

During this time, Nanette said she was "working deals, looking at options, buying stocks" with Bill, and was also helping him with a Mexican village development. Still, she said it wasn't like working a real job.

Nanette's ex knew something was up because she'd been

driving an old car and suddenly showed up in a brand-new red Infiniti. She claimed that she'd bought it with a commission from a really good deal she'd done with Bill.

K. Ross initially thought she was holding to their agreement because she'd introduced him to other men she was dating, who were all closer to her own age, such as Eric Naposki. Eric was around for multiple sports seasons, first as a friend, and later as a lover, a change that became obvious when she started sitting in his lap.

"I didn't see any that were fat and ugly," K. Ross said, listing off half-a-dozen men she'd brought to games or birthday parties while living with Bill.

One day, Kristofer had two games. She brought Eric to the one in the morning, then showed up with a different guy that afternoon. Eric came by for the second game as well and stuck around to watch. At the end of the day, Nanette said good-bye to the other guy and left with Eric.

Although he had no proof, K. Ross figured she was dating Bill as well "because of the amount of time they were spending together," he said. "I'm thinking, 'What's going to happen?'"

But as it turned out, Nanette had no worries about running into Bill while she was with Eric. After raising three kids of his own, Bill had told her that he had no interest in going to watch Kristofer's sporting activities.


While Bill was busy fighting his legal battle with Jacob Horowitz, and flying back and forth to Las Vegas, Nanette was playing both sides against the middle.

Eric was obviously not the first man she slept with behind Bill's back. Eric simply lasted longer than the others. In 1993, she was seeing a guy named Scott Weisman, who told detectives that she'd broken up with him to start seeing Eric.

By May 1994, things were going well enough with Eric that she secretly took him to Chicago to meet her grandmother and then on to Jamaica for a romantic vacation.

Two months later, she and Eric were house hunting at the Turtle Rock Summit Estates development in Irvine, where model home prices ranged from $800,000 to $2 million, completely out of the couple's range. Nanette came to look by herself the first time, and returned a week later with Eric, telling realtor Sharon Hedberg that they had a family with four kids. They never said they were married, but that was Hedberg's impression.

Nanette and Eric seemed excited about two particular lots, priced between $900,000 and $930,000, with a $25,000 down payment. The couple said they were looking for a home that would be ready by spring 1995, because they didn't have the money to buy just yet.

Nanette told Hedberg that she wrote business plans for money, and Eric was planning to form a security company. They asked if Hedberg knew anyone who needed security services, and Hedberg referred them to someone at Standard Pacific who might be interested. The realtor never saw or talked to them again.

On the nights that Bill was out of town, Nanette stayed at Eric's apartment in Tustin, hung out with him at the Seashore house, or went to dinner and clubbing with his friends. She also often picked up the check as she spun tales that made her seem wealthier, more educated, and more successful than she really was.

As the relationship between her and Eric grew more serious, he invited her and her kids to New York for Thanksgiving with his family. They left on November 14, shopped and saw the sights in New York City, and took photos of themselves with the Statue of Liberty and the Twin Towers in the background.

On the same trip, she took him to her sister's wedding in Baltimore, where she caught the bouquet, and in a very public display, Eric slipped the garter belt on Nanette's upper thigh. Typically, both of these wedding milestones are signs that the "lucky" guests are about to get married.

When Nanette was with her family back east, Eric was her boyfriend and Bill was a fatherly mentor. But at home with Bill, Eric was Nanette's six-foot-two, 250-pound, Polish-Italian secret.

Meanwhile, Nanette was also trying to work her family-planning wiles with Bill, presumably as a way to guarantee access to his assets for the long term.

"You've got to get that vasectomy reversed," Nanette said to him one Friday night in June 1994 as she ogled the babies at the next table at JACKshrimp, where they were having dinner with Kevin and Sandy. It seemed like a casual comment made in passing, just a blip in the conversation before they moved on to other topics, but Nanette could be subtle that way.

Bill clearly enjoyed the company of Nanette's children, and he treated Lishele and Kristofer with love and kindness. Apparently having no idea she was cheating on him, Bill seemed to give Nanette more latitude in his business affairs, or, perhaps, she was just taking it without his knowledge. He surely couldn't have known that she'd started pretending to *be* Bill McLaughlin, claiming that *she* had invented the blood-separator device, and telling people that she had hundreds of thousands of dollars to invest in various projects.

Bill's cousin Barbara LaSpesa said she thought Nanette

must have been a "smooth talker" and that the couple must have discussed Nanette's needs and wants. He probably believed he deserved to be happy, and if it "cost him a few dollars, it cost him," Barbara said, speculating that he gave Nanette what she wanted because he was scared of losing her.

Barbara said that because Bill had forced his ex-wife, Sue, to live so frugally, "I sometimes wonder if he felt guilty about that, because he did lose her and [tried] to make it up with this woman."

After Bill was so careful with his money while married to Sue, Barbara said, she couldn't believe how different he was with Nanette. "I remember he had a boat, and then he got rid of the boat, because it cost so much for gas and he wasn't using it."

He had to have known "what he was getting into when he answered the ad, because it plainly stated what this woman was looking for. I wondered if after he'd lost his wife, maybe it dawned on him, 'I have to pay for it.'"

Barbara speculated that some male ego was at work as well. "He's buying everything she's giving him, but he's going to believe it, because who's going to lie to Bill? He's so smart. That's what kills me about this whole thing. He puts her on a life insurance policy. . . . He ends up being with this woman who took all his money."

Nonetheless, she said, "he shouldn't have died for it. That's the unfortunate part. He had Kevin living with him. . . . The whole thing is tragic. I just feel bad for all of them. . . . There were red flags there—and, obviously, he didn't see them, didn't want to see them."

Bill's brother Patrick, however, believes today that Bill actually did have a clue. When the two men talked the night before Bill was murdered, Patrick sensed that Bill was on edge, angry, and "extremely shaken by what he thought was happening."

"He thought he was a wanted man or a guy who was a

targeted man, for whatever reason, and I think he also felt that he should try to be up for whatever came his way, and he was going to fight 'em off," Patrick recalled recently.

Bill never mentioned who was after him or why, but he did tell Patrick that night that "he'd stocked his home with firearms and ammunition."

"What the hell are you talking about?" Patrick asked his brother, confused because Bill had never mentioned his gun collecting.

"Broth, you have no idea," Bill said, using the nickname the two brothers had called each other since they'd started working together in business many years earlier.

Patrick said he also believes that Bill never disclosed any of this previously because he was too proud and embarrassed.

"Bill always prided himself with not pulling the wool over his eyes, and that may have been why we never discussed it," he said.

But he also wonders if Bill might have finally figured out that Nanette had been "helping herself to his checking account."

At least in the short term, Nanette's children got something out of their mother's double-dealing behavior, because they benefited from Bill's money, the lavish trips he paid for, and the extra fatherly attention that he gave them. And when Bill said he didn't want to traipse around to soccer, basketball, or baseball games, it didn't matter because Nanette had Eric for that, and the kids liked him too.

Nanette played the part of the soccer mom well, driving Kristofer and his teammates to games and bringing them sliced oranges to eat at halftime. She even went one better and became assistant coach to Kristofer's basketball team during the 1994 fall season.

But even then, Nanette didn't impress everyone with her Supermom act.

"She was trying to definitely let the world think she was a good mother with her two older kids," said Patricia "Tricia" Stearns, who lived down the street from the Seashore Drive house, which Nanette said was hers. Basketball star Dennis Rodman lived in a house somewhere in between them.

Stearns's boyfriend, Fernando Leguizamon, coached Kristofer's National Junior Basketball League team and chose Nanette—over the team fathers who were also interested in the job—to be his assistant coach.

"She's the best one of the bunch," Leguizamon told Stearns. "She really knows the game."

Nanette told Stearns that she was very pleased—and genuinely surprised—to be selected.

"She really sold herself well," Stearns recalled. "The guys teased Fernando, 'Oh, you picked her over all of us.'"

Stearns and her boyfriend, who had a boy and a girl about the same age as Kristofer and Lishele, thought Nanette had only one boyfriend—Eric Naposki, because he was the one who accompanied her to many of Kristofer's games and practices. Stearns knew that Eric had his own apartment, but she got the impression that he spent quite a bit of time at the Seashore house.

When Leguizamon's kids went down to play with Nanette's on the beach, Eric was often there as well, talking to the boys about working out.

"The kids loved him because he was a football player," said Stearns, who believed that this idolization also contributed to Nanette's landing the coaching position. "Fernando's son was just enamored with Eric."

Stearns, on the other hand, felt very different. "I couldn't stand him," she said. "He was an arrogant SOB. He's a ne'er-do-well, as it turned out."

Stearns met Nanette early in the season. As they chatted

during the weekly practices and games, Nanette told her that she had an MBA, that she wanted to start a professional women's basketball league, and that she wanted to play too.

"She professed to be an absolute fanatic on basketball," Stearns recalled.

But within just a few short weeks, Stearns had figured out that Nanette was not what or who she claimed to be.

"She always boasted about her background and her education and how smart she was," Stearns said.

Stearns worked in the health care field and was familiar with Baxter Healthcare and Bill's plasma-separator device. So when Nanette claimed to have invented it herself and described Bill as her business partner, Stearns immediately knew she was lying.

"It was to a point that I knew too much," she said.

Nonetheless, she didn't want to confront Nanette, especially after the murder, so she kept quiet.

"It was so obviously an inside job," Stearns said. "You had to have had a key."

# CHAPTER 17

On the morning of January 19, 1995, half-a-dozen detectives showed up with a search warrant at Eric's two-bedroom condo in Irvine, where Nanette, Eric, his twenty-five-year-old roommate, Leonard Jomsky, and a couple of Eric's visiting friends were hanging out after a night of partying.

As Detective Voth talked briefly with Eric outside the apartment, Eric said he'd heard the murder involved a love triangle.

"Why me?" he asked.

While several detectives searched the apartment, Tom Voth and Craig Frizzell interviewed Eric for several hours. Detective Dave Byington pulled Jomsky into the bedroom to question him, and Lieutenant Mike Jackson and Sergeant John Desmond took Nanette back to the Seashore house to interview her there.

Although Eric grumbled that he didn't want to talk without an attorney, he wasn't under arrest, they didn't read him his rights, and he kept on talking.

As Voth and Frizzell pushed Eric to talk more about his nine-millimeter, he became agitated, contending he had no idea where it was.

"That's my statement," he said. "I don't want to waste time talking about that anymore."

Pressed further, Eric hemmed and hawed, saying he'd actually purchased three guns: two .380s and the nine-millimeter.

"How could you confuse giving Joe David [Jimenez] a nine-millimeter, not a .380?" Frizzell asked.

"I didn't confuse it," Eric said.

"You misled us?"

"I misled you, yeah, 'cause I felt scared. . . . We played the old mind-fuck game between each other that night, okay? I mind-fucked you with the gun, and you mind-fucked me with what happened to me that night," he said, referring to their bringing him in at 2 A.M. on a traffic warrant arrest to question him about the murder.

He claimed again that he'd mailed one of the .380s to his father for protection after he'd been mugged, but he was concerned that his dad would get into trouble because it was probably illegal for him to have the gun at his house in New York. Growing confrontational, Eric said he bought the other Jennings .380 at the same gun shop in Dallas, but at another time.

Eric said he could get the gun from his father if the cops really wanted it, but his mother had been ill for years with ulcerative colitis, and he didn't want to worry her because stress worsened her condition.

"Do you want to verify that it's not the murder weapon?" he asked. "Is this it?"

"We want to verify he got the .380, and your story," Voth said.

As the interview went on, Voth noticed that Eric's time-line for the night of the murder kept putting him at a greater distance from the crime. Although Eric had originally said the nine-millimeter had gone missing in the summer of 1994, he said he always kept it "hidden very tightly in a cleaning box," even during the security job at an apartment complex in Lake Elsinore that Eric worked with two of his buddies, which turned out to be in December.

Confronted now with the fact that the detectives knew he hadn't bought the nine-millimeter until August 1994, Eric claimed that the gun was actually stolen around the same time that he lost the Jennings .380. He'd concealed the Beretta in a towel in the backseat of his Pathfinder, he said, and it went missing too.

For Frizzell, Eric's new story didn't make sense on its face. "You're going to leave a six-hundred-to-seven-hundred-dollar, nearly brand-new, Beretta nine-millimeter in the truck that night? And that location at that apartment complex, which is so despicable that they have to hire security guards?"

"That's the deal," Eric said. "I do not have my gun. I would love to give it to you, okay? Unfortunately, uh, I do not know where it is."

Later police called the Texas shop where he'd bought the .380 and learned that he'd only bought the one there. And as the police pointed out to Eric, he'd called Kevin McDaniel around Thanksgiving, asking what to do about reporting the loss or theft of his nine-millimeter.

"That is a gun that disappeared sometime back in July? August?" Frizzell asked rhetorically, calling out Eric on his lie.

Eric said he never bought ammunition for the nine-millimeter, but he'd heard from Nanette that they were reportedly seen buying ammo at the B&B gun shop. The detectives confirmed that yes, the couple had been ID'd in lineups at the gun store. Eric countered that either the gun clerk or the cops were lying.

"I'm not a liar, you understand. I'm not," Eric said. "I've got, you know, kids."

Moving on to the sad state of his personal finances, he admitted that his credit was so shot that he'd been forced to ask his parents for an American Express card, and then he'd run that up too. He also admitted that he was in debt and "didn't have a pot to piss in," whereas Bill had a lot of money, and much of it was flowing to Nanette. And yet he still denied that any of this gave him a motive to murder Bill.

"You can stay on my ass for my whole life and we will grow old together. . . . You will never, ever, ever find any reason to think that I had any motive to kill this guy."

As he had in the first interview, Eric continued to try to minimize the seriousness of his relationship with Nanette. But then he changed his story about the rest of that evening.

He said he got dressed for work, drove by his friend Leonard Jomsky's house, where the lights were out and no one was home, so he didn't stop. Then, Eric said, he got a page from the bar manager—"Mike Teresmo? Or, like, Mike something"—at the Thunderbird nightclub. So he stopped at a pay phone on Seventeenth Street in Tustin, most likely at the Denny's, to return the page.

"I know I made a phone call to work that night. . . . He said, 'I want to know what time you're going to be in.' I said, 'Yeah, I'm coming in.'"

Asked if he knew what time he was paged, Eric said, "I know, how about we go look at my phone bill and see what time exactly I made the call, and maybe then, if I made the call at a certain time, you guys can leave me alone."

"That might help," Voth said.

"Even if I rushed, then you're telling me I could have made it in time to do the killing?"

"Yeah, because Nanette made it all the way to South Coast Plaza and was buying something in time," Voth said.

Clearly feeling backed into a corner, Eric became even more agitated. "Do you guys think I'm a fucking idiot?

Would I do something like that and walk across the street to work? I mean, come on, man, give me a break."

Police contended that he did have a motive to kill Bill: jealousy. After falling in love with Nanette and finding out that she was having sex with another man, Eric got so mad that he killed Bill.

But Eric disputed that theory. "You guys are the first person ever to tell me that there was a relationship between Nanette and Bill," he said.

Nonetheless, Eric did seem rattled and all over the map emotionally, alternating between saying he didn't know or care—or even ask—what Nanette was doing with other men. He seemed surprised to learn from detectives that morning that she and Bill were having regular sex and that she bragged about it to Bill's friends.

Eric also claimed ignorance that she and Bill were engaged, that she didn't own the Seashore Drive house, and that she'd gotten all of her money, her nice car, and her expensive clothes just for being Bill's girlfriend.

"From looking at paperwork and businesses, she didn't get it for doing her business work," Voth told him. "I can guarantee you that right now."

"So you think he bought her?" Eric asked.

Eric didn't seem to want to buy any of this—or, if he already knew, he was a very good actor.

"I still don't think you're right about their relationship thing," Eric said. "Call me an idiot, okay?"

But he also seemed to want it both ways, acting cocky about this supposedly new information, as if he wasn't upset by it.

"Even if, like, I found out mysteriously, you know, some way that this was going on, am I a jealous guy to do something like that? Hell no."

"What do I have to gain when he goes?" he asked. "I had Nanette—I've always had her. There was no question in my mind. I talked to her every night, had her any night that she was free."

"You didn't have her living with you," Voth said.

"If she's doing some other dude for money, do you think I'd want her permanently? You're thinking a lot lower than I am."

"Maybe you just lose it," Frizzell said.

"Oh, please, I don't lose it. I've never lost it in my entire life."

After pointing out that Eric's former nightclub coworkers would argue with that statement, the detectives asked if he was sure that Nanette didn't shoot Bill.

"Of course I know that she didn't shoot him," Eric replied.

"You don't know if she's responsible or not?"

"How else would she be responsible?" Eric asked.

"A lot of other people will take money for doing that kind of thing," Voth said, referring to a hit man for hire.

Eric did not respond or react to this remark—an irony that would become clear when the topic came up again—sixteen years down the road.

Detective Byington spent forty-five minutes grilling Leonard Jomsky about Eric's relationship with Nanette and whether Eric had told him anything about the murder. Jomsky replied that he knew Eric and Nanette were a couple, but he knew nothing about the killing.

When Jomsky had moved to Orange County a couple of years ago, he said, he'd lived with Rob Frias, who worked as the front-door manager at Metropolis, where Eric was head of security. After that, Jomsky worked with Eric and Frias at the Roxbury, a nightclub frequented by celebrities in the 1980s and early 1990s, then later joined Eric at the Thunderbird.

Police had already interviewed Frias, who was also a

friend, former roommate, and business partner of Eric's. The two of them had started a security company called Harbor Security Management. After Frias moved to Miami, Eric formed his own company, Coastal Elite Security.

Frias said Eric owned one black and one silver semiautomatic handgun, which he thought Eric kept in his dresser drawer. He recalled that Eric had gone to a shooting range with Nanette, where she'd either bought or had been given a handgun.

Jomsky said the Thunderbird job came about at the same time that Jomsky was working nights for Coastal Elite at an apartment complex in a questionable area of Lake Elsinore, where they were supposed to ensure that people weren't breaking into cars or doing anything suspicious. The complex had had problems with gangs tagging the area, leaving graffiti, and breaking into apartments. Frias worked the Lake Elsinore job too.

When Byington was done with Jomsky, the detective listened to his colleagues interviewing Eric in the next room and became annoyed with the way things were going. He wished the detectives would get more aggressive with Eric, who kept trying to run the show.

*They are just getting ramrodded,* Byington thought as he searched through Eric's things. *Don't let him get away with this.*

Maybe it was Eric's overbearing personality or maybe it was just that he was physically imposing, but he had a habit of trying to steer the interrogation, and he was often successful. The detectives may have had a game plan to let him think he was in control as a way to elicit information from him, but it didn't seem to be working. Within a couple of minutes, Eric was the one asking the questions.

Byington was not part of the homicide team. He'd just been brought in to write the search warrants. However, he didn't like the way Eric was dressing down Voth and Frizzell, the latter of whom had the same type A personality as Eric. There was a lot of testosterone in the room that day, but it wasn't working for the detectives. It was working against them.

When he couldn't take Eric's attitude anymore, Byington decided to try to disrupt the balance of power and tip it back to the good guys. He couldn't stop himself from knocking down cocky suspects with his cutting, dry wit, and he saw plenty about Eric to poke at.

"Eric had rows of hair plugs back then, way down on his forehead," Byington recalled recently. "Nobody was buying that it was real. It was like it was drawn on. You could see the individual plugs."

Also, during the search, Byington found some paraphernalia for steroid use, including syringes in the bathroom, which were illegal to possess without a prescription. And even though Eric seemed excitable and aggressive, the detectives took note of Byington's find but didn't press charges.

"He was definitely juicing. He had the syringes," Byington said. "He was running a gym. He had to stay in shape."

But the most amusing find for Byington was a large, vibrating dildo in Eric's bedside table, which he waved with amusement in the suspect's face. "Is this on your side of the bed? Is this for you?"

"Fuck you," Eric retorted.

"Nice hair," Byington said, wondering if Eric was going to fight back and attack him.

*If this guy gets up, I'm going to have to shoot him in the kneecaps.*

Byington was getting dirty looks from Frizzell and Voth, who didn't see the humor in his interrupting their interview, so he left the room.

The detectives didn't end up finding anything else of use

to the investigation that day, but Byington certainly enjoyed the opportunity to take Eric down a notch.

Meanwhile, Lieutenant Jackson and Sergeant Desmond grilled Nanette for two and a half hours for details on her relationship with Eric, which she, too, played down.

"Did you ever spend the night at his place in Tustin?" Jackson asked, noting that people had described her as "the rich girl with the Cadillac who spends the night."

"Occasionally," she said, "but never the whole night, because I always came back to take care of Kevin." She admitted that she usually left at six or seven in the morning, but she apparently didn't consider that to be the entire night.

Nanette said she and Bill had been engaged for two years, but they were waiting to get married until he could settle the lawsuit with Jacob Horowitz "because of the liability if he, well, what he wanted to do is put everything in my name if he lost . . . and if we were married, then you couldn't do that."

She said they didn't tell everyone, just his family and his close friends. She hadn't told her ex-husband, for example.

"Did Eric know?" Jackson asked. When she said no, the detective asked, "Did you wear the ring with Eric?"

"I never wore it when I went to the gym and stuff, 'cause the first time I wore it to the gym, it broke. . . . I usually didn't wear it during the day."

She said she'd never really thought about why she didn't tell Eric about the engagement, but she seemed to know the answer. "Just because he would not like that, that's why."

"Were you afraid if you told Eric that you were engaged to Bill that you would lose Eric?"

Nanette skirted the question, saying that they started out as friends, when he had a girlfriend. Later, after they began dating casually, she never got around to telling Eric, and he never asked. She assumed that Eric thought she and Bill "mostly just did business together."

"So although you want to marry Bill, Eric somehow fills some kind of void in your life, yes?"

"Yes," she said.

She also admitted to seeing Glenn Sharp and Scott Weisman while she was with Bill, and Tom Reynolds before Bill.

"He was violent and he was a real jerk," Nanette said, referring to Reynolds. "I knew him for, like, a grand total of two months and he actually hit me one time and I was in the hospital in Newport Beach. . . . [He] threatened me, [and] I tried to get a restraining order against him, and the cops were of no help. . . ." She added that he finally left her alone after she threatened to tell his probation officer that he was bothering her, a completely different rendition of events from Reynolds's.

"Bill ever ask you about dating other guys?"

"No," she said. "Bill, in some areas, he knew where maybe there were some short things that weren't fulfilled, and he kinda knew, but didn't want to know, you know?"

"Yeah, it's the '90s," Jackson said.

"He never said anything. I mean, it's like we had a really good relationship, and there were certain things emotionally that really kept us together and where we were really good for each other. I'm sure if you talk to all his friends . . . they will tell you that we never fought. . . . We got along really well."

Because he knew he couldn't fulfill all her needs, she said, she and Bill had a "kind of unspoken" agreement that she could date younger guys on the side.

"We didn't sit down and say it that way, but yes . . . in a roundabout way . . . 'cause that's not the kind of thing you want to talk about."

In the beginning, she said, he wanted her to move in and quit her job, which she didn't want to do. So, instead, they made a deal: He would teach her the business and be "the brains" of it all. They would work together "and it will work well for everybody. . . . 'Just don't embarrass me . . . and be discreet, or just whatever you feel you need to do, but be here for us and the kids.'"

What Nanette described to the detectives went to the very heart of her personal ad. In essence, what Bill was saying, she claimed, was "I'll take care of you, if you take care of me." But she clearly had her own interpretation of the arrangement.

Asked what Bill knew of Eric, Nanette said he knew Eric was a friend she worked out with several times a week, but he knew nothing about their Jamaica trip. She didn't want to rub Bill's nose in it, so she said she let him think she was visiting her grandmother in Chicago the whole time.

She said she'd been using Eric lately as a "little bit [of] a shoulder," because she'd been having nightmares since the murder. He'd come over to the Seashore house to make the windows more secure because it had been broken into before and she was feeling nervous.

But as for Bill's murder, she said, "I know that I wasn't involved, and I feel pretty sure that [Eric] wasn't involved." She said she was "real nervous that maybe somebody could target me also, if it had anything to do with business or whatever."

Asked if she loved Eric and wanted to marry him, she said, "I don't know I would say 'love.' I would say I care about him a lot. I care about him as a person, I mean." However, she said she didn't want to marry him. If he'd proposed before the murder, she would have said no.

She sounded as though she had no idea he was going to propose, and had only learned from the police that his journal said something about it. If he'd asked and she turned him down, she said, he'd probably be upset, but she'd never seen him angry and they never argued.

"He seems pretty easygoing to me," she said. "I grew up with somebody who had a really bad temper."

The night of the murder, she said, she dropped Eric off at his apartment because he was in a hurry to get to work. "He was supposed to be at work at, like, eight, and our game ran him late. . . . He said he was going to take a shower and stuff because he . . . had a baseball cap on . . . and he wasn't dressed."

While she was Christmas shopping at the mall that night, she said, she stopped to look at sports coats in the men's department at Nordstrom, because Bill had said he wanted one. But "their prices are outrageous," so she didn't buy one. She went to Crate & Barrel, then to Bullock's, and then headed home when the mall started to close.

Asked if she ever threw her keys to Eric and let him drive her car without her, she said no. Nor had he ever driven any of Bill's cars, or been to Balboa Coves.

In long, evasive, and vague statements, she again minimized her interest in guns. She said she had no personal knowledge of Eric's "gun or guns or whatever guns he may or may not have had, other than what he's told me, you know, that somebody lost one or this or that . . . and that was only, like I mentioned, in passing."

"Has Eric ever told you he was going to go to a range to shoot or anything like that?"

"He mentioned going to a range one time," she said, neglecting to tell them that he took her with him.

"When was that?"

"I really don't remember, just a long time ago."

"Six months, a year ago?"

"He mentioned that he wanted to teach me how to shoot, you know, for, like, self-protection. . . . I don't like guns. . . .

I have shot one once, when I was young, and it scared me a lot 'cause my stepdad let me shoot and it, like, kicked me all the way back, so that was the context on which it came up."

"So, basically, you tell him you don't want to do that?"

"I don't have very much interest in that. I figure I don't have any need. My thoughts on that are if you have one in your house, you're more than likely to get shot with it yourself. So I had no intention of keeping one under the mattress."

"Did Eric ever ask you, maybe, about keeping a gun here or bring a gun over?"

"No, uh-huh."

"As far as you knew, he never had a gun when he was with you?"

"No."

Jackson pointed out that she wouldn't get any life insurance settlement if they found out she was implicated in this murder.

"Well, you're not going to find me implicated, because I'm not, so the only way you could find that is by fabricating it," she said.

"I'm not going to fabricate anything," Jackson said. "I don't want to have to yank you away from your kids, but if I find you're lying to us or you're an accessory—and 'accessory' can mean different things. You can plan the murder, or once you knew . . . this murder happened, you—in some way—don't tell us everything . . . because you feel for Eric. I know you do. It's obvious when you talk about him, your eyes get all misty, and that's fine. He means a lot to you. But if I find you are covering up for him somehow, we will come after you."

"Well, you won't because I didn't do anything," she said. "I have been trying to help you in any way that I can. . . . When Detective Voth told me, 'Oh, well, somebody ID'd

Eric in a gun store with a woman . . . ,' I'm, like, well, that's garbage because I was never in any gun store. If anybody ID'd me in any gun store, they're totally lying. Or you're lying. . . . I don't want to be railroaded into something because you're lacking leads in other areas."

Jackson warned Nanette that they would not stop working this case, and he urged her to try to help them solve it rather than lie to them. Then he made this prescient statement: "If you're hard-core and you think you're streetwise, and you're gonna pull the wool over our eyes . . . maybe you might for a little while, [but] we'll catch up to you."

The next day, Detective Frizzell called Eric to confront him about why he had Bill's license plate number scribbled into his notebook.

"It was about me doing some checking why the guy was knocked off, if my girl was in trouble," Eric replied.

Eric said he wasn't sure when he wrote down the number, "but I know I wrote it down, 'cause I got a phone call from a buddy of mine . . . soon after that."

Pressed further, Eric paused and said, "Ah, I don't want to go into my sources."

"So somebody gave it to you?" Frizzell asked.

"I don't want to talk about that."

In 2011, Eric told police that he'd had his friend Todd Calder follow Nanette back in October 1994, when he was having some trust issues with her, and Calder relayed the Mercedes plate number back to Eric. This statement was essentially an admission that before the murder, he did know where Bill had lived. How else would Eric have the plate number in his journal among items he wrote in December?

But when Calder was questioned by police about Eric's story, he told investigators that he'd never been to Bill's house for any reason. In fact, Calder got so angry that Eric had said he was involved, Calder wanted to go down to the jail and confront Eric about it.

Eric's response: Calder didn't want to get involved, so he lied to police.

# CHAPTER 18

In contrast to Nanette, who was not only secretive about her past but also fabricated much of it, Eric Naposki's life was much more open to scrutiny.

He was born in Mount Sinai Hospital in Manhattan on December 20, 1966, and grew up in the Bronx with his single mom, Ronnie. He never met his biological father, Joel Boyce, and had no father figure until he was nine, when Ronnie married John Naposki. After that, his family grew by one half sister, Angela, who was about twelve years younger, and two half brothers, John and Frankie—the latter of whom ultimately committed suicide.

Eric grew up as a standout athlete, playing baseball, football, and basketball with John Pappalardo, a friend with whom he forged a relationship that would last for decades. After Pappalardo became a defense attorney, their definition of "team strategy" took on a whole new meaning as their friendship was tested on a field bigger than any Little League diamond.

Eric and John met while playing pitcher and shortstop on the Navajos, a team in the Tuckahoe Youth Association. John was about seven, Eric was a little older, and Eric's stepfather

coached the team. The boys also played five seasons of Po
Warner football together with the Eastchester Blue Devils.

"Even back then, he was the most gifted athlete in the
league," Pappalardo recalled recently as he sat in the court
house cafeteria in Santa Ana, adding that he still had vide
of Eric carrying opponents on his back as they tried to
tackle him.

Eric attended high schools in Tuckahoe and Yonkers, finally landing at Eastchester High School, about twenty-five
minutes outside New York City, where he played linebacker,
tight end, and running back during his senior year in 1983
and 1984.

"He was an animal on defense," said Chris Fiore, who
was a year behind Eric in school, and played against him on
football, baseball, and basketball teams when they were
growing up. By 2012, Fiore had gone on to become Eastchester High's assistant principal.

The educator reminisced about Eric in almost sports-
hero terms. "He was always striving for greatness. He was
a very hard worker, kind of a blue-collar guy. He wouldn't
complain. He would just go, do his job, put in his time. He
knew success was going to take hard work, and he was
willing to put in that work. . . . He had a plan and he didn't
deviate from that plan. He didn't take shortcuts."

Off the field, Fiore said, Eric had a reserved demeanor
and a quiet confidence. "To people who didn't know him,
he really wasn't loud. He wasn't showy. He really didn't
look for attention. He wasn't trying to bring it on himself—
almost an unassuming kind of person."

Fiore said Eric was a popular, good-looking, and respect-
ful guy with a "laid-back, friendly nature" when he wasn't

suited up, a contrast to the powerhouse people saw during games.

"He didn't seem to have an anger issue in dealing with people or situations. You didn't really see it in him unless he was out on the field . . . where his aggression would come into play," he said. "He was so freakishly big and fast. [At a time when other players were] either big or fast, he was both. So he was kind of an anomaly. He was big enough to throw you down and fast enough to chase you down."

Eric's performance on the high-school team must have caught the attention of some scouts, because he was offered scholarships to the University of New Hampshire and the University of Connecticut (UConn). He chose to play for the UConn Huskies, a Division 1–AA team in the Yankee Conference, and became an "all-time letter-winner."

On a visit home, Eric went for a drink at Pat's, a neighborhood bar where high-school alumni hung out, hoping to catch a glimpse of former classmates. Chris Fiore, who had always looked up to Eric, noticed a few physical developments in him that night.

"Once he went to college, he really changed," Fiore recalled, noting that was when the rumors started that Eric was taking steroids. (Eric admitted in a jailhouse interview in 2012** that in college he'd "used steroids a little bit, and that was about it.")

Fiore had heard reports that Eric had also developed a temper. "He just became huge, an absolute monster. I don't know how you get that big. He had muscles. I'm sure that's where some of the anger stemmed from," he said.

In the years after that, Fiore said, Eric stayed very muscular. "When he had a brief stint with the Jets [in 1990], he was still pretty big," he said. "I think I came up to his chest. It was like standing in front of a wall."

During Eric's sophomore year at UConn, his girlfriend, Kathy O'Connell, whom he had known since the fifth grade in Tuckahoe, got pregnant. They were married in November 1985. The problem was that football players on scholarship, even fathers-to-be, weren't allowed to work.

"I don't know how I'm going to support myself," Eric told the head coach, Tom Jackson, who, according to Eric, promised to help find him a good summer job.

But Eric claimed he didn't get the financial help he needed, so he had problems putting food on the table for his wife and baby, Krista, who was born in June 1986.

After Eric suffered a separated shoulder during his third season, he took off one game to recover for the upcoming Homecoming match against Boston University. When he went back to practice, Coach Jackson told him he wasn't part of the starting roster anymore. His replacement had done pretty well—better, in fact, than Eric.

Eric spent most of the Homecoming game on the bench, because the coach didn't want to send him in until the last part of the game. By that point, Eric, who was still nursing his shoulder, felt there wasn't much point to chancing a reinjury in the closing minutes of the game. With that in mind, he said he didn't want to play.

The tensions between him and Jackson continued during the next practice, when Eric ultimately walked off the field, feeling like he was "being treated like shit" by the coach.

"Why are you home?" Kathy asked when he walked in the door early.

"I quit," he said. "I'm not playing football anymore. I have no money. I'm going to go out and get a job."

At the time, he said, they had about thirteen cents in the bank, and Kathy wasn't working because she was taking care of Krista. That night, Eric's team members came over and tried to persuade him to come back. It almost worked. That is, until he talked to his mother, who had called the coach to find out what was going on.

The message she relayed to Eric—or at least how he heard it—was "Your son isn't good enough to play anymore. The guy who took his place is better."

Eric was offended, not just by the message, but also because the coach had delivered it to his mother and not to him personally. When Coach Jackson asked him to come back, Eric said no.

"I've got to do what I've got to do for my family," Eric said.

In 2009, Jackson told the *Hartford Courant,* "[Eric] was a very good player, but at the time I had him, he was kind of immature and thought he would do it his way."

The day Eric quit the team in the fall of 1986, he landed a job as a trainer at a local gym. And that spring, he signed up for the U.S. Army Reserve to earn some extra money. He also enrolled in its college loan repayment plan.

"I wanted a challenge, a possible secondary career," he said.

He went through boot camp at Fort Benning, Georgia, for ten weeks that summer, where he learned "everything that's necessary to be a soldier," from firing machine guns, rifles, and rocket launchers to shining boots.

"They teach you how to shoot people," he said. "That's their job."

Tired of being yelled at in boot camp, he decided he wanted to be an officer, so he also joined the ROTC in

August 1987. Being in both the Reserve and the ROTC, known as the Simultaneous Membership Program, meant that he could graduate as a first lieutenant rather than a private first class or a sergeant, and earn more money doing it.

"You learn to tell people to blow people up," he recalled in 2011**, using words that would prove revealing later.

Still working as a trainer, he thought it would be smart to stay involved in organized athletics. In the fall of 1987, he tried out for the UConn basketball team—and made it.

So began the routine of getting up at 4:30 A.M. to run with the ROTC, then lifting weights and doing conditioning with the basketball team at 3:00 P.M.

But this regimen didn't last long. During practice one day, he sprained his ankle, "because linebackers shouldn't play basketball," he said. "I overburdened myself, but you can't say I didn't try."

In the spring of 1988, Eric still had NFL aspirations. When he saw a professional football agent timing players running the forty-yard dash, Eric bet the agent a cup of coffee that if he could run it in 4.5 seconds, the agent had to sign him. Eric won the bet.

Eric was never an All-American or an All-Conference player at UConn. But still smarting from his fallout with Coach Jackson, he felt he had something to prove.

When the annual open tryout for the New England Patriots came around that April at Sullivan Stadium in Foxborough, Massachusetts, Eric decided to go for it. But because he hadn't gone through the proper process of getting an invitation, he snuck onto the field through an opening in the fence, grabbed a number at the check-in desk, and pinned it on his chest. He ran a 4.52.

By the end of the day, he said, 205 guys had tried out. It came down to him and one other athlete, and Eric was chosen. His agent, who had been watching from the stands all day, was there to sign Eric to his first NFL contract.

"Went from college worker, student, cadet, basketball reject, father, to under contract with the Patriots," Eric recalled. He couldn't wait to call his parents to tell them the great news.

Base salary for a rookie back then, he said, was about $55,000—if you made the team. "If you get cut, you get nothing." But compared to his $6-an-hour job at the gym, this was the big time for this twenty-one-year-old, who was ecstatic to receive a $500 check for travel expenses at the end of minicamp.

When news of Eric's signing with the Patriots hit the newspaper, his former UConn coach told a reporter that *he* was going to suit up for the next open tryout, as if to say, "If [Eric] can do it, anyone can."

Eric's response: "Just tell him I'll look forward to playing with him next year."

Word had it that Eric's stepfather had moved him from high school to high school to give Eric the best possible leg up in getting a college scholarship. But John Naposki might have had other influences over Eric's life as well. It's unclear how old Eric was when this started, but John, who was a big, burly man, became abusive to Eric's mother, Ronnie.

In the summer of 2003, Ronnie was separated from John when she obtained a restraining order to stop him from harassing her. After John was arrested for violating the order, Eric moved Ronnie into his house for her protection. She didn't see John again.

"I don't take kindly to women getting abused, but it's not enough to convince me to kill somebody," Eric said in 2012\*\*, two years after his mother had died.

In November 2003, while John and Ronnie were going

through a divorce, he threatened to burn down his vacant house because she wanted to sell it. John, who owned an asbestos removal business in Yorktown Heights, doused the house with gasoline, flicked his lighter to start the fire, set off the fire alarm, and died of smoke inhalation. Firefighters found an empty five-gallon can, John's car keys, and a lighter on the floor near the alarm. Apparently, he'd tried to douse the flames in the first-floor bathroom, but the water had already been turned off.

By his own account, Eric had some shady associates in his past. He told a friend in Orange County that he'd once been arrested for beating up a guy while helping a loan shark collect a debt—an incident that involved a pushing match with the debtor and a confrontation with the debtor's bat-wielding son. Eric said the records of this incident had been sealed, which would explain why Newport Beach police couldn't find them.

Joe Naposki, Eric's uncle, also had a criminal history. In May 1989, Joe confessed to a priest at a church in Salem, Oregon, that he was tired of running from charges related to an attempted murder, robbery, and gunfight among cocaine dealers and undercover narcotics agents in 1984. The priest helped Joe find a lawyer. After a brief Naposki family reunion, Joe surrendered to police in New York, and like Eric, made the news.

# CHAPTER 19

In the years before and after Eric met Nanette, he tried to make something of himself in the world of professional football, going for the big time in the stressful and uncertain world of the NFL, an acronym that some people joke is short for "Not For Long."

During the off-season, each of the thirty-two clubs has a ninety-man upper limit on its roster, which leaves room for 2,880 players in training camp, plus an additional thirty-seven per team who may be in reserve. By the time the regular season rolls around, each team has room for only fifty-three players, or a total of 1,696 players in the league.

Competition is fierce, and when the best are playing the best, it's no surprise that players get injured. But in this high-stakes game, an injury can mean lost money, status, and hope. Some injuries can end an NFL career before it even gets started.

In Eric's case, he made the first cut with the Patriots in the 1988 season, but he played only three of the sixteen regular games. This would be the high point of his NFL career, and it didn't last long.

During the fifth game, Eric got hurt, and was hospitalized for ten days with two broken ribs and a liver contusion.

He went on injured reserve status, and was ultimately released from the team as a free agent, meaning that he was no longer under contract. This left him free to sign with another team.

In general, when a player under contract is on an active-team roster at the beginning of the season, but is released midseason, he would be paid for that full year, said Michael Signora, the NFL's vice president of football communications. But without seeing Eric's contract, Signora said he couldn't confirm how much Eric got paid.

In March 1989, Eric was back and ready for action. Signed as a free agent in the off-season by the Dallas Cowboys, he was released in mid-August after turning his right ankle before training camp. He was promptly picked up by the Indianapolis Colts, only to be released about two weeks later after playing just one game. He got a second chance with the Patriots, who signed him as their seventh linebacker on September 6, 1989.

"Right now, I'm feeling very Patriotic," he told *The Boston Globe.* "I'm not taking it for granted. I was lucky. I was lucky coming out of college. . . . It's been a long and winding road; now I'm used to this. But I think it's time to settle down and play football."

Eric's ankle gave out again and he was cut about a week later after playing what would be his last game in the NFL. His daughter Kayla was born about a week after that.

The New York Jets signed Eric as a free agent in March 1990, but he never got to play a game with them after fracturing his hand and spraining his ankle in training camp. He was released in late August with an injury settlement.

Rebuffed by the NFL, Eric did what many players over the years have done, and that is to try out for one of the less prestigious leagues, such as the Canadian Football

League, NFL Europe, United States Football League, United Football League, National Minor League Football, or World League of American Football (WLAF).

After recovering from his injuries, Eric was drafted by a team in the WLAF in its 1991 inaugural season. Playing outside linebacker for the Barcelona Dragons, he not only became a team favorite, but the first player with a fan club: La Penya Naposki, with five thousand members.

"I was just running onto the field and people started to scream," Eric told the Associated Press. "I didn't know what they were doing. I even looked around to see who was following me, to see who they were cheering for, but there was nobody. Suddenly, I realized it was me."

His ability to speak some Spanish helped his popularity rise, especially with the children who walked with him from the stadium to the practice field each day, asking for autographs or to hold his helmet. A crowd of kids even swarmed the twenty-five-year-old when he stopped at the local McDonald's.

The AP described Eric as "fast approaching superstar status," noting he was helping the Dragons "to fashion the league's toughest defense en route to first place in the European Division."

But when the team made it to World Bowl finals that year, Eric was on the sidelines with a pulled groin muscle.


While Eric's European football career was taking off, his marriage was dying. In March 1991, when his daughter Kayla was about eighteen months old and his other daughter, Krista, was almost five, his wife filed for divorce in Danbury, Connecticut, just a few weeks after he'd left for Barcelona.

Citing an "irretrievable breakdown" in their relationship,

Kathy asked for alimony and child support, saying she was "without adequate funds to support herself" and the children, whereas Eric, as a professional football player, had "considerable income and funds."

The judge ordered Eric to pay her $475 per week, but by mid-June, Kathy had already filed a motion for a contempt order, complaining that he owed her more than $3,800.

Eric returned to the United States from Barcelona that summer and was signed by the Washington Redskins in July. He arrived at camp, still injured.

Even after taking a month off, he bruised his shoulder and reinjured his groin during the second practice. He passed the physical, but he ended up pulling the same groin muscle again, and left in August.

The Redskins paid his doctor bills, he said**, and "we were even. They won the freaking Super Bowl that year. My luck. The doctor told me I'd probably never play football again. Probably my worst [injury], even worse than the ribs."

Nonetheless, he recovered enough to play a second season with the Barcelona Dragons in 1992, when his weight rose to 260 pounds.

"We all know where we are—we're in the WLAF. Now you can say that's only one step away from the NFL, but it's also one step away from a nine-to-five job somewhere," he told the AP that May.

Eric tried out with the Seattle Seahawks, and was signed in July 1992. But after wearing a cast all summer, he was the first player to leave training camp later that month because of his pesky groin injury and a torn arch in his left foot.

He dropped off his playbook at the front desk and announced he was retiring, walking away from the NFL in what one spokesman called Eric's "final transaction" with the league. The NFL declined to comment on anything further relating to Eric Naposki.

After he'd lost his NFL income in the fall of 1991, Kathy requested that he pay her a "suitable sum" for support each week. In the meantime, she had to live with and borrow money from her parents. With two small children and an estranged husband who wasn't paying any support, she couldn't make ends meet on a $680 welfare check and $160 in food stamps each month.

Kathy petitioned for sole custody in January 1992, saying that Eric had "shown no interest or inclination to visit the children in the past."

The couple's inches-thick divorce file in Connecticut contains a series of motions for contempt orders against Eric for not making his required payments, along with repeated pleas he filed to lower his payments because his "financial circumstances" kept changing.

By August 1992, Eric had relocated to Irvine, California. Court records show that his child support debt had risen to $20,400, that he claimed he owed $15,000 to his mother and other creditors, and had only $350 in cash.

The state of Connecticut had joined Kathy in her collection efforts by this point, which is typical when a spouse receives state-subsidized welfare benefits. A family court judge issued a capias—another term for a bench warrant—with a $5,000 bond for Eric because he wasn't paying support or attending required hearings.

In January 1993, the state tried to garnishee his wages with the World League, but it had suspended operations by then. Eric, who was working private security and jobs as a bouncer at popular upscale nightclubs in Orange County, submitted pay stubs to the court to prove that his net weekly earnings were only $567 a week. He said he couldn't even afford to travel to the East Coast to attend a hearing, let alone pay his support debt.

But some of this wasn't his fault, he wrote, blaming the court for sending the hearing notice to an old address. Calling the $288 court-ordered weekly payments "completely ridiculous" and "utterly devastating," he said there was "absolutely no possible way" he could afford them. Furthermore, he wrote, *I am quite anxious to have this matter resolved. I do feel, however, that I am being judged rather harshly. Please remember that I only got divorced, I did not commit a felony. And to be honest, I am very tired of being treated like a criminal.*

After his split with Kathy, Eric started dating a woman named Samantha, whose father was a big football fan. And along the way, he befriended an attractive woman he met at the gym named Nanette Johnston.

He stayed in Dallas for a few months to promote some videos. Then, after breaking up with Samantha, he and Nanette began dating around January 1994. He played football in Edmonton, Canada, for a few months that year before returning to live in Tustin.

# CHAPTER 20

Bill McLaughlin may have been worth $55 million on paper, but he'd been having increasing cash flow problems in the months leading up to his death, even after earning more than $2 million in annual gross income in 1993 and 1994.

Working out of his home office, he made his own schedule. He enjoyed exercising his biomedical and entrepreneurial muscles as he searched for a cancer cure and tried to adapt the blood filter to other consumer uses, such as water filtration and wine separation. He also liked to play with real estate and development deals, such as the property he'd bought in Palm Springs with hopes of building a Mexican-style village.

But by the fall of 1994, that project wasn't going well, and he lost money on his desert properties. He'd purchased the two homes in Las Vegas as an investment and to save a significant amount in personal income and corporate taxes, but he'd acquired them at the top of the market, right before the values plummeted. He'd also made a bad investment in Fiji in 1989, and had failed to repay a debt of at least $5 million to an offshore bank, which ended up going under.

As money got tighter, Bill told his daughter Jenny that

Nanette's routine of going to the gym and taking the kids to school every day was getting old. If some of his businesses didn't start producing some income, he said, he was going to have to tell her to get a job. Nonetheless, he took Nanette on a first-class tour of Europe, because he'd never been there before.

Bill told his friend Denis Townsend that he gave Nanette a monthly allowance, no questions asked, and he let her write checks to pay the bills. But Townsend said Nanette had very little to do with the desert projects or business decisions in general; she just did the books.

Townsend said Bill had been thinking about reversing his vasectomy in 1993, and never would have stood for Nanette seeing other men. Similarly, Bill's buddy Don Kalal said Bill told him that Nanette wanted a monogamous relationship.

In 1993, when Bill told his longtime accountant, Brian Ringler, that Nanette wanted to get married, Ringler advised him to wait.

"Why don't you give it some more time and see how it goes," he said. "There's no harm in waiting. You can always get married in the future."

Bill gave Nanette the diamond ring she'd been wanting, and by the fall of 1994, the couple was shopping for a bigger home. Bill told Jenny that he was thinking about trading four or five properties to afford a new one. And on October 27, 1994, realtor Betty Comegys showed the couple a property in South Laguna worth $5.5 million.

When Bill talked to his brother in late 1994, however, Patrick got the sense that Bill had already made up his mind that he wasn't going to marry her.

The question is, how much of this did Nanette know? Was she playing both of her men to see what or who would break first, or did she have a plan all along? And what, if anything, did Bill know about Nanette's various schemes?

After several years of legal battling against Jacob Horowitz, a decision in Bill's favor finally came down on October 3, 1994. Using some arcane calculations, the arbitration panel determined that Bill had $9 million coming to him from the holding account where Baxter had been funneling royalties, ruling that Horowitz had, in fact, breached the contract. The next $18 million in royalties would go to Bill and Baxter Healthcare, and Horowitz would give up his half, $9 million, before he got any more.

Bill was obviously pleased about the court ruling, but he told his attorneys, Paul Gale and Ray Bogucki, that he was frustrated with the holdup of the payout because he needed cash for his real estate deals in the desert. He'd been receiving $500,000 to $550,000 in royalties every quarter—or about half of the disputed royalties, which varied depending on sales—and the same amount had been going into the holding account.

Bill complained that he had to borrow money in November to meet his various obligations before the royalty check came in on the fifteenth. But the arbitration panel wouldn't allow him to move any cash until a final judgment was entered. The release of the money was also complicated by the fact that it had been placed into the investment pool run by Orange County, which filed for bankruptcy on December 6, 1994.

Not surprisingly, this long and drawn-out struggle with Horowitz had frustrated Bill to no end. He'd always believed that his former partner had breached their contract, and Bill believed that excused him "from paying Horowitz any royalties otherwise due him." Hearing that Horowitz's lawyer had made it his life's mission to keep Bill from getting his share of the money only made him more upset.

The antagonism between Bill and Horowitz came across in the interview that police conducted in Santa Barbara two days after Bill's death. Horowitz said the war wasn't over because the arbitration was "still active," and that he disagreed with the legal interpretation that Bill had been victorious.

"I won my royalties. I don't consider that having lost. . . . He didn't win against me, and I didn't win against him," Horowitz said, referring to the panel's October ruling that neither one had to pay the other's legal fees. "It's a complex litigation and it's still going on."

Horowitz appealed that ruling, so it wasn't until well after Bill's death that the courts confirmed the $9 million award to Bill's estate. After Horowitz lost his appeal, he was ordered to pay the $9 million to Kim McLaughlin, the estate's executrix.

All of Horowitz's lawsuits were ultimately dismissed with prejudice in June 1996. It was unclear from the court records whether Horowitz ultimately had to pay Bill's voluminous legal fees.


While Bill was working on his various investment projects, Nanette was pursuing a few of her own. In early 1994, she met a personal trainer named Robert Cottrill at the Sporting Club. As the year progressed, Cottrill saw her and Eric Naposki kissing and holding hands, working out three times a week together, so he assumed Nanette and Eric were boyfriend and girlfriend. She and Cottrill chatted from time to time, but it wasn't until the summer that they started talking business.

Nanette asked what else Cottrill did for a living. When he said that he was moonlighting as a software developer and looking for investors in a start-up business, she expressed interest. She told him she was an independently wealthy retiree after inventing a medical device that she'd sold to Baxter, and was now living on the royalties. Cottrill was impressed that she'd been able to retire so young. Hers was the kind of success to which he aspired.

She was also asking him all the right questions: How was he planning to structure his company? Was he planning to find other investors?

After she inquired if he had a business plan, he got to work on one and finished it a few weeks later. They met at his apartment to talk in November.

Nanette said she was interested in investing $100,000 to $200,000, but she didn't want to be active in the business. They would have to wait a bit, though, until she had the cash in hand.

"She wasn't liquid, so she couldn't readily get the money and get it to me," he said. "She said her money was parked offshore, and she had to manipulate the money around to get it, bring it onshore, and that's tricky."

He never heard from her again.


After the good news about the lawsuit came down on October 3, Nanette quietly made preparations for all the money she expected to be flowing in very soon.

On October 17, she filed articles of incorporation for Krishel, Inc.—a title that combined her children's names, Kristofer and Lishelle—in the state of Nevada. Nanette named herself president, secretary, treasurer, and director of the corporation, which could issue 25,000 shares of common stock by a board of directors. She also established a trust account with the same name, and had deposited $220,000 into it by January 26, 1995. On February 13, 1995, the trust paid $2,500 to Coastal Elite Security, Eric's private security business, and $15,000 to Julian Bailey, Eric's criminal defense attorney.

It appeared from these and other transactions that Nanette thought she stood to gain control of much more of Bill's money upon his death than he'd provided for in his living will, even though she insisted she believed the opposite.

By the time the NBPD detectives discovered the corporation and seized the balance in the trust account, which they believed she was using as a "funnel," it contained $192,000.

One of Eric's coworkers from the Metropolis nightclub ran into him and Nanette at the mall soon after Bill's murder. Seeing that their hands were full of shopping bags, he noted that Nanette didn't seem to be grieving about her fiancée's murder.

Bill's death also didn't stop her and Eric from celebrating over New Year's, when the couple took a two-day trip to San Francisco, to get away from it all. Nanette paid for their stay at the Amsterdam Hotel on January 2, 1995, using the credit card from Bill's "S" corporation.

# CHAPTER 21

Based on the notebook journal that police found in Eric's car, he was well aware of his past mistakes, character flaws, and financial weaknesses, as well as his need for self-improvement.

In an entry dated February 13, 1994—the day before Valentine's Day, and soon after he'd begun dating Nanette—the twenty-seven-year-old wrote up a list of ten rules to live by, pledging to build a better relationship with his two daughters and to support them both financially and emotionally; to be honest with himself; to stay disciplined in pursuing his short- and long-term goals, and to remember that money isn't important or necessary to have fun. (*Enjoy the free things life has to offer. Go back to the basics!*) He pledged to keep his body "strong and perfect" so his soul could "prosper"; to develop a strong spiritual life without any excuses; to avoid being "sidetracked by bullshit"; to stay positive, and not to fear success or failure.

Despite Eric's claims that he'd never hurt anyone or lost his temper, his coworkers said he sometimes had a hard time keeping his anger and frustration under control.

He was fired from the Metropolis nightclub, where he worked as a bouncer, after becoming unglued during a skirmish with a patron in the parking lot. Roy Rauschklob, who had hired Eric, told detectives that Eric was a good employee, but he had a temper and a difficulty brushing off verbal attacks from patrons, which contributed to his termination.

Eric admitted to Newport Beach police that he'd gotten aggravated at work one night, when a guy he'd thrown out of the club a month earlier came up to him, got into his face, and said, "See you later, motherfucker," then took off. Eric said he told the guy to wait, but he didn't, so Eric followed him into the parking lot, where the guy ran to the passenger side of his car, and Eric grabbed him.

"I hold him in a hold, didn't hit him once, didn't hurt him," he said. "Why did I go after him? Well, for the same reason, I wanted to see why the fuck he was coming in my face, swearing at me, and leaving the club."

Eric noted that he was trained in hand-to-hand combat in martial arts, and yet, "I've never raised my hand to anybody."

In late 1992, while he was still working at Metropolis, Eric attended an eight-hour training session run by Combative Concepts, a company that taught "close-quarter battle" or combat tactics, to local police departments, the DEA, SWAT, and other special-ops teams. The company was run by two former Navy SEALs and a private investigator named Joseph "Joe" Stoltman Jr., who did security for nightclubs in Orange County, including Metropolis.

In an interview with Detective Voth in February 1995, the PI said that Eric, Roy Rauschklob, and other Metropolis bouncers participated in a training session for Irvine's SWAT team, in which Eric pretended to be a terrorist during a paintball skirmish. Eric, who told the participants he'd been trained in handguns in boot camp, did so well that he was complimented on his performance.

The paint guns they used that day were tweaked to inflict pain. "If you're coming around a corner and you get shot, and you think it's a game, no big deal," Stoltman explained. "If it actually stings, leaves a welt, or maybe breaks the skin, then they're not going to make the same mistake twice."

Stoltman's experts taught the trainees a number of different shooting techniques that day, including the "double tap," which involved taking two shots at the target in the lower-chest area—*pop pop*, *pause*—drawing back to evaluate whether you hit the target, then taking two more shots—*pop pop*, *pause*, *pop pop*, *pause,* and so on, until the target was no longer a threat.

They also taught the trainees the "two-man rule" (always stick with your buddy, don't leave him behind), to stay out of fatal funnels (dangerous areas like hallways, where you can't hide, all you can do is engage or retreat), and to "clear," "corner," and "pie." The latter technique, also known as "slicing the pie," involved peeking and then slicing around a corner, keeping about an arm's-length distance from the wall so as not to get shot.

When Stoltman first met Eric at Metropolis, he remembered how Eric used to talk longingly about getting a 9mm Beretta.

"Beretta's the gun, man," Eric said. "I want to carry a 'nine.' Joe, look it up. Sell me your Beretta."

Eric also wanted to be a part of Stoltman's company and handle the security together for the Roxbury South nightclub. When Stoltman applied for a license, Eric said he'd already told the Roxbury that they were licensed, which was a lie. When Stoltman said he wouldn't lie, Eric told him to forget it. Stoltman found out later that Eric got the contract.

Witnesses told police that Eric grabbed a manager one night at the Roxbury. When questioned later by Newport Beach police about the incident, Eric denied it, saying he'd simply stated, "Get out of my face," and pushed the manager away.

"He was a guy that worked for me that stabbed me in the back," Eric explained. "It cost me my account, and I still didn't hit him. Do you know anybody that wouldn't? . . . Instead of looking at me as the aggressor in the situation, I would say, 'Damn, Eric, you did a pretty good job of holding your fucking temper, 'cause if someone did that to me, I would've killed him,' right?"

Eric told Stoltman in 1993 that he was engaged to Samantha, who had moved to Texas. Eric later told Nanette that he broke up with Samantha because she didn't want him sending money to his kids.

In June 1994, Stoltman said, Eric told him he was seeing Nanette, and that she had paid for his toupee. Nanette wanted to support him, Eric said, but he didn't want that. He wanted his own business.

In October 1994, Eric told Stoltman that he was having second thoughts and some trust issues with Nanette. He said he was planning to ask her to marry him, but he wanted Stoltman to follow her while she was on a business trip in Palm Springs to see what she was up to. But after Stoltman quoted him a price of $1,500 to $2,000, Eric never called back.

Later he told Stoltman that he'd taken care of the situation himself. Whatever issues Eric had with Nanette must have been resolved before he took her home to meet his family that Thanksgiving.

Still trying to get to the bottom of Eric's gun stories, the detectives interviewed other friends and former coworkers, including Roy Rauschklob, cross-checking their statements with other evidence.

Eric practiced at a firing range at least twice that fall and winter. Rauschklob told police he went with Eric during a September trip, noting that Eric didn't have a gun with him so he used his friend Tony Diaz's, who had a Beretta 92F. Diaz, a former Metropolis bartender, said Eric had told him he was planning to buy a similar model, and by mid-1994, he'd done so.

Rauschklob also saw Nanette, Eric, and his friend Jamsheed "Jayme" Amirie at the Firing Line range in the next month or two. Eric told Amirie that it was Nanette's first time shooting.

Rauschklob recalled that Eric said Nanette didn't like the trigger pull of the .380, so he'd bought her a 9mm Beretta for Christmas in 1993. Eric also told him he'd been carrying his nine-millimeter during the Lake Elsinore security job.

In Eric's journal—on the page *before* he wrote Bill's license plate number—he noted that the Lake Elsinore job took place over three weeks of evenings in December 1994. An invoice for the job said it lasted from December 3 to 17.

If Eric was carrying his nine-millimeter in Lake Elsinore, how could it have been missing since the summer, as he'd originally told police? Detective Voth ran a gun ownership database inquiry on Nanette and found no gun registrations for her, and no record of a second 9mm gun for Eric.

Eric's off-and-on roommate, Leonard Jomsky, said he went shooting one Saturday afternoon in late summer 1994 with Eric, Nanette, and Todd Calder. They fired at targets—including the silhouette of a person and a set of concentric rings—for a little more than an hour with Eric's .380 and Calder's nine-millimeter.

They each went through two or three clips, or a total of twenty or thirty shots, which they bought at the range. Nanette stood with the gun in front of her, with one hand

supporting the other. When Eric tried to show her a certai
technique, she said, "I know," as if she didn't need to be
instructed.

Jomsky and Nanette both struck the targets, but Jomsky
said that "hers was a little bit better than mine. It was the
second time I shot a gun. She made a point of that, once
we returned back to the house, to let everybody know that
she shot better than I did. She mentioned that someone else
had taught her how to shoot a gun, so it wasn't her first time
shooting."

Jomsky said Eric loaned him the same .380 in December
1994 when they worked the Lake Elsinore job, and he gave
it back when the gig was over.

# CHAPTER 22

In the summer of 1994, Eric Naposki met an attractive blonde named Suzanne Cogar while lying out at the pool at the Newpointe Apartments in Tustin. Cogar, who worked for a high-end shoe distributor, lived in a mirror-image studio on the ground floor near his. Cogar and Eric became friends, hanging out at the pool and taking Jacuzzis together. They went out for some food with his friends one night, and to a movie together another night.

Cogar appreciated that he was nice-looking, had a muscular body, and seemed likeable and charming, but she didn't see any romantic potential.

"As far as intellectualwise, I kind of thought he was a meathead," she said in 2012. "I'm more the brainiac type and he's not. I knew it was going to be a friendship thing as soon as we started talking."

She added that she didn't feel like Eric was pursuing her either, even though she did sense an attraction between them.

"Otherwise, I don't think he would have given me the time of day," she said. "So it worked being friends."

From her only window, a sliding glass door onto her patio, Cogar could see him coming and going from his apartment. Sometimes he was with a blonde who often had two children in tow, and they all hung out by the pool. She usually saw the woman on weekends during the day, never on a weekend *without* the kids, and some weekends Cogar didn't see her at all. If she ever came over at night, Cogar didn't notice.

*What's the deal?* she wondered. *Why is she here only part of the time?*

Curious, she asked Eric about their relationship. "Is that your girlfriend?"

"We hang out sometimes," he said vaguely.

He talked a bit about the woman—Nanette—but he wouldn't give Cogar a straight answer whether they were actually dating. Cogar didn't feel the need to push for clarification, but did wonder why Eric was being so evasive about it.

One weekend in early September, Cogar showed up with a girlfriend at Eric's door around midnight, after a night of clubbing.

"Do you want to come to the Jacuzzi?" she asked, surprised to see that Eric was naked when he answered the door, groggy with sleep.

Looking first at Cogar's friend and then at Cogar, he said, "I don't know you, but I do know you." He took Cogar by the wrist, pulled her inside his apartment, and closed the door on the girlfriend. He started to kiss Cogar and began backing her toward his bed, which was only a few feet away in the small studio.

As he bent her over the bed, she didn't resist at first. But after quickly determining that she didn't want to be kissing a naked linebacker, she tried to push her hands against his shoulders to signal that she wanted him to get off her. However, she couldn't budge him. He was just too big.

She felt completely defenseless. She didn't feel as if he was going to force himself on her, but she feared that if he did decide to get more aggressive, she wouldn't be able to stop him.

Thinking fast, she said, "Oh, my God, it's so cold in here."

"Is it too cold?" he asked.

"Yeah, it's like a refrigerator."

"I can turn it down," he said, getting up to check the thermostat, mounted on the wall a few feet away.

Taking advantage of the opportunity, she jumped off the bed and bolted out the door. She wasn't in fear for her life; she just wanted to get out of there.

The next evening, Eric stopped by her apartment to apologize. "I'm sorry about last night," he said. "I hope I didn't scare you, because you ran out."

Cogar didn't want to hurt his feelings so she made up an excuse. "That's okay," she said. "I had to get going. My friend was waiting for me and we wanted to go get changed and go to the Jacuzzi."

Cogar accepted his apology, and they went back to chatting occasionally around the complex.

Then, in the middle of the night in October, Eric came banging on Cogar's door, around 2:00 A.M. "I wanted to warn you," he said in a voice other than his usual calm, smooth tone. He wasn't in a panic, but he seemed genuinely alarmed. "Some guys just tried to get into my apartment."

"You scared the crap out of me," she said, annoyed that he had overreacted to the situation and then jerked her out of a sound sleep. "Why did you have to come and tell *me* if they were banging on *your* door?"

"I just wanted to warn you because they ran down this way and I was wondering if you saw them," he said.

"No," she replied.

Later, Eric told police that he'd chased a man out of the complex after seeing the handle on his front door jiggling at 3:00 A.M. in December (either he or Cogar misremembered the month and time of this incident). At first, he thought it was Nanette trying to get in. But when the jiggling got harder, he grabbed a big jacket and a sword—the only weapon he said he kept in the apartment—and ran after the guy who had been trying to break into the apartment.

"Now, if that was the case and I owned a gun, any gun whatsoever . . . I sure as fuck wouldn't have chased him with my sword," he said. "If I had a gun, I still would have shot the motherfucker if he came into my house."

Cogar, however, told police she didn't recall seeing him holding a sword that night. A sword wasn't something she'd miss.

In early November 1994, Eric showed up at Cogar's one evening as if he wanted to talk. Things clearly had changed between him and Nanette. He revealed that he felt stronger about her than he had about any other woman. In fact, he wanted to marry her. So he was quite incensed, he said, when Nanette told him that her wealthy, older business partner, Bill, had come into her bedroom and tried to force her to have sex with him.

"She's living with this guy?" Cogar asked with surprise and disbelief—this being the first time she'd heard about Nanette's living arrangement.

Cogar couldn't believe that Nanette wouldn't be involved with *any* man she was living with. It sounded like Nanette was seeing Eric on the side, a case of "money here, body there," and that she was trying to pacify Eric by claiming that she wasn't romantically involved with Bill. Only later did Cogar decide that Nanette had said this to Eric intentionally, to get him riled up and jealous.

Although Eric seemed to sincerely believe that Nanette's so-called roommate was forcing himself on her, the story made no sense to Cogar.

"Do you really believe that?" she asked. "Why doesn't she just leave?"

"Because of the kids," he said. "She has to stay because of the kids."

Eric said that the kids didn't belong to the older guy, and Cogar knew from previous conversations that they weren't Eric's.

"She's feeding you a line of bull," Cogar replied, thinking that any woman in her right mind would move out of the house if something like that had happened.

*Doesn't she have a mom, siblings, Eric, or a hotel that she could go to?* she wondered.

But Eric was angry. So angry, he said, that he was going to do something about it. Bill had his own private jet, which he often flew to Las Vegas, and he was planning to go there over Christmas.

"I'm going to have him killed," Eric said, "blown away. . . . I'm going to have his plane blown up."

"Blow his plane up? That's crazy," she said. "What are you talking about?"

"I know how I would have that done," he said.

Eric sounded so serious that he scared her.

"That's not something that you go around saying to people, that you want to have someone's plane blown up," she said.

But Eric didn't seem to be paying attention to what she was saying, and Cogar lost all interest in continuing the conversation *or* their friendship.

Suzanne Cogar went home to visit her family for Christmas. When she came back in early January 1995, she walked by Eric's apartment and saw that it was vacant. One evening a couple weeks later, he knocked on her front door.

He said he'd moved out on December 22, but he'd apparently come back to the complex specifically to have this talk with her.

"Have you seen any cops around here?" he asked with a profoundly curious tone.

"No, why?"

"Well, if you see any, just don't talk to them, and don't tell them that you know me," he said. Eric added that he was worried the police might talk to the manager, who would tell them that he and Cogar were friends, and then they might try to question her.

"Did you hear that man is dead?" he asked.

"What man?" she asked. Remembering their earlier conversation, she asked, "You mean that man you told me about?" *Surely, he's not going to tell me* that *man was killed.*

"Bill McLaughlin, the guy that Nanette was living with," he said. "Somebody shot him and he's dead."

Now Cogar really didn't know what to think. First, Eric had told her that he was going to have this guy blown away or his plane blown up, and now he was telling her that the guy had been shot? Was he getting off by shocking her? Was he trying to impress her somehow? Or was he for real?

"I don't even want to know if you did it," she said, shaking her head and trying to push away the information.

"I didn't do it, but I might've had somebody do it," he said, smirking.

Knowing he had a security company and the resources to pull this off, Cogar felt the weight of this grim possibility on her chest and shoulders. She'd known others in the security business and to her they seemed like "hotheaded wannabes." Why had he laid this knowledge on her? What was she supposed to do with it?

"I don't even want to know if you did it," she said again, still unsure whether he could have done it himself or had someone else do it.

"Maybe I did, maybe I didn't," he said, still smirking.

That remark made her think that he really *could* have done it himself. "Why [else] would he leave himself in the pool of possibility?" she said later.

On the other hand, she still wasn't sure if any part of his story was true.

"His demeanor was creepy," she recalled. "The expression on his face was unnerving."

Then Eric told her about the key the killer had left in the entryway of Bill's house, a key copied at a store right down the street from their apartment complex in Tustin.

And as if that weren't enough, Eric knew about the killer's gun too. "The gun that was used was the same kind of gun that I own, but they're not going to find it on me because I don't have it anymore," he said. "I loaned it to a buddy of mine."

All these incriminating statements were making her very uncomfortable, but given that she hadn't read the newspaper or watched the TV news lately, she was still skeptical that there had even been a murder. (At this point, the detectives didn't know where the keys had been made, so those details hadn't been released to the public, including what type of gun the killer had used.)

Trying to avoid any conflict with Eric, Cogar pretended to agree not to talk to the police and tried to encourage him to leave her apartment without letting her true feelings show. The last thing she wanted to do was to provoke or upset him, but she didn't think she'd be able to deny anything he'd said to anyone.

*If he's capable of having someone killed, then he could do the same to me.*

Eric called a few months later to chat and touch base, and perhaps, she thought, to check to see if she'd spoken to the cops, which she still had not. During the conversation, which seemed to have no other particular purpose, he reported that his relationship with Nanette was flagging.

"Things aren't working out," he said.

Cogar figured they were breaking up, but that it wasn't "one hundred percent over." All she could think was *Well, you got yourself into this, and for what?*

By this point, it seemed to her that Eric had left Orange County. This gave her a little more peace of mind, and she felt safer about reporting his comments to the police. Especially after she had watched the news and confirmed for herself that Bill McLaughlin had actually been murdered. Nanette, to whom they referred as Bill's fiancée, was also featured. Cogar recognized her walk, with those short, quick, confident steps.

Cogar dialed the NBPD and got a woman on the phone. Cogar said she had information about a murder, and wanted to give a statement. However, no one was in the detective bureau to talk to her, so the woman asked her to call back.

"It took so much nerve for me to make this phone call that I will likely not call back," Cogar replied.

The woman didn't seem to know what to do—and as Cogar had warned, she didn't have the nerve to call back.


Three years later, in March 1998, Cogar was living in a different apartment with a roommate, and they had gotten nearly twenty hang-up calls in the past month. As the two women wracked their brains, trying to figure out who the caller could be, Cogar thought of Eric.

*Maybe he's checking up on me.*

After having pushed his disturbing comments out of her mind, this harassing episode brought them back to the forefront of her conscience.

*I can't live with suppressing this anymore. I'm going to call the police again.*

This time she reached a detective, Tom Fischbacher. As she recounted her story, Fischbacher took an edgy tone with her, as if to say, "Why should we believe you?"

When she said she was scared, he also didn't reassure her that she would be protected from Eric if she was ever called to testify. So, after mulling it over, she left a message canceling the appointment to meet with him.

About five days later, Sergeant Pat O'Sullivan called to apologize for Fischbacher's abrasive manner and asked if she would meet with him instead. As she elaborated on her story, she found him much nicer and easier to talk to, but she still wanted to remain anonymous. He told her that her information was important, but "it isn't enough to make an arrest."

*After all that, it just goes to show that I know nothing about law enforcement.*

Nonetheless, she felt as if she had done her part, and that her safety was intact.

# CHAPTER 23

Tricia Stearns would never forget the night of December 15, 1994. She and her boyfriend Fernando Leguizamon were in bed asleep when the phone rang, sometime around midnight. It was Nanette, which took them by surprise.

Leguizamon picked up the receiver and put the call on speakerphone. In her usual monotone voice, Nanette delivered some sad news.

"There's been a death in my family, and I'm very sorry, but I won't be at the game tomorrow," she said, referring to a Lakers game to which she'd been planning to take Kristofer's team.

"That's fine. We'll take care of it," Leguizamon said.

But Nanette wasn't finished. "I was at [the mall] and I was Christmas shopping, when I got the call that somebody died," she said. She didn't mention any names, or what relation this person was to her.

Stearns and Leguizamon went back to sleep and got quite a shock when they saw the article in the *Daily Pilot* that Saturday morning, describing the murder and mentioning Nanette as Bill's live-in girlfriend.

"We were like, 'Wow. Oh. My. God,'" Stearns recalled.

"It blew our minds, because it couldn't have been further from what we thought we knew."

Stearns and Leguizamon decided pretty quickly that Nanette's midnight phone call must have been part of her plan to establish her shopping trip as an alibi. As they began to put the whole thing together, they both felt frightened.

"You know, the kids can never go over there again," Leguizamon said. "I don't care who has the gun. The kids are never going to be around any of this. Ever."

Luckily, the basketball season was coming to an end, so they were able to distance themselves and Leguizamon's kids from Nanette and Eric without making a big deal about it.

Stearns said she and Leguizamon each called separately and left messages with the police, but no one ever called them back. Stearns couldn't understand why.

"We thought it was important that she'd called us at that time," she said.

Leguizamon subsequently developed cancer. And even on his deathbed at the City of Hope, a cancer center in Orange County, he kept bringing up Nanette's call. It was odd, Stearns said, that the sicker he got, the more he seemed to want to talk about it. As he lay on life support, he kept saying that the police needed to know what he and Stearns knew about Nanette and Eric.

"Honey, you need to call the police again," he insisted.

After Leguizamon died in May 1998, Stearns said she tried to call the NBPD again, to honor her dying boyfriend's request, and asked to speak to a detective or whoever was involved with the Bill McLaughlin case.

"Someone will get back to you if they need the information," she was told.

But still, no one called her back.

"It always bothered me," Stearns said. "Personally, I think the police did a pathetic job. I felt like I was being a pain in the ass, which is why I didn't call back more. . . . I think they made mistakes all the way along."

After seeing that Nanette and Eric had been arrested and were going to trial, she forwarded a written statement to the department in 2010. Stearns really wanted to attend the trials, but she couldn't see flying all the way back from San Antonio, Texas, where she'd since moved.

"I wanted Nanette and Eric to see me," she said in 2012. "I've lain awake nights, thinking about this."

# CHAPTER 24

In interviews with Bill McLaughlin's children, Detective Hartford asked if their father had ever given them permission to sign his name. They all said no. Nor did they think Bill would have let anyone else sign for him on a document or check. All three of them also denied knowing anything about business plans that Bill had with Nanette. In fact, Jenny recalled Bill telling her that he planned to divest himself of the majority of his investments because they weren't profitable. The only area in which he felt knowledgeable enough to make money was the biomedical field, something about which Nanette only pretended to know.

In February 1995, the police began to receive anonymous calls and packages of information that put Nanette in a negative light, such as a copy of the "Wealthy Men Only" singles ad, which arrived at the NBPD in a yellow envelope. The police later learned that the packages and anonymous calls had come from K. Ross Johnston's girlfriend, Julia, who also told detectives that Nanette had been fired for forging customers' signatures at the company that published the Donnelly phone directory. Julia wanted to stay anonymous because she feared that Nanette would sue her.

Julia said that after Nanette broke up with Tom Reynolds, she was driving a late-model Mercedes, wearing a Rolex watch, and throwing around details about a trip to Europe. Julia also said that Nanette had been bragging about owning a residence on Seashore Drive and being "a millionaire on paper."

When Voth followed up with Donnelly, he learned that Julia was telling the truth about Nanette being fired. She was terminated on May 14, 1990, after less than six weeks of working there.

Tom Reynolds also supplied the singles ad to police, claiming that he was due some of the reward money, but Voth told him he'd already received that information from another source.

Nanette and Eric were named as suspects in Bill's murder in search warrant affidavits that were released to the media in early February 1995. After keeping this information to themselves for fear that the McLaughlin family might confront Nanette, who would then flee, the detectives notified Bill's daughters that the information was about to hit the papers. The McLaughlins, in turn, sat down with Kevin's girlfriend, Sandy Baumgardner, to fill her in.

Recalling the gist of Kim's words, Sandy said: "Nanette is absolutely nasty. She's dated a bunch of other guys. [There was] something about getting into a car accident and breaking her nose. She told Bill a different story, but she was out with some other guy. She was dating this guy Eric Naposki. She didn't have custody of her kids—she had joint [custody]. She's not educated. Everything she said was a bunch of BS." There was also the cockamamie story she'd told Bill about taking her grandmother on a cruise to Jamaica, when, in fact, she'd taken her boyfriend Eric.

As expected, front-page stories came out over the next couple of days in the *Daily Pilot* and the *Orange County Register,* in which Nanette denied, denied, denied. The *Los Angeles Times* also covered the story.

"It's all garbage. It's been a living nightmare," Nanette told the *Register.* "I'm in limbo. I've lost somebody and now I'm being pointed at as being involved somehow."

As soon as K. Ross Johnston read the stories describing Nanette as Bill's "fiancée," he asked her about it.

"The reporters got all that wrong," she told him. "I'm going to sue them."

The news stories prompted various people who knew or recognized Nanette and Eric to call the NBPD with possible leads.

Sharon Hedberg, the sales rep for Turtle Rock Summit Estates, for example, told Voth about the couple's house-hunting trip to the Seven Oaks development in July 1994.

Voth and Hartford checked with Bill's accountant, Brian Ringler, who said that Bill had never mentioned any interest in buying a new million-dollar home. More important, he said, Bill never would have been able to purchase such a home, because of his cash flow problems.

The detectives also checked with Marjorie Taft, one of Bill's business partners in the desert development project, and learned that she and another partner, Lou Glisan, had taken a $20,000 loss on the project and had been forced to relocate to Colorado. She described Bill as a pleasant person to deal with, but said Nanette had appeared cold, antisocial, and didn't participate in their business dealings.

Voth said that Taft and Glisan were cleared of suspicion once the detectives learned that Bill had rolled over the $1 million insurance policy on the project to cover Nanette instead.

The day in February 1995 that the news stories came out, the McLaughlin family got a call from a neighbor on Seashore Drive that the garage door to the beach house was wide open. Sandy immediately drove Kim, Sue, and Kevin over there to secure the property.

As soon as they walked inside through the open garage, they didn't like what they saw. Upstairs, Nanette had set up an office with a new and rather expansive wraparound desk. They recognized the fax and copy machines she'd snagged from Bill's office while they were in Hawaii. It looked like this woman had been busy.

*What the hell is she doing?* they wondered. *She's never had a job before.*

As they wandered into Nanette's bedroom, they were greeted by a poster-size, silhouetted image of her, which was resting on an easel and revealed the outline of her naked breasts as she arched her head and her back with abandon. And shut away in the walk-in closet was Goldie, who emerged, wagging her tail.

The police had asked them to retrieve a recent photo of Nanette in case she decided to flee, so they were on a mission to pluck one of the many shots Nanette had once displayed throughout the dining area at Balboa Coves, which were now arranged around the beach house. The one they grabbed subsequently made its way onto a news broadcast.

After about twenty minutes of snooping around, they went outside. Sandy and Kevin were standing in the alley when a man driving Bill's Cadillac pulled up and motioned for them to move out of the way so he could pull into the garage. He did so, then closed the door from inside.

It was Eric Naposki, and the fact that he was driving the Cadillac directly conflicted with Nanette's claim that he never drove her car or had access to her keys when she wasn't with him.

A few days later, Nanette left Sandy a pissy message on her answering machine, complaining, ironically, that they had rifled through her things and had stolen something of *hers*.

"You took that picture," she said. "That's theft."

In early March, the Orange County crime lab asked the NBPD detectives to obtain a sample of Eric's blood to see whose blood was on the towel found in his car. Eric agreed and gave them the sample on March 7. The test came back positive for Eric's blood, but there was no sign of Bill's.

At the request of the NBPD, a Yorktown Heights police officer went to chat with Eric's mother, Ronnie Naposki, about Eric's claims that he'd sent his father the .380 to protect himself. Immediately defensive, Ronnie stuck up for her son, saying he didn't kill Bill McLaughlin. It was fifteen degrees out, and yet Ronnie didn't ask the officer to come inside.

Eric never had anything to do with guns when he was living in New York, she said, although he did buy some when he was living in Texas. She said she never saw those weapons and she had no clue what type they were, but there were none in her house now.

She seemed to be familiar with Nanette's engagement to Bill, but she said Nanette was seeing Eric now.

"Because she is some kind of slut who was living with some rich old man, they think my Eric killed him," she said.

Shortly after the officer's visit, Detective Craig Frizzell got a call from Eric, who was incensed that the police had bothered his mother. Frizzell said it was necessary because Eric still hadn't given them the information they needed about the weapon. Eric said he would call back with it.

Four hours later, he called to say that he'd given his father a Davis Industries blue steel .380 semiautomatic, model p-380, with the serial number AP074982, which he'd bought two or three years before he'd bought the Jennings .380 in Dallas.

Upon checking, Detective Hartford found no legal record of Eric or his father ever owning a gun in New York.


On April 9, 1995, Eric and Nanette went house shopping again, this time in Lake Forest, with her two kids, saying they had four kids between them.

The couple contacted Richard "Dick" Kurth, a former deputy finance director for the city of Newport Beach, about buying a four-bedroom home that Kurth was selling for $375,000. The deal would have been $50,000 down and $3,000 per month.

Nanette told Kurth that she had the use of the Seashore Drive house for a year, but she still wanted to move out in August. She said that she was expecting to receive some insurance money or a trust within a year, and that she alone planned to take title of the Lake Forest property, adding Eric to it later. Eric said he played football for the National Football Conference (NFC) and that he would be playing in the Canadian Football League (CFL) in Memphis the following season.

Two days later, Nanette called back. When Kurth asked about her finances, she said her attorney would call to discuss the deal. Kurth never heard from her attorney, but he did hear from Eric, who called about two weeks later to say they very much liked the house and were still interested in buying it, but they would have to wait until the controversy reported in the media had died down.

Failing to persuade Nanette to return their father's Cadillac, Kim and Jenny McLaughlin called upon a friend, Jason Gendron. Gendron was living with a woman named Krissy, who had been Jenny's best friend since kindergarten, and whom he later married. They asked if Gendron would go into the garage at the Seashore house and take the car with a key, but Gendron said he was uncomfortable doing that while Eric was hanging around.

"I think it would be better if we would just wait till she goes somewhere, and we take the car there," he said.

Gendron asked another friend to help him. For three hours before work every morning, the two men sat in a white Toyota truck across from the house, waiting for Nanette to drive away.

They were about to give up when the garage door opened three days later, on April 14, and they saw Nanette loading her kids into the car, with Eric standing by.

As they were pulling away, Gendron called the Newport police to inform them about the Cadillac repossession. Noting that it was a civil matter, a detective said he wanted to look in the car as soon as the McLaughlin estate had possession of it once again.

"Just call when you get the car," he said.

Gendron followed Nanette to Interstate 5, heading north to the 57. He had no idea where she was going, but he hoped it wasn't on a long trip.

She got off at the Brea Canyon Boulevard exit, headed west, and stopped at a private Christian school on Brea

Canyon Road, where she dropped off Kristofer. From there, she drove to a McDonald's in the Diamond Bar/Walnut area, leaving the car near the double doors while she and Lishele went inside.

Acting quickly, Gendron hopped out of the truck, unlocked the Cadillac, and started up the car. Hearing the engine noise, Nanette turned around. As Gendron was driving away, she ran outside and waved her arms, but he kept right on going.

Assuming she would report the car stolen, Gendron called to arrange to meet the Newport Beach detectives in Costa Mesa and headed for the southbound 57. Given Nanette's response, he wanted to deliver the car to the police right away, so he wouldn't get pulled over in a "stolen" car.

In the trunk, the police found five banker's boxes of the financial records Nanette had taken from Bill's office at Balboa Coves. The cops seized them as part of the investigation.

Gendron went to work from there. On his way home, his girlfriend called to warn him that he had voice mail messages waiting from a very upset Nanette Johnston and an angry Eric Naposki.

"They were extremely hostile and extremely agitated about the car being gone," Gendron testified later.

Gendron had no idea how they'd gotten his home number, but he didn't like it. Later he figured that when Nanette reported the car stolen, the Newport Beach dispatcher had told the Walnut Police Department that Gendron was the repo man, so they probably broadcast his phone number over the police radio and also gave it to Nanette.

As Gendron and his girlfriend were discussing options, the phone rang. It was Nanette, screaming about "stuff that she needed in the car, and how could I take it and leave her stranded in Walnut," he explained later.

"Hey, I just was asked to do this," he told her. "I have nothing to do with it. I returned the car to its rightful owner."

Then Eric got on the phone and threatened to find out where Gendron lived. The gist was "Give us back the car. We'll do this the easy way or the hard way. It's only a matter of time before I find you."

Gendron was so scared that he immediately called the phone company to have the line disconnected and get a new number.


That same day, Detective Voth asked Jenny to call Nanette and tape the conversation, hoping that Nanette would say something incriminating. Jenny started the call by letting Nanette vent about the day's events.

"Well, they left me, like, up in Diamond Bar," Nanette said, "with four kids. . . . All Kristofer's sports equipment is in the car. My camera . . . just everything."

"I understand that you thought that we weren't supposed to take the car," Jenny said.

"Well, obviously, it was *my* car."

Jenny said they didn't have any records to that effect, noting that Bill's will specifically left Nanette the Infiniti, not the Cadillac.

Nanette countered that she was the only one who ever drove the Cadillac—and, besides, Jenny *knew* it was Nanette's car.

"Well, no, I don't know," Jenny said.

"You know your dad bought that car for me," Nanette repeated, as if that would make it so.

"So it was his intention to leave it to you?"

Nanette said that was her impression. "I have the title that he signed that you guys were supposedly disputing, saying that I signed it myself."

She said she'd faxed a copy of the title to the McLaughlins' attorney, but Jenny said he needed to see the original, because it hadn't been filed with the DMV.

Nanette had an excuse for everything. She said she didn't file it with the state because she wanted to talk to the McLaughlins first and went through her attorney so it wouldn't look "suspicious," an odd choice of words. She also said she didn't file the DMV paperwork because Bill's insurance rates were one-third of hers.

Jenny countered that if it really was Nanette's car, didn't it make sense that she file the pink slip with the DMV?

"I didn't know he was going to die," Nanette replied defiantly.

Moving on to the questionable bank checks the McLaughlins had been trying to discuss with Nanette, Jenny said, "If we have those analyzed, they're not from my dad's signature."

"It *is* your dad's signature," Nanette argued.

Asked when he'd signed them, Nanette was evasive. "Which one are you talking about, the big one?"

"Well, there's one for two hundred and fifty thousand dollars," Jenny said, "and then there are a couple other ones where the signatures don't check out."

Nanette claimed she often signed for Bill, with his permission. When Jenny expressed her skepticism, Nanette stood firm. "Oh yeah, I signed his name on many things."

"Huh," Jenny replied in disbelief. "He never let *us* do that."

"Whenever he was out of town and something needed to be done, he told me to sign for him, and I've signed on so many things, you could be checking my signature against his."

"So, did you sign his name, then, on that two-hundred-and-fifty-thousand-dollar check?" Jenny asked.

"No, I did not sign that one. He signed that one."

Asked when, Nanette said there were so many checks

that she wasn't sure, but she thought it was about a week before his death.

"Oh, really?" Jenny asked. "When did you put it through the bank?"

"Not until afterward, because it was supposed to go in the corporation, but I hadn't opened the checking account yet."

"If it was supposed to go in the corporation, then why was it made out to Nanette Johnston Trust?"

"Because he had signed it and written it, then I went after he died, 'cause I hadn't made it. I had not opened that account yet. I wrote that part."

"He signed a blank check for two hundred and fifty thousand dollars?"

Nanette proceeded to concoct a scenario where Bill was supposedly signing checks every week, leaving the rest blank for Nanette to fill in as she paid bills or transferred funds among his various accounts. They wrote so many checks, she said, that she and Bill had been in the process of setting up a system so she could wire transfer funds between accounts on her own.

When Jenny told Nanette that they'd already found a couple of checks where they'd noticed that the payee had been changed to Nanette's name, Nanette played ignorant.

"I don't know what you're talking about—on that you have to show me," she said. "I can't remember every single thing. I signed so many things for him and I did tons of . . . that."

Jenny said she also couldn't find any paperwork on the McDonald's or Burger King franchises that Nanette claimed they'd been thinking of buying. Furthermore, Jenny said, she'd never heard anything about those deals from her father.

Nanette replied that the paperwork was in those boxes in the Cadillac's trunk, which had since been confiscated by police. "So I have no idea where anything is now." Besides, Nanette added rather cattily, "he doesn't tell you guys everything. We looked at many things. Every time, we . . . he told you something we were looking at, you always scoffed at it."

As for Nanette's personal belongings in the Cadillac, Jenny said, Nanette could go to the NBPD station to pick them up. But Nanette wanted them brought to the Seashore house.

"Why can't you get it from the police station?" Jenny asked.

"Well, I'd rather not," Nanette said, claiming that she was worried about theft. "There's a lot of expensive stuff in there."

"The police station seems like a pretty good place to me," Jenny retorted. "I mean, at least somebody will be there and your stuff is sure to be safe."

Although Nanette claimed she was concerned her things would get stolen from the yard where they took the cars, it's more likely that she simply didn't want any more contact with police.

Once Nanette realized she wasn't going to get the Cadillac back, she started asking when she could get the Infiniti. Jenny explained that Dave Mitchell, Bill's friend and realtor in Las Vegas, was in a coma after having a heart attack, so they couldn't make the transfer at the moment.

Nanette volunteered to go to Las Vegas to get the car. "I have a key to the house, unless you changed the locks."

But Jenny was one step ahead of her. "Yeah," she said, "we changed the locks."

# CHAPTER 25

After determining that Nanette had stolen at least $497,000 from Bill McLaughlin's bank accounts by forging his name on fifteen checks, Detective Bill Hartford obtained an arrest warrant for grand theft and forgery, at 1:45 P.M. on April 17, 1995.

Four hours later, a lieutenant, two detectives, and an officer arrested her at the Seashore Drive house. Taken to jail, she was held on $500,000 bail, a figure based on the amount she allegedly stole from Bill's accounts.

Searching her wallet, police found a State Farm Insurance check for $133, issued to Nanette Johnston and the McLaughlin Estate on April 6, 1995, along with $1,412 in cash. She also had an American Express corporate executive gold card, issued to Nanette Johnston and Bill Mac Development on March 3, 1995, and a regular American Express corporate card, issued in March 1994 to the same parties.

After Bill's death, she still had the authority to sign on the PriMerit trust account, to which she'd been illegally transferring money, but she had no control or signing authority on any of his other accounts or credit cards, nor the authority to obtain a credit card in his companies' names.

Those assets and accounts were under the purview of Kim McLaughlin, as the estate's executrix.

Nanette also had a plastic envelope that contained a single passport photo. The detectives thought one must be missing, because they typically come in pairs. The items were booked into evidence, and she was allowed to call her attorney, Barry Bernstein.

Deputy District Attorney Debbie Lloyd said recently that she never supported the NBPD's decision to split the detectives' work into separate fraud and homicide investigations, and she'd made her feelings known at the time.

With the help of Bill's accountant, Brian Ringler, the McLaughlins compiled a binder of financial records that showed Nanette had been embezzling money, saying "they suspected that [Bill] found out about it and he was going to cut her off," Lloyd recalled.

"We definitely had a good case, so then the police immediately wanted to go arrest her on the fraud," she said, because they thought they could strong-arm Nanette into talking about the murder.

Lloyd said she and Joe D'Agostino, a fraud prosecutor, tried to dissuade the police from taking this approach.

"She's not going to talk. She did it," Lloyd said. "Don't do it."

After the NBPD went ahead and split the case, she said, D'Agostino handled the fraud portion and Lloyd held on to the murder case.

"I still wanted to do the homicide," she said. "I thought it was the more important."

Around eleven o'clock on the night of Nanette's arrest, one of the detectives called her.

"We arrested her," he said.

"What did she say?"

"I want my attorney."

*Perfect,* she thought facetiously. *Now she'll never talk.*


The day Nanette was arrested, Kim McLaughlin decided to change the locks on the Seashore house to ensure that Nanette couldn't cheat them out of anything else. Kim called a locksmith to meet her there, and she and her brother showed up half an hour early to look around.

"We thought, who knows who's been in the house? Who knows who has had keys to the property?" Kim recalled. "We don't know what kind of condition the house is in."

Not knowing if Eric or someone else might be there, they knocked before entering. That's when Goldie started barking, and they heard a man yell, "Hush, hush."

Kim and Kevin looked at each other with surprise, wondering, *Who is that in the house?* If it was Eric, neither of them wanted to confront him, especially after his threatening calls about the Cadillac. The police had already labeled him as a murder suspect, and that was enough for the McLaughlins to know he could be dangerous. So they headed back to Balboa Coves, called the police, and let them know what was going on.


Nanette was set to be arraigned Wednesday, April 19, which turned out to be the same day as the Oklahoma City bombing.

An *Orange County Register* article that morning quoted Eric's attorney as saying that his alibi could be proven by records of the call he made with a calling card, a type of credit card, at 8:52 P.M. from a Denny's at Seventeenth

Street and Tustin Avenue, while on his way to work at the Thunderbird.

By this time, Eric had hired Julian Bailey, a well-known criminal lawyer, to help him deal with the NBPD's well-publicized suspicions about his involvement in the murder. Bailey noted that Eric had cooperated with police by agreeing to the tests that showed the towel in his car didn't have Bill McLaughlin's blood on it.

"We are aware of a number of other persons who have a motive, either personal or financial, to want Mr. McLaughlin dead," Bailey said.

In court that day, Nanette's attorney, Barry Bernstein, asked the judge to delay Nanette's arraignment for a few days so he could get up to speed on the case. He complained to reporters that the police had arrested Nanette in front of her children, instead of arranging for her to surrender. He also said that her bail of $500,000 was too high and he hoped to get it reduced to a more manageable $70,000.

Eric complained to reporters that he and Nanette had been publicly named as suspects, proclaiming that he never knew Nanette had been romantically involved with Bill McLaughlin.

"Do I look like the kind of guy who would need to date someone who already had a boyfriend?" he asked rhetorically.

Eric said he had a phone bill to prove that he was in Tustin around the time of the shooting, and that he didn't even get to Newport until 9:30 P.M., twenty minutes after Bill was killed. Faulting the police, he said, "I think they went public before they really knew the facts of that evening. . . . It was like they were ignoring the truth."

The police laughed off the criticisms. "That guy is a media whore," one of the detectives said, laughing with his colleagues in the captain's office after the hearing.

Later that day, Eric called the Yamaha dealership in

Costa Mesa, where Nanette had bought the motorcycles the day of Bill's funeral—the same ones Eric had been keeping in his storage unit. Eric proposed to sell the items back, but when he was offered only $3,500, he yelled at the dealer and hung up, saying he would call back later.

While Nanette was in jail, Eric began calling the McLaughlins on her behalf, trying to get the Infiniti back. Advised by the police to tape one of the conversations, Jenny did so when he called again, the morning of April 20.

Eric said he was acting as a middleman because Nanette couldn't make these calls herself. Trying to defend himself and Nanette, he said he'd been working with private investigators to compile information, clear himself as a murder suspect, and "point some fingers" in another direction.

His directive from Nanette's attorney, he said, "was to watch the house and protect the belongings," take care of the dog and her kids' stuff. So when Kim and Kevin had come over to try to change the locks, he explained, he'd just wanted to make sure they had "the right paperwork with them," because no one had the right to enter the house at that moment.

"I thought that was kind of weird that the day she goes to jail, someone tried to get in the house and tried to take it over," he said, apparently missing the point that this "someone" was the murder victim's son and daughter—the executrix of Bill's estate.

Eric said he'd never met Bill, and yet he'd almost gotten thrown in jail for his murder, "something I totally had nothing to do with."

And now that the police had ruined his life, he was going to sue everyone involved. "They're going to pay for it," he said. ". . . I should be away playing ball right now. They totally screwed that up."

Playing devil's advocate, Jenny said it was a shame that he'd gotten dragged into this situation. It wasn't fair that Nanette had never told him she was trying to marry Bill and have his children, while she was also having a relationship with Eric.

"Are you sure she's giving you a straight story?" she asked. "How come Nanette didn't come to your defense on that and then try to help you out? . . . It sounds like, you know, you got screwed in this whole thing."

Eric agreed, but he said that didn't mean he was going to walk away when he didn't even know if she was guilty, or if she'd lied to him. To his knowledge, people were making accusations against her without asking her where the money was.

Jenny said they had asked those questions and she'd lied to them, so they'd given up.

"She's lied to everybody she's been involved with. According to my dad, you know, she's lied to her family all along. . . . She's just not trustworthy at all, as far as I can tell."

"Yeah, but that doesn't make anybody a criminal," he replied, griping that the police had been asking him to come down and make a statement against Nanette, a single mom who was just trying to take care of her kids. And they'd tried to throw him in jail too.

"I have two kids. I have a family. I have a life," he said, neglecting to mention that he'd left that family and had failed to keep up with his child support payments for the past four years. "You want to take that life away from me and now, all of a sudden, you're going to be my friend?"

Jenny tried to educate him about Nanette's parenting techniques. "Yeah, but at the same time, I mean, how do you explain having two and three boyfriends at one time to your kids too? How healthy is that?" she asked, adding that she also didn't think Nanette set a very good example by displaying nude pictures of herself around the house.

Eric said he didn't want to debate the nudity issue with her. His first priority was to get Nanette out of jail, "because there's no reason for her to be in there. . . . She had no family. She has nothing," and no way to pay her bail bond.

Jenny noted that Nanette had passport photos in her purse because she was about to go on a cruise, which meant she had to have some money. Eric said she had the photos because she was part of a travel agency, and it made him nuts when things like this were misconstrued. (Police found no affiliation between Nanette and a travel agency.)

From there, the conversation turned nasty. "You know, she has things that can hurt you guys," Eric said. "You have things that can hurt her."

Jenny told Eric that Nanette had been siphoning their money, trying to operate under their corporate names, and was ruining their credit. "That's just pure criminal. That's not right," she said. "She just doesn't give the straight story on anything."

But nothing seemed to get through to Eric, who was on a mission to get Nanette out of jail, where she didn't belong because of "this bull-dinky material stuff."

"Well, I don't call a half-a-million dollars 'bull-dinky,' especially when it's not your money," Jenny said.

Insisting that no one had been hurt by these activities, he overlooked the simple and very relevant fact that he was arguing with a murder victim's daughter. "No one is suffering," he said. "No one has been beaten up. I think people that rape people should go to jail forever because they hurt someone. . . . I'm going to try to get her out of jail because no one . . . belongs in there."

"I just hope that she's not leading you down the wrong path," Jenny said.

"Forget all the relationships, I'm still her friend," he said, "until she proves totally otherwise that she did something to hurt me deliberately."

Jenny thought it was odd and surprising that Eric had called her on behalf of a woman charged with stealing money from Jenny's family, and that he was now demanding even more from them. Especially after he and Nanette had been named as suspects in Bill McLaughlin's murder.

While Nanette was in custody, Eric tried everything he could to get her out of jail, including asking his parents to put up their house as collateral for Nanette's bail bond.

Nanette apparently wasn't handling her incarceration very well, but with her assets frozen, she had nothing to leverage to make bail, and no one to pay it for her.

When Jenny and Kim got wind that Eric had asked his parents to help, they approached Sandy Baumgardner to give his mother a call. If they tried to do it themselves, they figured Ronnie Naposki would hang up as soon as they uttered the name "McLaughlin." In their minds, the longer Nanette was in custody, the more likely she was to crack.

Sandy was scared to call, but she agreed, knowing she needed to be gentle or Ronnie would shut down.

Ronnie seemed surprised to hear from Sandy, but she didn't hang up.

"I'm a concerned person who is close to this family, and I heard you might be putting up your house as collateral for bail for Nanette," Sandy said. "I don't think you know who Nanette really is. She was engaged to Bill McLaughlin, and she may have portrayed herself as something else."

"I thought she was a successful businesswoman," Ronnie said.

"I've never known her to work," Sandy said.

"She came over for Thanksgiving and she gave everybody in New York the impression that she was a successful businesswoman," Ronnie countered, apparently trying to reconcile what she'd seen with what she was now hearing.

Careful not to bash Eric, Sandy said, "I just hate to see good people get sucked into her schemes. She's not what she says she is, and I don't want to see you guys get burned."

"I don't know what to believe any more," Ronnie said, sounding exasperated. "I'm hearing all these different things."

"Please, please, it's your house. Don't put that up because she will find a way to make you regret that. Your son has been duped."

Ronnie sounded very sad as she thanked Sandy for calling. "I don't know what I'm going to do," she said.


Once Nanette's bail was reduced to $250,000, she managed to cover the bond, and she was released on April 24, after spending nearly two weeks behind bars.

Nanette wasted no time before buying a new car, but she was not about to give up her luxury tastes even though her sugar daddy was gone. On May 2, she decided she needed a black 1988 BMW 750iL, with 65,000 miles on it, formerly owned by actor Dennis Quaid.

Her credit application for the car listed Eric Naposki as a reference and her sister, Stephanie King, in Scottsdale, Arizona, as the nearest relative.

Nanette claimed once again that she owned the Seashore house, listing it as her current address, with a market value of $1.2 million. She also cited two employers, saying she'd worked for Johnny's Burgers since March 1995 and for Krishel, Inc., since 1990, claiming she earned a monthly income of $11,000 as a "consultant to people starting up new businesses, writing business plans for companies." (Krishel wasn't formed until October 1994, and Nanette told police that she was unemployed.)

Detective Voth got a tip about the BMW purchase from

someone who saw Nanette driving it. Voth tracked down the car, and seeing *Cove Motoring* on the plate frame, he paid a visit to the dealership, where he learned that Nanette had come in with a big guy, six-foot-one, 250 to 270 pounds, with dark hair and a "bad hairpiece."

"Did you fill out the application?" Voth asked the salesman, who identified Eric from a photo lineup.

"No, they did," he said.

Chase Manhattan Bank and California Thrift and Loan had initially denied the loan application because Nanette had no proof that she owned the Seashore house. She left the dealership and came back with State Farm fire insurance paperwork that listed her and Bill McLaughlin as the policyholders.

She also attached 1993 and 1994 federal tax returns to the application, showing adjusted gross income of $197,089 and $222,271, respectively. California Thrift approved the loan, financing the entire $19,869 price of the BMW, which came to $20,398, and Nanette drove off in her new car.

Seventeen-year-old Bill McLaughlin with a date in Chicago, the year he enlisted in the U.S. Marine Corps. *(Photo by Barbara LaSpesa)*

Bill and his three kids (from left) Kim, Jenny and Kevin, on Kevin's birthday in March 1994. *(Photo by Andy Baumgardner)*

Aerial view of the house in Balboa Coves (second house from left) in 1994. (Photo by Newport Beach Police Department

Nanette swims with Lishele an Kristofer. This picture was take while she was married to her fir husband, Kevin "K. Ros Johnston, in Arizon

Nanette met Bill through this "Wealthy Men Only" singles ad i early 1991. (Courtesy of Newport Beac Police Department)

Several months after Nanette and Bill started dating, she moved into his two-story house (shown in 2012), where her kids each had a bedroom. *(Author photo)*

Nanette told people she owned or co-owned Bill's beach house on Seashore Drive in Newport Beach, where she brought men to have sex. *(Photo by Newport Beach Police Department)*

Nanette forged Bill's signature on this $250,000 check to the Nanette
Johnston Trust the day before he was killed in December 1994.
*(Photo by Newport Beach Police Department)*

Tom Voth (shown in
2012) was appointed
lead detective on the
case in 1994. He came
out of retirement to
help bring the case to
trial. *(Author photo)*

The killer left behind this newly copied key, stuck in the front door lock at the McLaughlin home. *(Photo by Newport Beach Police Department)*

In his haste to flee, the killer also dropped this newly copied key to the pedestrian access gate on the doormat. *(Photo by Newport Beach Police Department)*

On the day of Bill's funeral Nanette used his credit card to pay for three motorcycles, later claiming one was his Christmas gift. She signed the bill "Nanette McLaughlin." *(Photo by Newport Beach Police Department)*

After learning that Nanette had been dating Eric Naposki on the side, detectives arrested him on a traffic warrant for questioning on December 23, 1994. *(Photo by Newport Beach Police Department)*

Eric was a football star at Eastchester High School in New York. He later played as a linebacker in the National Football League. *(Senior yearbook photo)*

Police found this license plate number written in a notebook in Eric's car on the night of his arrest in December 1994. *(Photo by Newport Beach Police Department)*

The plate number was for Bill's white Mercedes, which was parked in the garage at Balboa Coves. Eric insisted he'd never been to the house. *(Photo by Newport Beach Police Department)*

Detectives learned that Eric had recently copied keys at a Tustin hardware store, where he also had a fake silencer like this one made for his Beretta 92F, reportedly as a movie prop. *(Author photo)*

Authorities believe that Eric shot Bill, ran out the pedestrian access gate, along this bike path, and over the Newport Boulevard bridge to the Thunderbird nightclub, where he worked. (Author photo)

In 1994, it took less than three minutes to walk across the bridge from Balboa Coves to the Thunderbird. (Photo by Newport Beach Police Department)

After Eric and Nanette broke up, he remarried and had two more children. Here in 2000, Eric swims with his son in Yorktown Heights, New York. (Photo by Angie Naposki)

Nanette lived the high life in Orange County with her second and third husbands, chartering this boat for drinks and dinner in 2005.

Nanette (shown in 2007) had a sizable collection of pricey designer dresses, which she wore to eat lavish meals and dance at nightclubs every weekend.

Orange County District Attorney Investigator Larry Montgomery helped bring this case to trial. *(Author photo)*

NBPD Sergeant Jo Cartwright (left) an Sergeant Dav Byington, no retired, worke together on the 200 arrests. *(Author pho*

Eric was arrested in a "felony stop" by Greenwich, CT, police detectives and their SRU team on May 20, 2009. *(Photo by Newport Beach Police Department)*

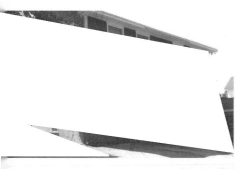

Eric was stopped just down the street from this duplex, where he lived with his fiancée. *(Author photo)*

Nanette was arrested the same day at the $1.3 million home in Ladera Ranch, California, she shared with her third husband, Billy McNeal, and their baby son. *(Author photo)*

Senior Deputy District Attorney Matt Murphy was the winning prosecutor at both trials for Eric Naposki and Nanette Packard in July 2011 and January 2012. *(Photo by The Orange County Register)*

New York attorney Angelo MacDonald gave the defense's opening statement in Eric's trial. *(Photo by The Orange County Register)*

Orange County attorney Gary Pohlson delivered the closing argument. *(Photo by The Orange County Register)*

Bill McLaughlin's older daughter Kim showed her joy at hearing the guilty verdict for Eric Naposki. *(Photo by* The Orange County Register*)*

.im and her sister Jenny hugged after Eric's verdict. *(Photo by* The Orange County Register*)*

Nanette, whose trial began in January 2012, flashed a brief and rare smile the day of the prosecution's opening statement. *(Photo by The Orange County Register)*

Nanette's attorney, Deputy Public Defender Mick Hill, painted her as a liar, cheat and thief – but not a killer – during his opening statement. *(Photo by The Orange County Register)*

Kim McLaughlin Bayless hugged Nanette's third husband, Billy McNeal, while her first husband, Kevin "K. Ross" Johnston, waited in line for a hug after the jury found Nanette guilty. *(Photo by* The Orange County Register*)*

Nanette was led into her sentencing hearing in handcuffs in May 2012. *(Photo by* The Orange County Register*)*

Matt Murphy gave a news conference with the McLaughlin sisters after Nanette's sentencing, which drew national media attention.
*(Author photo)*

At the end of Eric sentencing hearin in August 2012, h leaned toward Murphy and said, "You blew it."
*(Photo by The Orange County Register)*

# CHAPTER 26

Slowly but surely, Nanette's relationship with Eric began to unravel as the clamp came down on her financial shenanigans, although it's unclear exactly when or why they finally broke up.

As Eric tells it, he had a stop-and-start relationship with Nanette in 1995—mostly off—because he didn't trust her once he realized she was involved in Bill's murder. He claimed he was mostly away playing football before he returned to Connecticut, where he'd started dating a new woman by October.

However, authorities say the couple was still communicating and spending time together for up to a year after Bill's murder, based on the following facts:

After Kim and Kevin ran into Eric at the Seashore house, the McLaughlins filed paperwork to evict him and Nanette—and anyone else associated with her—from the house in May.

In mid-May, the Canadian Football League's Baltimore Football Club signed twenty-eight-year-old Eric, who then headed off to training camp. A month later, he left for the Ottawa Rough Riders' practice fields, another CFL team.

(Detective Tom Voth's notes say Eric was in Memphis on June 14.)

But on August 10, 1995, Newport Beach police took a photo of Eric's Pathfinder parked in the garage of Nanette's newly rented house on Foxhollow in Dove Canyon. Eric claimed he'd left town by then, and had only flown back into town for Nanette's preliminary hearing, which started August 7. At the close of the prelim, the judge bound Nanette over for trial on charges of theft and forgery.

During a search of her house, however, investigators found typed instructions on Nanette's computer to her attorney, dated August 1995, in which she stated that Eric should get $50,000 if she died.

Prosecutor Matt Murphy also pointed out that Eric, Nanette, and Kristofer posed for a photo with a soccer trophy at the end of the 1995 season—further evidence that Eric was still in contact with Nanette in December 1995, when the trophy ceremony was held, a year after the murder.

Despite Eric's claims that he didn't trust Nanette and wanted nothing to do with her, the police also found evidence that the two of them were conducting business deals together that summer.

One proposal involved a friend of Eric's from the nightclub scene, a movie producer named Juan Gonzales (pseudonym), with whom he entered into a limited liability corporation called Midnight Moon Productions (MMP).

A fifteen-page business plan for MMP, also found on Nanette's computer, stated: *[The corporation] was established for the purpose of producing projects for film, video cable and television, acquiring rights to marketable film and television properties.* Eric was the producer in charge of television production, and Gonzales was the executive producer in charge of film, television and commercial production. Gonzales listed credits including feature films starring Clint Eastwood and Quentin Tarantino.

Gonzales's phone number, which had an 818 prefix and was noted on the business plan, was found on Nanette's car phone records on December 8, 13, and 14, 1994. Although police obtained those records with a warrant in early March, there is no documentation that detectives explored that particular connection at the time.

Eric and Nanette were also working on launching a professional women's basketball league with Art and Dominic Menaldi. The four of them were to be equal partners, each holding 25 percent of the shares.

On a parallel track, Nanette was launching some nefarious schemes. She sent out letters from the Dove Canyon house, asking people for guaranteed loans. She said she was awaiting life insurance payouts totaling more than $10 million from one company alone, but she needed money right away.

*To Whom It May Concern,* she wrote, *I am making this offer as an investment opportunity due to my need for immediate cash to fund my current business venture.*

As her "current business interests," she cited annual income of "just under $200,000" for the past two years working for Krishel, Inc., half the rights to a patent for a filtration device through Gelman Sciences (this was Bill's device, and why she mentioned a connection to Gelman, a legitimate company, is unclear), and a 10 percent ownership share of a $21 million Mexican village under development in Rancho Mirage, scheduled for completion in early 1997 (Bill's desert project).

At her arraignment in October 1995, Nanette pleaded not guilty to the charges of forgery and theft. Then, on December 12, she had the audacity to file a palimony lawsuit against the estate of Bill McLaughlin and its executrix, Kim McLaughlin.

Nanette alleged that she'd had an oral agreement with Bill, dating back to August 1991, that she would get half his assets if he died. She said this was based on the fact that she'd been living with him as his fiancée, and had quit her regional sales manager job at Racine Industries, Inc., because he'd asked her to spend time with him instead. Jenny had to admit that Bill had confirmed the last claim with her.

But Nanette went even further. She claimed that Bill had created a living trust in November 1991 "to shelter certain assets from creditors because of a then-pending lawsuit," assets that included the Seashore house, which "was bought by decedent for plaintiff," and two pieces of Las Vegas real property purchased "by plaintiff and decedent together," among other properties. As his fiancée, she also claimed she was owed half the $9 million in forthcoming Plasmacell-C royalties, $1 million from a nonmarital support agreement, a $5,000 monthly stipend retroactive to the day of his death (presumably for serving as a trustee), half his properties and shares of stock, and more than $1 million in damages for breach of contract.

The battle grew more complicated as the life insurance company, parties to the McLaughlin estate, and the McLaughlin family engaged in all kinds of legal maneuvering, arguing that Nanette had violated the intent of Bill's living will.

The McLaughlins filed a countersuit in the name of the Seashore Drive house's official owner, W.F.M. Newport, against Nanette Johnston et al, in an attempt to evict her and Eric from the house.

It worked. Under the final judgment, Nanette and anyone connected to her were ordered to vacate the premises.

Ultimately, Bill's friend Don Kalal got possession of

the Infiniti, and he continued to drive it for many years in Bill's honor.

Nanette was arrested again, on March 7, 1996—this time, on suspicion of filing false financial statements to obtain the BMW and the loan she'd taken out to rent the $575,000 five-bedroom home in Dove Canyon in July 1995.

Held on $100,000 bail, she was accused of lying on a credit application, using two fake Social Security numbers (her father's and an ex-boyfriend's, because her credit history showed debts and a repossession), inflating her income, and lying about her tax returns. She was released from jail a week later after family members posted her bail, and was now looking at eight years' prison time for the two criminal cases combined.

"I should write a book when this is all over," she told the *Daily Pilot,* saying that she wouldn't talk about the case until then.

Later that month, Nanette and the McLaughlins entered into a settlement to resolve their legal battle, which incorporated the civil and criminal cases against her. It appears that all the attorneys hammered out a resolution together, because the plea bargain she signed on March 22 stated that restitution for her crime was also part of the civil settlement agreement, which was attached to the plea.

In the plea agreement, Nanette stated under penalty of perjury: *In O.C. between 1-1-94 and 1-30-95 I willfully and unlawfully embezzled more than $150,000, the property of William McLaughlin. On 12-14-94 in O.C. I forged another's name on a $250,000 check with the intent to pass and defraud.*

The life insurance company said it was legally required to pay her the $1 million claim because she hadn't been convicted of murder, so the McLaughlins subtracted the amount accountant Brian Ringler had identified that she'd stolen from the estate ($341,272), then added the taxes the estate would have to pay on the $1 million life insurance payout she was getting. In the end, the family had to suck it up and pay her a final negotiated amount of $220,000.

On April 3, Nanette signed another agreement pleading guilty to criminal charges of grand theft and forgery, admitting: *In O.C. between 10-95 and 3-96 I did willfully and unlawfully make a false statement in writing respecting [sic] my financial condition for the purpose of obtaining credit. This occurred while I was on bail.*

On May 13, 1996, she was sentenced to a year in jail, with five years' probation, and was sent to the James A. Musick Facility, a low-security camp in Irvine known as "the farm."

Nanette's ex-husband, K. Ross Johnston, accepted her collect calls from the camp so she could talk to Kristofer and Lishele, who were staying with him and Julia. He also took the kids to visit her every week.

After serving a little more than half her time, Nanette was released on December 23, 1996, just in time for Christmas.

# CHAPTER 27

Eric Naposki rejoined the Barcelona Dragons in the World League during the spring seasons of 1996 and 1997, leading the team in his last year with 165 tackles and 16.5 sacks.

The Dragons coach, Jack Bicknell, told the *Hartford Courant* that Eric was one of his favorite players, describing him as "a guy who basically was in the right places at the right times, but just couldn't stay healthy."

Fox analyst Matt Millen also expressed admiration for Eric, saying, "With his size and the way he plays, he could have played in any league. This guy is scary and will hit you."

Although Millen was referring to Eric's on-field performance, court records show that his ex-wife Kathy filed a petition for a restraining order against him in Milford, Connecticut, in 1996. The records have since been destroyed, along with whatever allegations Kathy made against Eric, and the reasons for dismissal. A court clerk said a judge may dismiss a petition simply because no one shows up at the hearing.

The state of Connecticut was still attempting to garnishee Eric's wages in 1997, when it notified the WLAF that Eric owed a whopping $76,300 in support payments to Kathy. But that year's season with the Barcelona Dragons was Eric's last. He retired his #91 jersey midseason after suffering more injuries.

"Well, I'm not coming back here," Eric told a *Courant* reporter in June from Barcelona. "I'm going to step aside and let some of the younger guys get a chance. If something happens where I can get into an NFL camp, sure I'll give it a try, but if not, it's all over for me."

The Dragons hosted—and won—the World Bowl that year, but Eric, a team captain, missed that opportunity as well.

"I never got the chance to prove what I could do at the next level," he told the *Courant.*

By September 1997, the momentum had been lost on the McLaughlin murder investigation, and Eric's relationship with Nanette appeared to be over for good.

*Suspect Naposki left the United States shortly after Johnston was incarcerated, and according to our investigation, either ended or seriously curtailed his relationship with Johnston,* Detective Tom Voth wrote in his final report, dated September 18, 1997. *A $100,000 reward was offered by the victim's family for information leading to the conviction of the perpetrator(s). No information was ever received in response to that reward. I have maintained contact with the victim's family and other involved subjects but no workable leads have been developed at this time. Pending further information this case will be held in abeyance.*

At the time, Voth said, he felt pretty frustrated to have to shelve the case.

"You never want to take a homicide case and put it in that type of criteria, because that basically means unless something comes to you or you stumble on something, that case will just sit there and not get any work done on it. . . . You really can't get angry at it. It's nobody's fault that it's not getting prosecuted."

He said K. Ross Johnston continued to call him for quite some time, but much of the information he provided seemed "vindictive" and unusable.

Memories markedly differ about the reasons why murder charges were never filed in the 1990s. It's evidently a sensitive subject, involving reputations, high emotions, and strong personalities—not to mention recollections that are imperfect after the passage of nearly two decades.

Voth recalled that at least a year before he wrote that last report in 1997, he and Detective Bill Hartford "hand carried the case to [prosecutor] Debbie Lloyd in her office. We were told that absent the murder weapon, a corroborated confession, or some other strong evidence against Eric or Nanette, she could not file the case."

Voth said he felt so strongly about the case that he subsequently approached a second prosecutor, Laurie Hungerford, but she passed too.

"I thought I had a better chance when I took it to her because we'd just finished a big case [together]," Voth said.

A former NBPD official, who didn't want to be named, backed this recollection. "I think the police department had more than enough to go to trial then. The DA elected not to," he said, adding that the prosecutor passed because "it wasn't a slam dunk, tie-it-up-with-the-bow [case]. We ended up settling with the ugly sister," referring to the charges of theft and fraud, which were easier to prove in court.

That said, the official acknowledged that the detectives' overall effort "could have been more aggressive." Given that this was Voth's first murder case, he said, "someone should have taken Voth by the hand, and they didn't."

At that time, the forensic tests of the bullet casings were

not as sophisticated as they are today. They showed that the Beretta was a possible murder weapon, but so were twenty-seven other types of guns. (Neither the Taurus nor the Astra, owned by Bill McLaughlin, however, were on that list.)

Debbie Lloyd, who retired in 2009 after being promoted to assistant district attorney, has a dramatically different recollection of the case history. As she told prosecutor Matt Murphy and DA investigator Larry Montgomery, she always believed that this case was "solvable." But the message she got from the NBPD, she said recently, was that "Newport just didn't want to be told what to do, and they would handle it without me." When she offered suggestions on how to move the investigation forward, she said, "they laughed at me."

Frustrated as the months and years passed with no action, she repeatedly asked around her office if she could resurrect the case and get it "worked up." If the detectives had ever gathered strong enough evidence to prosecute, she said, they never shared it with her.

"It was never, ever presented for filing to me. Ever," she said. "This is the irony. For twenty years, that case bothered me."

Was this simply a matter of semantics, that certain forms weren't filed to make this an official "presentation" of the case? Lloyd insisted she never saw any such document, and Voth said his case notes don't cover that period. But he said he was never offered any help from or approached by a DA investigator until Larry Montgomery came along many years later.

It's possible that Voth believed Lloyd had ultimately "rejected" the case for prosecution when she was simply telling him he needed to investigate further and to come back with better or more detailed evidence so she could file charges and win the case. Whatever the reasons, it's clear that communication broke down between the NBPD and the DA's office, and the case went cold.

Lloyd, who was honored as California's "Prosecutor of the Year" in 2001, had a reputation for having a strong personality and knowing what she needed to win a case beyond a reasonable doubt, but she said she was never known for being too scared to try a tough case. As she pointed out, she prosecuted three murder cases in which the victims' bodies were never found, and even one case in which a bloodhound was her primary witness.

"Before DNA, *all* our cases were circumstantial," she said.

Investigator Larry Montgomery confirmed that as he was transferring from the DA's Homicide Unit to its TracKRS Unit (Taskforce Review Aimed at Catching Killers, Rapists, and Sexual Offenders), Lloyd personally pulled him aside and urged him to take a look at the McLaughlin case. She'd known Montgomery since his days at the Irvine Police Department, when they'd worked the bloodhound case together.

"I just think if you have the time, you can solve this thing," she told him.

The bottom line is that she and the detectives all felt this case was winnable—with the right evidence.

Back in the 1990s, Voth acknowledged that the evidence "wasn't all there and maybe wasn't presented properly. . . . Maybe I didn't have the proper experience to convince the DA to do it. But I think they both wanted smoking-gun kind of cases."

"I put some blame on myself as not being as experienced as, say, Larry [Montgomery], but what do you do? You do what you can," he said recently. "Without Suzanne Cogar, I don't know how the case would have gone."

Ultimately the case did move forward, but the planets needed to align and the timing had to be right for Matt Murphy, a master prosecutor of complex circumstantial cases, to have Montgomery review the cold case and get it ready for trial.

# CHAPTER 28

Using a method that had worked for her before, Nanette Johnston returned to the personal ads, where she'd found her first rich, older man. This time, she landed a catch who would prove to be just as wealthy, if not more so, than Bill McLaughlin.

In April 1997, only four months out of jail, Nanette answered an ad placed by real estate developer John Packard, who, like the other men in her life, fell for Nanette's mystique and her tried-and-true Supermom con. Almost immediately after they began dating, he later testified, "we started interacting like a family."

She told him a variation on the same story, that she made a living writing business plans for medical ventures developed by her former business partner, Bill McLaughlin.

Nanette had started calling herself "Annette" Johnston, and had mail sent to her under that name to her home. John not only knew about this practice, he made light of it. In a letter dated May 11, 1997, he began, *Dear Annette, Oh, My Gosh! Now you have me saying it. What's next?*

It's unclear why she decided to use a different first name

(her middle name is Anne), although it's not uncommon for someone with a criminal record to use an alias.

Nanette told John that her ex-husband, K. Ross Johnston, was a bad man, and John believed her because K. Ross kept pestering him after they met in September.

"He was constantly calling me up, saying Nanette was a murderer," John said. "It was oppressive."

John finally had to ask a friend to write K. Ross a "cease and desist" letter to force him to back off.

Nanette and John were engaged by October 1997. Nearly fifteen years her senior, he stood head to head with her at five feet six inches.

She immediately started trying to get custody of her kids away from her ex-husband. In court papers, Nanette claimed she'd had no input into the original divorce decree and was "coerced" into signing the paperwork. *Respondent is 6'2" and weighs approximately 220 pounds,* she wrote. *He was far more intimidating to me in 1989 than he is today, but I still am intimidated by him.*

She said neither of them ever followed the original court order for custody and visitation, claiming that when he moved to California, he'd left the kids with her. She wrote that she came out in mid-1990, *with the thought in mind that we might reconcile. However, that was short-lived and we only lived together less than a month.*

Since then, she wrote, they'd been sharing custody of the kids fifty-fifty, but the kids now wanted to live with her and attend regular school, not be homeschooled by K. Ross and his girlfriend, Julia. Nanette didn't like the homeschooling, she wrote, nor did she condone K. Ross's use of "corporal punishment" on the children. Besides, she said, K. Ross and Julia had a baby who was almost two years old, and they were expecting a second child in the spring.

K. Ross countered that Nanette had gotten violent with him during an argument at his house on January 17, 1998, triggered by her attempt to exchange custody days so she and John could take the children skiing.

"You never do anything with the kids," K. Ross quoted her as saying. "All you do is make them clean the house and hang out at home."

"That's not true," K. Ross said.

"That's why the kids want to live with me. I go places with them. I do things with them. I buy them things. They have fun with me. I'm sure they would have more fun skiing with me than staying here with you."

"Nanette," he said, "how can I compete with someone who is unemployed and has half a million dollars of stolen money to spoil the kids?"

*[That] is when she began punching me in the face, leaving my lip swollen, yelling bad language and then drove away,* K. Ross wrote.

---

Nanette and John were married on Valentine's Day in 1998 at the Westin Hotel, only ten months after they'd met. And it didn't take long before the thirty-three-year-old femme fatale got herself—and her husband—in trouble with the law again.

Still on five years' probation, Nanette was prohibited from writing "any portion of any checks." She also was to "have no blank checks in possession . . . not have a checking account nor use or possess credit cards or open credit accounts unless approved by probation."

On April 2, 1998, four Newport Beach police detectives conducted a surprise probation search of her house in Lake Forest, where they found a number of receipts for wedding-related purchases, including some freshwater pearls at Zales jewelry store and some flowers at Greenworks, Inc., all made by check.

Asked if she had written the checks, Nanette said no, it was her husband John; she'd only delivered them to the businesses. After finding John's letter to "Annette," Detective Tom Fischbacher's antennae went up and he called John for more information.

John said he'd written and signed the checks. However, after further investigation, the detectives learned that he and Nanette had lied to detectives, trying to cover for her.

John also faxed over copies of canceled checks on which he'd "fraudulently altered the information" in an attempt to "conceal" his wife's connection to the check so she wouldn't be sent back to jail on a probation violation, the police report noted.

*Packard related that suspect Johnston was very well aware of the terms and conditions of her probation,* the report said, noting that John also contradicted earlier statements to the police about the matter. Packard's offering of fraudulently altered checks to the NBPD during the course of this investigation constituted a violation of 132 PC (Section 132 of the Penal Code) for being an accessory after the fact; Packard also provided false statements to investigators, the report pointed out. (John, however, was never charged with a crime.)

As it turned out, these personal wedding items were charged to John's business account for Pacific Housing and Development Corp., on which only John and his partner were authorized signees.

By the time the detectives finished getting search warrants, obtaining copies of other checks, and going over the accounts again, they found she'd written more than two dozen checks. When confronted, she said she called John "most of the time" to tell him what the checks were for, but she admitted that she'd lied to detectives because she was "nervous," and they had caught her "off guard." She then claimed that she hadn't written any checks after the wedding, which the police also found to be false.

*This investigation revealed that suspect Johnston, while on formal probation for two separate felony cases, wrote portions of at least twenty-five (25) checks, totaling $17,695.03, in direct violation [of her probation],* Detective Jeff Lu wrote in an October 1998 report. Lu submitted his conclusions and evidence to the Orange County Probation Department and to the DA's office for possible prosecution and punishment for the probation violation.

Deputy District Attorney James Marion subsequently called Lu to tell him that the DA's office had decided not to prosecute the case after meeting with Paul Meyer, Nanette's new attorney. Marion told Lu that Nanette's probation conditions had been modified such that only future violations would count against her. The case was "exceptionally cleared."

In 1999, Nanette got pregnant with their daughter, Jaycie, who was born in March 2000. Having a rich man's child was a pretty good way to assure his financial commitment in the long term—and plenty of cash in the short term to feed Nanette's frenzied materialistic taste for clothing, shoes, cars, and cosmetic surgery.

That said, John Packard was clearly no innocent. He and his partner in Pacific Property Assets (PPA) were accused in a consolidation of investors' lawsuits of defrauding and soliciting $90 million in investments from elderly folks in an alleged Ponzi scheme of condo developments.

Packard and his partner denied the allegations, which they chalked up to the poor economy, claiming to have operated successfully for more than a decade and acquiring more than one hundred properties, refinancing the buildings and selling 40 percent "for very significant gains." However, the two cofounders testified that they misled investors by reporting investment funds received as revenue on their income statements, which allowed them to appear profitable. According to the WTF Finance news site, these activities weren't all that different from the practices of big banking corporations that overstated their assets during the recent Wall Street mess.

But Packard's legal troubles didn't stop there. In 2012, the Securities and Exchange Commission (SEC) filed a complaint in federal court against him and his two partners, alleging they'd "engaged in a scheme to defraud potential investors" by boasting a false track record of a 60 percent return and $100 million in net equity on their previous venture, PPA, when they launched a new corporation, Apartments America, in 2009.

In fact, Apartments America was formed only three months after PPA had filed for Chapter 7 bankruptcy and had defaulted on $91.6 million in promissory notes held by 647 investors whose investments had been pooled to buy apartment complexes, according to the SEC complaint.

The complaint was still pending when this book went to press. Attempts to reach John Packard for comment on these allegations and others by Nanette, detailed in this book, were unsuccessful.

Before John Packard lost big in the real estate market collapse, he was quite well off, and Nanette took full advantage of his healthy income. That continued even after their marriage went south.

*We had a very lavish and extravagant lifestyle,* Nanette later wrote in divorce papers, noting that during happier times in the marriage, she'd never wanted for anything. It wasn't uncommon for her to spend $10,000 to $15,000 at a time on designer clothing.

He'd always bought her jewelry and had been "very generous" with her older children, she said, estimating that they'd spent $37,170 per month for basic expenses, not including vacations. *[But] to punish me for divorcing him,* she wrote, *petitioner has essentially cut off all available funds to me. He has canceled all my credit cards and refuses to put any significant money in my checking account.* And yet, she said, he'd just bought himself a $125,000 Mercedes.

Nanette spoiled their daughter, Jaycie, and volunteered at her school, all the while still fussing over Lishele and Kristofer. She never missed one of Lishele's dance recitals and still took birthday cupcakes to her class, even during college.

Still unsatisfied, however, Nanette remained out on the hunt. On July 13, 2002, she met a handsome young man named Billy McNeal, a senior financial analyst for PepsiCo who was in his last year of graduate business school at the University of Southern California (USC). Billy, who was six years younger than Nanette, was also married.

In court, Billy described his first interaction with Nanette as "a social meeting, chance encounter up in L.A." He later elaborated to say that they were both out in Hollywood, with respective groups of friends, and noticed each other while passing through a hotel lobby. They stopped and struck up a conversation that resulted in the two groups leaving together for cocktails. After that, he and Nanette began dating—and cheating on their respective spouses.

"It was a little complicated, because there were marriages involved," Billy testified in 2012. "We dated for quite some time," but it "got serious rather quickly."

Billy said he'd already "checked out" of his marriage

about six months earlier and had been "looking elsewhere" ever since. He and his wife formally separated on August 14, 2002—only a month after he'd met Nanette—and his wife filed for divorce three months later, citing "irreconcilable differences." With no children, the claim went uncontested. The divorce was final on December 20, 2003.

Billy said some of the problems in his marriage stemmed from the difference in their personalities and conflicting interests in how they spent their free time. Billy's first wife liked staying home; Nanette and Billy both enjoyed going out. Even so, he said, he was pretty busy with school and working full-time when he met Nanette, so he didn't have "a lot of time to gallivant."

"We both were high-energy people, type A personalities, who like to be out with friends, having fun," he said. "It was refreshing, and that's how it started."

Nanette told Billy that she was a successful business-woman who made her living by writing business plans for friends, companies, and colleagues. Embellishing her credentials, she told him she'd started out at a young age in sales of athletic club memberships and bought her own Mercedes. Then, adopting her usual tactic of claiming Bill McLaughlin's accomplishments as her own, she said she went into pharmaceutical sales as a rep for what is now Baxter International, Inc., in Orange and Los Angeles Counties. She soon became their number one rep, she said, and got promoted to regional manager. While traveling to various medical offices for work, she identified an opportunity for a new and improved heart valve. She presented it to the executive board, but her boss squashed the idea. She tried going over his head, but she got nowhere.

"She wasn't happy with that," Billy testified. "She wasn't going to be told no."

Determined, she told Billy, Nanette found a doctor in

Orange County who believed in her product. She found some engineers to produce a prototype, then sold it to Baxter, which bought her out for millions in profits. And that is when she met John Packard.

"That's the story I understood, and that's the story I told people in front of her and she told people in front of me," Billy said.

In turn, Billy told Nanette that he was "an up-and-comer," still in school, but he didn't have anywhere near as much money as she and John Packard. Billy earned a comparatively modest $50,000 annual salary.

But that did not seem to deter her. "I think she knew I had a good career," he said recently.

The fact that he was also handsome and athletic surely helped make the physical attraction between them part of the package, because this, too, had been part of Nanette's MO.

He also was able to help her spend her and John Packard's money on things she wanted. Besides designer clothes and shoes, she had a serious thing for motorcycles. But she didn't want just any motorcycle. She had to have a special custom-built one. So Billy found a builder in Boca Raton, Florida, and commissioned him to build her a purple chopper to her specifications for $50,000, a model that normally would have cost $100,000.


Citing "irreconcilable differences," John Packard filed for divorce from Nanette on July 17, 2003, when their daughter was 3½ years old. He asked the court for joint legal and physical custody of Jaycie.

A week later, Nanette filed for sole physical custody and joint legal custody, claiming that she and John had been separated since March 1—eight months after Nanette had met Billy and five years and one month after she'd married John. He claimed they'd separated December 27, 2002.

A few months later, Nanette filed paperwork accusing John of being "a severe alcoholic," who bought sixteen year-old Lishele and her friends a half gallon of vodka at Albertsons. Nanette said she had to take Lishele to the emergency room, where she was kept overnight for alcohol poisoning.

*I can honestly state that in the last two years, I have never seen petitioner go a day without a drink,* she wrote. *This is a way of life for him.*

She complained that she found their toddler, running around in her underwear on John's front lawn, and that the child had reported some pretty alarming comments to Nanette, such as *"Daddy is teaching me how to make a martini for him."* (None of these allegations could be confirmed.)

In a rather ironic filing, dated November 2006, Nanette accused John of being "incapable of setting rules."

*[He is] negatively impacting the co-parenting relationship and is the primary cause of the problems,* she wrote.

# CHAPTER 29

Between seasons playing in Europe, Eric Naposki met Natalia Algorta in 1996 at Polyester's, a bar in Stamford, Connecticut, where they both worked. After returning to Barcelona for the 1997 season, he married Natalia in Sitges, a Mediterranean coastal town about twenty-two miles outside of Barcelona, in June 1998.

Finally done with football, Eric came back to Connecticut to finish his college degree and opened a gym in Milford.

In 1998, Eric was granted visitation rights to see his two daughters, despite owing more than $75,000 in back support payments, for which a portion of his wages was being withheld.

According to Eric, he was working by that time for a security company, where he said** he ran the ESPN account and claimed to have "caught the mailman stealing." While at that job, he also claimed to have been honored as "Supervisor of the Year," although he listed his position in court records simply as "security guard," earning $480 a week. (ESPN couldn't confirm this information, noting that even if he had worked security there, his records would be

with the private contractor.) Later, Eric said, his boss aske
him to work security for a property management company
which he did until 2004 or 2005.

Eric occasionally made $800 payments to the famil
court, but he missed numerous hearings, prompting the is
suance of a series of bench warrants with bonds as high a
$25,000. When the self-described unemployed physica
trainer asked the court to decrease his support payments, h
was ordered to prove that he was looking for a job.

In spite of his outstanding child support debt, he and hi
new wife decided to have two children of their own—Eri
Junior, in April 1999, and Susanna, in June 2002.

Eric's marriage to Natalia ultimately went bad as wel
During an argument in a parking lot, he said**, he punche
and shattered Natalia's car windshield. She called out t
some cops driving by, who subsequently issued an arres
warrant for him. He said the case was dismissed, and n
court records of any such incident could be located in 201:

Natalia and Eric separated after almost seven years, o
April 30, 2005, and she filed for divorce in late June. Th
estranged couple initially agreed to share joint legal custod
and for Eric to pay child support, based on his "uneven
earning potential. Two months later, Natalia went for so
custody, because Eric wasn't visiting the children or payin
support.

At this point, Eric was not sending money to either of hi
ex-wives for his three minor children, ages three, six, an
fifteen.

In July, Eric said he was so poor he couldn't even affor
to pay the court fees for his second divorce. Nonetheless, h
filed a separate set of divorce papers in November.

Meanwhile, Eric still owed more than $75,000 to Kath
for his older daughters. Contending he had only $70 t

his name, he complained that his debts were now up to $104,000, including credit card bills and student loans.

Not surprisingly, Natalia also filed a number of contempt motions after he failed to make his payments to her as well.

*I never know what I am going to get and when I am going to receive it,* she wrote in March 2007, prompting judges to issue bench warrants with $5,000 bonds when he failed to show up for hearings.

"Defendant to be arrested any weekday between nine-thirty A.M. and four P.M.," a judge ordered in April 2007.

By this point, Eric had moved on to another woman in his life, a pretty blond schoolteacher named Rosemarie "Rosie" Macaluso, of Greenwich, Connecticut, whom he met in a bar in Stamford. Rosie's uncle was a police officer.

Eric continued to work security, opened a gym in Westchester County, New York, and also trained high-school athletes at a gym in Chappaqua, but he still had the massive support debt hanging over his head.

As a result, Eric was picked up in August 2007 on one of the bench warrants, and had to fork over $5,000 to the state of Connecticut as bond forfeiture.

As proof that he was trying to earn a living, he submitted a flyer to the Danbury court to show he was running a six-week $850 training camp: *Increase your speed, strength, endurance, flexibility and quickness. Learn proper weight training techniques, speed drills, boxing skills, plyometric exercises and vertical training programs,* it stated.

During the spring of 2009, Eric and Rosie moved in together and got engaged.

Based on photos of the couple posing with his two

younger, giggling children, it looks like he did spend some
time with them.

On May 20, 2009, at 9:00 A.M., Eric was supposed to
appear at the umpteenth hearing on one of Kathy's contempt
motions. She showed up, but he did not. For reasons he
never saw coming, he had more pressing matters to deal
with that morning.

# CHAPTER 30

Nanette had moved on as well. She registered to vote as a Republican, and after three years of dating, Nanette and Billy McNeal got engaged in April 2005. He gave her a three-carat diamond ring, and was disappointed when she insisted that he buy her several diamond-studded bands to wear on either side of it.

"For me, as her husband, it never seemed like it was enough," he said.

At first, it was hard for Billy's parents to warm up to her, but eventually they came around. "She was very cold, hard to know," he recalled.

Nanette, who was working at a real estate office in Ladera Ranch, still had dollar signs in her eyes. She bought two homes in Lake Forest, which Billy said he and his father helped her renovate and flip, but he had no idea how much she made off the sales.

In 2006, she told Billy she was helping a wealthy property owner sell big lots to real estate developers, such as Lennar and Standard Pacific Homes. For the next six months, she traveled to Palm Desert every six weeks to meet for a few hours with this wealthy man, whom she said she'd me through a mortgage broker friend. She was always home b three in the afternoon.

Nanette claimed to have earned a 3 percent commissio by working with this man on a $20 million transaction involv ing 1,200 acres, and Billy had no reason not to believe her

A few years later, Billy learned that this man had been i his mid to late fifties and his wife was dying of cancer. T man had indeed made some big deals, but when Billy look into it, Nanette's name was nowhere to be found on th public documents.

"I think she was trying to weave her way in there," h said, speculating that she'd been searching for another ric mark like Bill McLaughlin or John Packard, whom sh could entice into marrying her.

Instead, Nanette married Billy on a boat in Newport Beac on August 25, 2006, and they honeymooned in Greece.

With the financial portion of her divorce to John Packar finalized, Nanette continued to fight for a bigger share o John's complicated asset portfolio, a quest that continue for years.

But she never shared her financial paperwork with Bill They had a postnuptial agreement, he said, and "never com mingled" their money. She also declined to take his last name

"I never asked her about money," he said, noting that h wrote checks to pay for the mortgage for their house, whic was in her name. She'd bought the $1.27 million house o Illuminata Lane in Ladera Ranch with her half of the pro ceeds from the sale of the home she'd shared with John.

The only time she and Billy discussed finances, he sai was seven years into their relationship when she couldn' afford to send her daughter Jaycie back to the Stoneybrooke Christian School. Nanette was upset and Billy wanted to help, so he offered to sit down and create a budget for her.

Billy built her a spreadsheet of her expenses, based on her word alone. She told Billy that she was receiving $6,500 a month from John for child support, which had never gone into the communal marriage pot.

"I never saw a bank balance," he said.

This exercise seemed to make her feel a little better, but it didn't slow her shopping for the walls of shoes and designer clothing that filled her closet. Her extensive collection of dresses included three dozen in the $100 to $600 range and three dozen in the $700 to $2,000 range. She rarely, if ever, wore the same dress twice.

Nanette also insisted that Billy pay for lavish trips, and expected him to spend as much as $600 each weekend for nights out with drinks, dinner, and clubbing (averaging about $400 per weekend, depending on whether they went out both nights). They even chartered a yacht one evening to drink champagne, eat dinner, and cruise around. Billy drained his own bank account and bounced a few checks trying to keep her happy.

"It was always lopsided," he said later, noting that this was "a point of contention in our relationship. She always wanted more."


Sandy Baumgardner wouldn't let go of this case. Surfing around on the Internet one day in 2005, she decided to look up Eric Naposki. She found him—teaching Tae Kwon Do and boxing at the Westport Boxing Gym in Westport, Connecticut, just outside of New York City.

Cold-calling Sergeant Dave Byington, who was now in charge of the NBPD's robbery-homicide unit, they chatted about the case and she sent him a link to Eric's latest whereabouts, trying to keep the case alive and on the cops' radar on behalf of the McLaughlin family.

"We're bringing in someone to look at cold cases," he told her, confiding that they'd always been pretty sure that Eric was the shooter.


Nanette came to Billy for help again in December 2007. After fighting John Packard over finances for more than four years, she was in debt to experts she'd hired to help her make sense of his expansive and complicated asset portfolio.

"I'm buried," she told Billy. "I owe the forensic accountant, like, seventy-five to a hundred thousand dollars. If I don't pay it, I'm going to lose my butt."

"I don't have the money," Billy said.

Billy talked to a friend to see if Nanette could borrow some money, not knowing the details about how much Nanette wanted, which turned out to be $150,000. When the friend came by the house with the paperwork, Billy signed the promissory note, but he didn't read the fine print.

"That was probably one of the worst decisions I ever made," he said later.

Although she received sizable regular monthly payments from John each month, Nanette still managed to chalk up tax liens on the Ladera Ranch house. Starting at $1,188 in July 2006, they'd grown to $37,252 by March 2009.

Nanette didn't have to borrow any money, Billy said, but she did so nonetheless. In June 2007, she got a $100,000 loan from a friend in her real estate office. Although Billy never knew anything about this loan, the friend came after Billy years later and sued him for it. Billy said it cost him

$30,000 in attorney's fees to fight, and they finally settled out of court.


Although some saw Nanette as a good, loving mother, she secretly exercised some parenting techniques that certainly wouldn't win her a "Mother of the Year" award. For one, she used her daughter Jaycie as a pawn in a scheme to defraud their neighbors out of $8,000.

Seeing that Jaycie loved fashion, Nanette and Billy enrolled her in a sewing class. Then Nanette had an idea. She told her daughter to design outfits and make them herself. Jaycie and her friends could model and sell them at a fashion show, she said, then donate the proceeds to charity. Nanette had a website designed especially for the event while Jaycie got to work.

In the end, Jaycie didn't end up designing all the dresses. Nanette had some of them tailor-made. During the fashion show, some of the attendees noticed. Even worse, Nanette wrote on the website that the $8,000 in proceeds had gone to orphans in Africa when, in fact, the cash had gone into her own pockets, Billy said.

Nanette's eight-year-old daughter was learning from the master how to lie, deceive, and steal.


In the fall of 2008, Billy and Nanette were working at either end of a long desk in their home office, when he stopped to listen to her type. He was surprised and confused when he realized that she was hunting and pecking on the computer keyboard.

*If she types that slowly, how in the world can she write a business plan? It would take years to complete.*

But her poor typing skills and phony career weren't all

that she'd been hiding from him. When they decided to have a child together, he still had no idea about her sordid past.

"At the end of the day," he said in 2012, "had I been in-formed, given the choice" to move forward while they were dating, or even while they were engaged, "I can certainly say today, and [even] in late 2009, I wouldn't have stayed with her."

Yet, on December 19, 2008, Nanette gave birth to her fourth child, Cruz William McNeal.

# CHAPTER 31

In 2002, on Senior Deputy District Attorney Matt Murphy's first day in the Homicide Unit, he took over the caseload for Newport Beach, Costa Mesa, Irvine, and Laguna Beach from Debbie Lloyd, the original prosecutor on the McLaughlin case.

"There's a bunch of cases you're going to want to review," she said. "You're going to want to take a look at McLaughlin, because I think it's solvable."

Murphy didn't have time to get into the case right away, because he had a full plate and much to learn. But, luckily, he was a quick study.

Born to a U.S. Air Force doctor and a nurse in Taiwan in 1967, Murphy attended an all-boys Catholic prep school in Los Angeles. He studied political science at the University of California, Santa Barbara, where he became vice president of his Phi Sigma Kappa fraternity house, and worked with disabled kids.

The rape of a close friend inspired him to start a mandatory program on campus called Greeks Against Rape, which aimed to educate pledges about the possible consequences of drinking too much and getting into inappropriate sexual situations with female students. This experience sparked his motivation to go to law school at the University of San Diego in 1990. He began clerking at the Orange County DA's Office in the summer of 1992, and was hired full-time after graduation.

Along the way, he accrued victories in the juvenile gang, felony and sexual assault units before he was transferred to homicide at age thirty-four. As of 2012, he hadn't lost a single homicide case, although he did have his first hung jury in the penalty phase of a trial that year.

Over the years, Murphy made a name for himself in Orange County for his cutting and sarcastic cross-examinations, persuasive opening statements and closing arguments, and for artfully handling complex circumstantial cases involving intricate financial and legal machinations. He took pride in annihilating defense witnesses' credibility on the stand, exposing hypocrisy and pointing out inconsistent testimony. He also enjoyed ripping apart those criminal defendants who claimed to be innocent because they were good, practicing Christians—or, in this case, a churchgoing pathological liar who claimed to be innocent of murder because she was a loving mother.

A career bachelor, Murphy watched his single friends get married as he took trips to Indonesia to go surfing or to the desert to play golf with his buddies, because becoming submerged in a case—and winning it—was enough for him.

His successful prosecutions have been chronicled in several true-crime books, including *Dead Reckoning* by this author, about the murder of Tom and Jackie Hawks. Murphy also chalked up face time on national TV crime shows for winning convictions against Skylar Deleon and Insane Crips member John F. Kennedy, who tied the Hawkses to the anchor of their yacht, then threw them overboard—alive—in 2004. Skylar Deleon and Kennedy were sentenced to death row in 2009, and Skylar's wife, Jennifer, got life without the possibility of parole. The couple was dubbed the "Bonnie and Clyde of Orange County."

Murphy also put serial killer Rodney Alcala back on death row after Alcala, known as "The Dating Game killer," successfully appealed his two previous convictions. Even though he'd won a date as a contestant on *The Dating Game,* Alcala creeped out the woman so much that she refused to go out with him. Good choice.

In late 2007, while Murphy and NBPD Sergeant Dave Byington were preparing for Skylar Deleon's trial, they discussed the McLaughlin case and agreed it was worth resurrecting with the help of Larry Montgomery, a DA investigator who had already proved invaluable on the Hawks case. Montgomery was now conducting case reviews as part of the TracKRS Unit.

Murphy and Byington had first met on the prosecutor's virgin homicide call in May 2002. In late 2004, Byington called Murphy to report his suspicions that the Hawkses were not only missing, but most likely dead, and that Skylar had been identified as the prime suspect. After three years of putting that "murder for financial gain" case together, Murphy and Byington had become close friends and didn't want their self-described "man love" working relationship to end.

The Hawks case proved to be similar to the McLaughlin case in more ways than just the capital charges. Both involved conspiracies, and some of the killer-couple suspects' acts prior to the murders were also parallel: Nanette Packard and Jennifer Deleon both used their children as pawns in schemes to manipulate their victims, and both couples went shopping for million-dollar homes they planned to purchase with their victims' money.

"The last time someone writes a quarter-million-dollar

check and then someone dies," Byington said, "that's a clue in this business."

Bill McLaughlin must have thought something was amiss, he added, or at the very least, he'd changed his mind about getting married to Nanette.

"She was going to get caught. It was just a matter of time. He wasn't a fool."

Byington and Murphy figured that because quarterly tax payments were due in January 1995, Nanette realized that she had to kill Bill before he noticed the missing money and checks with his forged signatures. If the timing of the murder had been random, Byington said, Nanette would have bought Bill a Christmas gift and had it ready for him under the tree. Instead, "she bought stuff for everyone else" *but* him.

Sergeant Byington assigned Detective Joe Cartwright to work on the case with DA Investigator Larry Montgomery. Cartwright, a former marine who had cut his detective's teeth on the Hawks case, was feeling inspired and gratified by the department's success.

"Definitely something I wanted to keep doing, keep bringing that kind of closure to people," he said.

The first thing he did was go downstairs to the property/evidence room and look through the items collected during the three years the McLaughlin case had been open: the blood evidence in the freezer, the keys the killer left behind, Bill's bathrobe, riddled with bullet holes and steeped in blood, the expended shell casings, the photos, the financial documents, and the binders of police reports from the homicide and fraud investigations. He made two copies of all the paperwork, one for him and one for Montgomery.

Byington was "blown away" by Cartwright's thorough

and meticulous work on the case. "He was just awesome," he said. "He did a great job on it."

During several initial meetings, Murphy, Byington, Cartwright, and Montgomery went through all the files and evidence together. They had never seen these materials before, so the significance of certain aspects of the case was not immediately clear. As they continued meeting, their strategy evolved as the overall puzzle came together.

"The checks were a big thing, trying to figure out what the scam was," Murphy said, noting that Nanette had also written a number of checks to Eric and his security company.

Detective Tom Voth, who had retired in 2006, was asked to come back part-time to help. As the lead detective on the original case, he was also expected to testify and be on call to answer questions if the case made it to trial.

Just because this was a cold case didn't mean that Murphy was any less involved in monitoring the investigation. As things progressed, he often discussed developments with Montgomery three times a day; they went no longer than a couple of days without talking.

Montgomery, who had worked thirty years as a police officer—twenty-three as a homicide detective with the Irvine Police Department—often conducted interviews with Cartwright as they followed new leads and reexamined old ones.

Over the next eighteen months, Montgomery listened to sixty-three audio interviews with witnesses and the primary suspects, Nanette Packard and Eric Naposki, and reviewed two thousand pages of documents. He conducted his own driving-time trials as well, including several he videotaped with Voth.

Early on, Murphy asked the team of investigators to run new DNA tests, given that the technology had improved so much since 1994. So they retested Bill's robe as well as the shell casings and the keys.

"I was very confident we'd get DNA off that key and also off the shell casings," Murphy said, acknowledging that he hadn't realized at the time that no one had ever retrieved DNA from a shell casing.

Cartwright was hopeful as well. "Back then, you had to cut a piece of material and soak it to get DNA," he said. "Now you can take a swab to get DNA. So maybe, we thought, the killer got close enough to leave DNA on the robe or grab it."

While they waited the eight weeks for results, Montgomery made some headway in other directions, but the DNA and fingerprint tests both came up empty. They figured the killer must have worn gloves.

Wondering if they still had a case, Murphy asked Montgomery to weigh in.

"What do you think, Larry?" Murphy asked. "Can we win it?"

"They absolutely did it," Montgomery said, "and we absolutely can win it."


Twice a year, Jenny McLaughlin had been making regular calls to the NBPD, urging them not to forget about her father's murder.

"Please always keep my dad's case open," she pleaded. "We're still hopeful."

After being forced into the deep, dark world of Nanette Johnston, the McLaughlin sisters had learned far more than they'd ever wanted to know about her lying and stealing ways. They were sure she'd murdered their father.

But they couldn't stay in that darkness. Instead, they tried to focus on the good in their lives, surrounding themselves with positive people and avoiding negative activities.

Kim stopped watching TV and reading about crime in the newspaper, for example.

"We've really tried to live in our dad's honor and remember the good times and try to put all the evidence, and, ugh, that horrible tragedy behind us," Kim said in 2012. If they'd continued "to go on with anger in our hearts," she said, then Nanette would have stolen their ability to be happy too.

Kim and Jenny both moved out of Orange County to escape the memories. Kim and her husband relocated and got a teaching job on the island of Coronado in southern San Diego County, where her husband had grown up. Jenny and her husband landed on a horse ranch, running an equestrian business in Valley Center, in northern San Diego County.

As if losing their father weren't enough, the McLaughlins had to endure another tragedy seven years after Bill's murder. While living with Sue in Hawaii, Kevin drowned in the ocean one evening after going to church on October 23, 1999.

Kim theorized that Kevin got carried out into deep water, where he swallowed some of it, and was unable to cough it out because of the scar tissue from his tracheotomy. A couple walking along the beach under the full moon pulled his body out of the water later that night.

Some months after the cold-case investigation was under way, the detectives contacted Jenny because Murphy wanted to meet with the McLaughlin sisters to ask them some questions. But, not wanting to give false hope to the sisters, the detectives didn't mention the explicit purpose of the meeting.

When Jenny told Kim about the request to bring to the OC whatever relevant financial documents they had, Kim couldn't help but get her hopes up once again. But after all these years without an arrest, she tried to temper her emotions.

"Really? They want us to come up?" she asked Jenny. "That means it's still open!"

When the McLaughlins arrived, they saw none of the detectives who had originally worked with them on the case and had become like members of their extended family. The faces at the table—Murphy, Montgomery, Cartwright, and Byington—were all unfamiliar.

That's when Murphy told them they were taking another look at the case.

"I just want to let you guys know that we're pursuing this as a murder investigation," he said.

By this point, these men had already been working the investigation for most of the year, but they didn't elaborate, just in case they didn't make it to trial. However, just hearing that the case had been reopened made the McLaughlins so happy, they cried.

When months went by and they didn't hear anything more, however, the sisters felt as if they'd been left hanging once again.


On one of the many audiotapes Montgomery listened to, he heard a reference in a phone conversation between Detective Jeff Lu and a woman who had called the station to report that she thought Eric and Nanette had killed Bill McLaughlin. Claiming to have founded a medical company that was going to make her a millionaire, Nanette had expressed interest in investing in the software business of this caller's fiancé, who knew Nanette from the Sporting Club.

When Lu asked the woman to put her fiancé on the phone, she called him by name. It was so faint that Montgomery had to put on a high-quality headset to enhance the sound: She called him "Robert."

Robert, who didn't identify himself to the detective, said Nanette claimed that she was living on the royalties from a medical device she'd sold to Baxter Healthcare, and in November 1994 she said she might want to invest $100,000 to $200,000 in his company.

Robert said his call was prompted by news reports about the murder, which named Nanette as a suspect, saying his suspicions were raised as soon as he heard how Bill had made his fortune. The original interview tape ended midsentence, however, so Montgomery called Detective Cartwright to tell him about the promising anonymous caller.

Cartwright called the Sporting Club in Irvine, asking to search their member records from 1994 and 1995, with the hope of finding this man named Robert something.

Meanwhile, Montgomery checked Irvine police records from the same timeframe at the department's business license division, searching for software companies with owners by that name. He found two, but neither said he'd called the NBPD.

On July 22, 2008, Montgomery pulled Nanette's cell phone records from the evidence. If she'd been having secret meetings about investing Bill's money, he thought she might have used her cell phone, rather than the victim's home phone, to avoid getting caught.

The next day at the Haines Publishing headquarters in Fullerton, Montgomery searched through the Orange County Criss+Cross Directory from 1994, looking for matches on Nanette's phone bill with anyone named Robert or any computer software company. (The Criss+Cross Directory lists published phone numbers with associated street addresses and residents' names.) But he found nothing.

After that, he flipped through the 1995 directories, and came across a number listed for an R. Cottrill. Although the directory didn't list an address, Montgomery recognized it as an Irvine number and got a rush, hoping he had a match. Excitedly calling Cartwright, Montgomery told him he might have a lead.

Cartwright ran the name of Robert Cottrill through the DMV database and found a Robert T. Cottrill in San Clemente, which is in southern Orange County. Checking other databases, Cartwright saw that Cottrill had headed a software company in 1994, had lived in Irvine, and had married a woman named Dori in 1995. The lead looked even more promising.

On July 24, the two investigators drove to Cottrill's house, where they spoke to a woman house-sitting for the vacationing homeowner. By the time Montgomery got back to his office that afternoon, he already had a message from Cottrill, so he called him immediately.

By all appearances, Montgomery was generally a low-key guy. But that day he was jumping on the inside, frankly ecstatic that all this legwork had proved fruitful. Cottrill indeed was their man.

"That was pretty big," Montgomery recalled later, remarking how much he enjoyed his job. "You can't get that thrill from doing too many other things."

Cottrill told the investigators again that Nanette had claimed she couldn't invest any money in his business right away because it was offshore, noting that she'd also told him that she'd just broken up with a bodybuilder boyfriend who worked out at the same gym. And that ex-boyfriend wasn't very happy when she started dating Eric Naposki.


In January 2009, Montgomery listened to a taped call between Detective Tom Fischbacher and a woman named Suzanne who said she'd been too scared to call the NBPD before because she feared for her safety. The call was on March 3, 1998, six months after the investigation had officially been shelved.

Suzanne told Fischbacher that she'd been Eric Naposki's neighbor at an apartment complex in Tustin in 1994. She'd called police in 1995, but the case detective wasn't available and a woman who answered told her to call back. She said she didn't call for the next three years because she was worried that Eric would seek revenge. She then proceeded to recount Eric's comments about blowing up Bill McLaughlin's plane, the keys, and the gun, and the "maybe I did, maybe I didn't" remark. She said she still wasn't willing to testify against Eric, but she did agree to meet with Fischbacher.

On the same tape, Montgomery heard Fischbacher calling Suzanne two days after she'd canceled. A receptionist answered, "Charles Dunn" before transferring the detective to Suzanne's voice mail, where he left a message. The next call was a conversation between Suzanne and Sergeant Pat O'Sullivan.

Montgomery and Cartwright were unable to find any other tapes involving this witness. Montgomery searched online for Charles Dunn and found a company in Newport Beach, while Cartwright went through the case files and located one labeled *Suzanne Cogar,* detailing a woman born November 24, 1964, who had a driver's license with an Irvine address. It had to be her.

O'Sullivan had since retired from the NBPD and was now an investigator for the DA's office. Because O'Sullivan was the last one to speak with Cogar, Montgomery asked him to call her and relay the message that Montgomery wanted to discuss her statements from thirteen years ago.

When Suzanne Cogar got the call from O'Sullivan, she was pleased that the police hadn't forgotten about the case after all these years, because it had continued to bother her.

By this time, Cogar felt safe and was 100 percent "willing to testify." She regretted not meeting with the police all those years ago, she said. After telling O'Sullivan so much about herself before, she wanted to look him in the eyes "so he would see that I was credible, that what I was telling him was on the level."

When they met at her house, O'Sullivan asked her to review the tapes of her statements from 1998, then meet with Larry Montgomery. She agreed.

"Why has it taken all these years?" she asked Montgomery, who explained that the case had gone "cold" some months before her call in 1998, but he was taking a new look and applying "fresh eyes" to the evidence.

In March 2009, she met with him a second time. Montgomery also brought along the prosecutor, Matt Murphy. Both men could see that Cogar's testimony would be very important to the case, so Murphy tried to reassure her.

"I don't want to scare you, but your testimony is really key here," he said.

Cogar, who could tell that Murphy wanted "to close the door on this horrible injustice," told him she wasn't surprised.

"I figured as much," she said.

# CHAPTER 32

Detective Joe Cartwright tracked down Eric Naposki in Greenwich, Connecticut, and spoke with the local police department there in early May 2009 about the NBPD's plans to arrest Eric for murder.

Cartwright and his boss, Sergeant Dave Byington, worked together on the arrest and search warrant affidavits, with Byington contributing the evidence gathered in the 1990s, and Cartwright adding the new evidence that he, Larry Montgomery, and Tom Voth had collected.

In a strategy largely dictated by Matt Murphy, Cartwright coordinated a game plan with Sergeant Tom Kelly and Detective Jeff Stempien, of the Greenwich Police Department, who agreed to watch Eric for a couple of weeks to learn his habits and schedule.

After scoping out the situation, they learned that Eric lived with Rosie in a duplex owned by her father, a two-story brick building at the end of a long driveway off a windy two-lane road. Eric usually left between 6:30 or 7:00 A.M. in a bright yellow truck that had the name of his gym emblazoned on its side. He stopped at a gas station down the street for a newspaper and coffee; then drove to work in Mount Kisco, New York.

Cartwright went through the same exercise monitoring Nanette's comings and goings in Ladera Ranch, California. Sitting in a van with dark windows, parked a block from her house, he watched Billy McNeal leave for work. From there, Cartwright followed Nanette to a private school nearby and saw her drop off Jaycie. Most days Nanette stayed close to home, though, because she'd only recently had baby Cruz.

The plan was to keep both suspects "in pocket" until the DA investigator, Larry Montgomery, could arrive in Connecticut with Newport Beach Detectives Cartwright, Steve Rasmussen, and Elijah Hayward on May 18. The police would arrest Eric and Nanette simultaneously on May 20, and make it a competition between the detectives on both coasts to see if they could get one suspect to turn on the other.

"We wanted one of them to flip," said Byington, who was staying in Orange County to make the drop on Nanette with his team in Ladera Ranch.

The hope was to get one suspect to cooperate by calling the other on a taped line and elicit incriminating statements.

Cartwright took the search warrant affidavit for Eric's house to the Connecticut Chief State Attorney's Office for approval, and the affidavit to search Eric's gym to the New York State Attorney General's Office in Westchester County, New York. But both warrants were denied.

"It had been too long," Cartwright said. "The expectation was 'Hey, maybe we'll find the gun. Maybe he's stupid enough to keep it.' We don't catch the smart ones."

Because Eric's house was set so far back from the narrow, twisty street, the Greenwich police wanted their

Special Response Unit (SRU, similar to a SWAT team) to arrest Eric in a "felony stop" after pulling over his car.

"If we were to arrest him at the house, we had the challenge of Rosie possibly being there, the father-in-law possibly being there, and going up the driveway," where Eric would be able to see them coming, Cartwright said. "We'd lose the element of surprise."

Instead, Detective Stempien dressed in a Greenwich patrolman's uniform to take advantage of "Click it or ticket" week—a time to remind drivers to buckle up. He parked across the street, then stood at the top of Eric's driveway, stopping cars as if he were routinely enforcing the ticket law.

When he saw Eric driving his truck down the driveway, he would radio the other officers—a team of six waiting to nab him down the road, rifles ready, in a marked car and a black SUV with dark windows.

While the Connecticut team waited for Eric to leave the house, the California team waited for Nanette to show up at hers, thinking she was out.

Eric started down his driveway at eight-fifteen that spring morning, only he wasn't driving the truck. He was in a sporty black Nissan 350Z two-seater, a nice ride for a guy who couldn't afford his child support payments.

Detective Stempien stopped a car so Eric would have to stop behind him. Eric cruised up and rolled down his window to talk to the officer.

"Love to see the enforcement out here," Eric said. "They're always speeding through here like it's a highway."

"It's 'Click it or ticket' week. Make sure you have your belt on," Stempien replied.

"Yes, I have it on, officer."

But Eric surprised them again, by driving in the opposite direction from the gas station.

"He's not going south. He's not going south. He's going north," Stempien repeated into his radio.

The Greenwich detectives and patrol supervisors sped to catch up to Eric a quarter mile down the road and pulled him over. They ordered him to throw his keys out the window, show his hands, kneel on the road, and lie facedown in the middle of the street.

"What's your name?" Stempien asked, standing over him with Cartwright.

"Eric Naposki."

"Joe," Stempien said to Cartwright, "is this Eric Naposki?"

Cartwright confirmed that it was, in fact, the bulky former linebacker, who had shaved his head and grown a goatee since the NBPD detectives had last questioned him in Newport Beach in 1995.

"What is this about?" Eric asked. "This is a mistake. I haven't done anything."

"You're being placed under arrest as a fugitive from justice," Stempien said.

"What are you talking about?"

"The state of California has a warrant for you for the murder of Bill McLaughlin," Cartwright said.

"Bill McLaughlin?"

The Greenwich police brought a very defiant Eric Naposki into the interview room back at the station, where Montgomery and Cartwright were waiting.

While the two men conducted the interview, Newport Beach Detectives Rasmussen and Hayward questioned Eric's fiancée at the elementary school in Greenwich, where she was teaching.

"When did you guys get here?" Rosie asked.

"A couple of days ago."

"Why couldn't you have done this yesterday?" she asked. "I just sent out all the wedding invitations."


Although Eric said he was on his way to court to pay his child support, Cartwright didn't believe that he would have gone there wearing gym clothes.

During a search of Eric's car, the detectives found a gym bag containing vitamin supplements and what Eric later described** as "AndroGel. It's a rub-on for men who want a little boost to their, whatever, testosterone [levels]." He said it was nothing like full-blown steroids, as the detectives had suggested. Even so, the clear odorless topical gel, which comes in a pump bottle, does require a prescription, so it's also not a harmless, over-the-counter supplement.

The interview room was about eight feet by ten feet, but Eric's imposing stature made it feel as if the three of them were in a cramped two-foot-by-two-foot space.

"Eric takes up half the room, with one arm hooked to a bar on the wall," Cartwright recalled, noting that he'd imagined Eric jumping across the table and grabbing one of them. "He's got the other arm in front, leaning forward, pointing at us, threatening that he was going to sue the police department."

Once Eric got to trial in 2011, Cartwright said, "he looked kind of pudgy. But at the time of the arrest, he was really muscular, really cut up, didn't have much fat on him. Larry and I were sitting across from this guy, and we were going, 'Wow.'"

After listening to Eric's police interviews from the 1990s, they were prepared for him to try to dominate the questioning. Although they'd hoped to thwart that effort, Eric was still very aggressive as Montgomery and Cartwright tried to get a word in edgewise.

Knowing that Eric hated the NBPD, Cartwright dressed

in street clothes. Montgomery, who wore a suit, introduced himself as an investigator from the DA's office and Cartwright as his "partner."

Eric was just as cocky as ever. "You kidding me?"

"Nope," Montgomery said matter-of-factly.

"I'm under arrest for murder?" Eric asked, demanding to see the warrant. "If you've done your homework—"

"Yes, I have," Montgomery said.

"I haven't done shit," Eric said, asking what new evidence they'd gathered since deciding not to arrest him all those years ago. "I have all the respect in the world, but you're about to fucking kill me. . . . You're about to ruin my life again. And I worked hard to build what I have back up. All right? I'm not a criminal. I've never done anything wrong, anything. I have no record, nothing. I don't know why I'm arrested."

When Montgomery told him about Suzanne Cogar's statement, Eric leaned toward him. "All right," he said, "I'm going to give you a straight-ass answer. Look into my eyes."

"Okay."

"I did not kill him back then. I did not kill him now, you understand me? . . . I think you know I didn't do it. . . . Look at me, don't look down. You know I didn't do it."

"I know you did," Montgomery replied.

"Come on, all right, you know, let's go to court. I want you to put me on a plane to California today. I want my trial right now."

Cartwright was thinking that if Eric had nothing to do with this, "who volunteers to go to jail in California, with no bail, and sit, for a couple of years at least, [waiting] for a trial?"

Asked why Cogar would say such things about him if they weren't true, Eric replied, "I don't know. . . . I made out with the girl one time and, you know, the whole time we lived together, we sat in a hot tub once and we went to the movies once. I don't know why, and, to be honest, I don't think she said that stuff, 'cause I never said that stuff."

Eric said it was impossible for him to have killed Bill because he was at the soccer game and then Nanette dropped him off at Leonard Jomsky's house, where he was living with Jomsky at the time. (This was the first time he said this to explain why he had driven by Jomsky's when it was in the opposite direction from work. Back in 1994 and 1995, he and Nanette originally had said she dropped him at his apartment in Tustin; then he changed his story to say he was driving by Jomsky's for some other reason on his way to work when he got paged.)

But clearly confused about which stories he'd told all those years ago, Eric said that maybe his car had been parked at Jomksy's house, after all.

"Now I remember," he said.

As he repeated the rest of his previous story—that he'd gone from Jomsky's to Denny's, where he'd answered the page with the 8:52 P.M. call on his way to work—it became clear to Cartwright that Eric thought his phone record was a "Get Out of Jail Free" card, the reason that he hadn't been arrested back in the 1990s, and that the alibi would set him free once again.

But when Cartwright asked him to describe what the phone bill looked like, Eric shrugged off the question and tried to change the subject.

"If you understand it, are you going to unhook me and let me out of here?" Eric asked.

"No."

"So what the fuck's the difference?" he said.

Eric grew increasingly agitated as he went back and forth with Montgomery about why he'd lied about the 9mm gun fifteen years ago.

"This is bullshit. You guys are fucking with me. . . . Let's all get famous on fucking TV for nothing."

The investigators could see they were getting nowhere, so they decided to see if they could trick him into admitting that he'd been to Bill McLaughlin's house, even though they'd never found any of his fingerprints, clothing fibers, or DNA there. But when they told him they'd found his DNA on the keys and bullet casings at the crime scene, Eric didn't go for it.

"There's no way," he said.

On to the next ploy, Montgomery told Eric that he had a chance to be the first to turn on his partner in crime. If he called Nanette and got her to talk, they would record the call. However, he only had so much time to do it.

"Within the next three hours, four hours, she is very possibly going to know that you're in custody and then there's nothing we can do," Montgomery said. "I mean, she's not going to believe you or any kind of phone call. . . . I know you're in a pickle."

While Eric rejected their overture, he also didn't implicate Nanette in the murder.

"On my children, on my parents, on my life, I've not talked to the girl since that shit went down," he said. "Did she lie to me? Yes. Is all that shit? You know, yeah, yeah, yeah. But I didn't kill anybody. . . . I ain't got no blood on my hands, ever. You got the wrong guy."

Around 11:00 A.M., after the Newport Beach detectives had left the Greenwich station, Eric complained that he didn't feel well. He said he was sweating, and he felt extremely hot and nauseated. He was taken to a local hospital, where he was treated and released, thereby missing his arraignment in court.

After being held overnight at the Greenwich jail, which Stempien said was like the Holiday Inn compared to state prison, Eric was taken to court in Stamford the next day.

From there, he was transferred to the state correctional facility in Bridgeport to await his extradition hearing. In the meantime, he was held on $2 million cash-only bail, which meant that no one could get him out on a bond, which only required a 10 percent payment.

After the arrest, Montgomery and Cartwright wanted to share the good news with the McLaughlin family, one of the more gratifying parts of their job. They tried to reach Jenny first, but got no answer, so they called Kim, who was in Hawaii on sabbatical from her teaching job, helping her mother take care of Kim's grandmother. The time difference made it six hours later in Connecticut than in Hawaii.

Sue McLaughlin answered, handed the phone to Kim, and told her who it was.

"Do you know where I am?" Cartwright asked.

"Um, no."

"I'm in Connecticut."

"Okay. What's this about?" Kim asked as her heart started racing. After getting her hopes up before, she didn't want to let herself go through that again. Still, she couldn't help but hope just a little bit.

"We need to let you know, we've just arrested Eric Naposki," he said.

Kim erupted with a scream. "*Whaaat?* You're kidding me! You guys are unbelievable!"

Crying with joy, Kim paused for a moment, then asked, "What about Nanette?"

"We have patrol on Nanette and we will be arresting her," he said. "We're hoping to do it today. We'll call you after we make the arrest."

Later, Kim recalled how happy she was to receive the good news so many years after she and her sister had thought the case had gone stone cold.

"It was way too surreal and way too much of a beautiful shock and a huge surprise," she said.

* * *

Surrounded by five detectives and a couple of uniformed officers, Sergeant Dave Byington walked up in his raid gear to Nanette's tree-lined stone-and-wood house in Ladera Ranch. After all these years, he wanted to be the one to arrest her and watch her reaction.

When he knocked on her door at 1:45 P.M., Nanette opened it just a bit and peered out cautiously.

"Nanette, remember me?" he asked.

"No," said Nanette, who was dressed in a casual T-shirt and sweatpants. Her dyed blond hair fell just above her shoulders and she looked a little scruffy, harder in the face and nowhere near as attractive as Byington remembered.

"I remember you. I'm Sergeant Byington, Newport Beach Police Department," he said. "I have a warrant to search your house and a murder warrant for your arrest."

"What murder?"

"Well, I'm not sure how many you've committed, but this one is for the McLaughlin homicide," he said.

Nanette's legs buckled slightly, but she quickly regained her composure and righted herself.

"Why would I want him dead? He was worth more to me alive. Can we do this later?" she said, trying to close the door. "My baby is asleep upstairs."

"No, this is the program," Byington said firmly. "We're coming in. We have a warrant. I don't want you shutting the door. I don't want to embarrass you in front of your neighbors. My biggest concern is the welfare of your baby. You're going to cooperate with us. If you do, we'll do everything in our power to leave the baby with either a family member or friend as opposed to having the kid taken into custody by child welfare."

"You're not taking my baby," she said like a lioness guarding her cub.

But Byington's veiled threat got her attention, and she let them inside the house, which was clean and nicely decorated.

"The interior matched the neighborhood. High-end, wealthy," he recalled. "Except for the stripper pole."

Byington had hoped that the shock of them showing up years later like this would catch her off guard and that she would just blurt out, "Yeah, Eric did it."

But that didn't happen, even when he tried to prompt her and give her an out. "I know, you've had a lot of husbands," he said. "I can't even keep track of your boyfriends, but back in the day, I know Eric is overbearing, physically imposing. . . ."

She still didn't bite. "I didn't have anything to do with that murder, and as far as I know, neither did Eric," she said.

Trying another tactic, Byington laid out possible scenarios for her to want to kill Bill, such as the claim she'd told Eric, that Bill had sexually attacked her. But she wouldn't give in. He even tried telling her that Eric was getting the same offer on the East Coast.

"Clock is ticking, kiddo. Eric is in custody right now and my detectives are telling him the same thing I'm telling you."

"I can't tell you what Eric is going to tell you, but I don't think he did it," she said. "Why now? How did you find Eric?"

Curious, yes, and a little concerned, but she still wouldn't budge.

Before they took Nanette out to the police cars in handcuffs, she asked if she could change into something else, knowing that the TV cameras were outside.

"Can I please get some clothes out of my closet?"

But Byington wasn't going to give her that. He did, however, agree to send the officers upstairs to fetch her something to wear from her closet, which contained some of the most expensive designer clothing to be found in Orange County.

"She had racks and racks and racks and racks of clothes that still had the tags on them," he said.

Just to mess with her, they picked out the ugliest pieces they could find, so she wouldn't wear them. They were right.

Then they searched her house. Under her bed, apparently so her husband wouldn't find them, the detectives found a stash of credit card statements in a box, with tens of thousands of dollars past due.

And, to their amusement, they found the stripper pole that Byington mentioned, along with a homemade DVD of her and her girlfriends flitting around like strippers. They later learned that Nanette worked out at S Factor, a "striptease fitness" company that teaches women how to do pole dancing and lap dancing for exercise.

The detectives seized her computer, where they found some correspondence with Eric, which contradicted the former couple's claims that they had stopped communicating.

Billy McNeal was at his desk at his company, Custom Blow Molding in Escondido, when his cell phone rang around 2:00 P.M.

"Hey, it's me," Nanette said in an unusually serious voice. "I need you to come home."

"Okay," Billy said, wondering what was up. "What's going on?"

"Well," she said, "you know that murder I told you about [from] fifteen years ago?"

"No," he said. "What do you mean?"

"There was a murder fifteen years ago and the police are here to arrest me, because they think I did it."

Billy sat silently in disbelief with the phone against hi

ear, not knowing what to say or think. Figuring there had to be a simple explanation, he was finally able to form a few words.

"Okay, I'll get there as fast as I can."

*We'll talk this through. They'll go away and everything will be all right again,* he thought. *There's no way this could be true. It's just craziness.*

Before they hung up, a detective got on the phone and tried to make sure Billy didn't do anything stupid or reckless.

"Don't drive crazy," he said. "It's fine. Just get here when you can. Your son is fine. We'll wait here for you."

When Billy arrived, he saw the news vans outside and assumed the police or the DA's office had leaked the story. As he ran inside, Byington and another detective stopped him in the foyer. About eight guys with badges around their necks were going through the house, carrying out computers and other belongings.

"We already took her away," the detective said. "Do you know what's going on?"

"No, I have no clue," Billy said.

As the detectives told him the story of Bill McLaughlin's murder, Billy shook his head. It sounded so crazy he couldn't even process what they were saying. All he could think of was taking Cruz in his arms.

"I just want to be with my son right now," he told them. "Take me to my son."

Upstairs, he found one of the neighbors sitting next to the crib in which Billy's son was napping. Billy leaned over and just stood there, staring at the baby, until his mother and sister arrived. They joined him in feeling at a loss for words, and just looked at each other. They finally sat down together on the floor to let the news sink in while Cruz slept the sleep of the innocent.

\* \* \*

Detective Cartwright and Investigator Montgomery flew back to Orange County, leaving behind the other detectives to take Eric to the extradition hearing later that week, and bring him back to California.

When Cartwright returned to his desk, he was delighted to find a huge bouquet of balloons and a card signed by the McLaughlin family.

*Thank you for making justice prevail,* the message read.

Cartwright was touched. "They were overjoyed, and their patience was to be commended," he said.

Attorney John Pappalardo got a call from his childhood friend, Eric Naposki, the day of his arrest.

The next day, Pappalardo drove up from New York to the Bridgeport Correctional Center in Connecticut, along with another attorney, who had a license to practice law in that state.

"This is crazy," Eric told Pappalardo. "We went through all of this fifteen years ago."

"Let's get you back to California," Pappalardo said. "We'll deal with it. Let's find out what's going on."

"Don't leave me alone out there," Eric pleaded.

"I'll come out and find you the right person."

At the time, Pappalardo planned to help his friend with the extradition process and then find him an attorney in California. But Eric begged Pappalardo to take his case for the long haul.

Pappalardo told Eric it would be difficult to defend Eric by himself. He had no license to practice law in California, and it would be expensive and time-consuming to put together a fifteen-year-old murder case.

As time went on, however, Pappalardo decided that he could work it *pro hac vice*—for this one particular occasion—meaning that he or an affiliate of his firm could serve as co-counsel with a California attorney who had the chops to handle a potential death penalty case.

When he spoke to Julian Bailey, Eric's attorney from 1995, Bailey said he was no longer a practicing attorney because he was on the bench. But more important, he no longer had a copy of Eric's file. Bailey recommended that they get in touch with Gary Pohlson, an attorney with a solid reputation for representing murder defendants facing the death penalty.

# CHAPTER 33

The next day at Eric's hearing in Stamford, he winke
and blew a kiss to his family and friends in court, wher
Judge William Wenzel ordered that Eric's $2 million bail b
revoked so he could be transported to Orange County fo
trial.

"Do you consent to return to the state of California fo
the purpose of facing the charges against you?" the judg
asked.

"Absolutely," Eric replied.

As he was being led out by a marshal, Eric turned towar
the gallery and said, "Good-bye, everyone."

"We love you, Eric," his friends and family called to him
"We're here for you, bro!"

After the hearing, John Pappalardo defended his frien
to reporters.

"He looks forward to getting out to California to addres
the charge against him," he said. "He is one hundred percen
innocent."

Pappalardo hooked up with Gary Pohlson by phone
then the New York attorney flew out to the OC with Angel

MacDonald and Richard Portale to "get a lay of the land" before the arraignment. As the attorneys walked through the Santa Ana courthouse together, Pappalardo could see that everyone knew and respected Pohlson, who had handled so many murder cases he couldn't remember if this was his ninety-third or ninety-fourth.

Pohlson started his college education at St. John's Seminary in Camarillo, but changed direction after three years because he decided he wanted a family. He finished his bachelor's degree at Santa Clara University, then attended law school at the University of California, Los Angeles.

From there, he landed a prosecutor's job at the Orange County DA's office in 1975. After three and a half years of public service, Pohlson left to pursue his goal of becoming his own boss. Forming a firm with a friend, he began trying death penalty cases in 1981.

Pohlson was a ruddy-faced man who wore nice suits, but he exuded the spirit of a man who could just as easily have worn a monk's robe, the benevolence shining through his kind eyes and easy grin.

"I see it more as a vocation than a job," he said. "I'm doing what I should be doing. God gave me some talents and I'm just doing the best I can."

Modesty and self-deprecating humor are two Pohlson trademark characteristics that make him a likeable attorney who can garner goodwill in the courtroom even while defending some of the most hated criminals.

"I really love it," Pohlson said. "It's really important to make sure a person's rights are protected. They are the underdogs in these situations. The DA's office has all the resources, the money, and the evidence, usually. So if nobody is going to fight for these people, they're always going to go down. . . . They're people too."

Among his professional honors, he has been dubbed a "Super Lawyer" by *Los Angeles* magazine every year since

2006 and was named "Criminal Trial Lawyer of the Year" by the Orange County Trial Lawyers Association in 1999. He was a Court TV commentator during the OJ Simpson trial, was chosen to be president of the county bar association in 1995 and served for a decade on its board of directors. Pohlson has appeared on *48 Hours, 20/20, Snapped,* and various shows on Investigation Discovery.

Pohlson was such a nice man that even victims' families couldn't help but like him. He knew what they were going through. After losing his father to murder and his niece to a fatal drunk-driving incident, he was always polite and empathetic with these families, so his words came across as sincere and genuine.

Another advantage in using Pohlson was that he'd gone up against prosecutor Matt Murphy in a high-profile case once before—quite recently, in fact—when Pohlson represented Skylar Deleon at trial in 2008. Deleon had just been sentenced to death row at San Quentin when Pohlson agreed to take Eric's case.

Once Pohlson was on board, Pappalardo committed to sticking with the case until the end. Although he didn't sit at the counsel table, he was usually part of strategic discussions and sat in the gallery for support during court proceedings.

"You don't have to do this," Eric told him. "I know you guys are away from your families."

But Pappalardo, who Pohlson described as "an unbelievably loyal friend" to Eric, said he felt strongly about seeing this through.

"We're committed," Pappalardo said. "This is what I do. This is what *we* do."

Pappalardo ultimately entrusted the litigation of the case to his mentor, Angelo MacDonald, one of the lawyers affiliated with his firm with whom he went back a long way—to the Bronx County District Attorney's Office, where they both rose to be senior attorneys.

MacDonald knew that Pappalardo went back even further with Eric Naposki, and that was good enough for him.

"We're fighters," MacDonald said in 2012. "We believe in what we do. We're very principled people. We believed in [Eric]. I still believe in him."

MacDonald had prosecuted more than sixty homicide cases before going into private practice, while Pappalardo had prosecuted homicides, robberies, burglaries, and assaults before leaving in 1998 to work with his father, another attorney.

"Apparently, [Pappalardo's] father is a really upstanding guy, so the acorn really didn't fall far from that tree," Pohlson said.


Born in Detroit, Angelo MacDonald graduated from the University of Michigan and went to law school at Villanova University in Pennsylvania. His dark good looks, affable personality, accessibility, and charismatic oratory style made him a media-darling as a regular commentator on the former Court TV, now TruTV, who has also been featured on MSNBC and *Nancy Grace* on Fox. In addition, he served as legal consultant to Robin Cook, who has authored more than two dozen best-selling medical thrillers since *Coma* in 1977.

In 2011, MacDonald split his time living in New York City and Toronto, where his wife worked as a TV reporter. She had previously headed the investigative unit at Fox News and also was a reporter for *A Current Affair*.

MacDonald left law for a while to run an Internet company, which he ultimately sold, and then did business development for a number of client companies in the World Trade Center. September 11, 2001, was a defining moment for him because so many people he'd worked with died that day.

A short time later, John Pappalardo called and asked him to get involved in a case. MacDonald slowly found himself getting sucked back into practicing law, and eventually became officially affiliated with the firm of Pappalardo & Pappalardo and two others.

The Pappalardo firm, located in Westchester County, New York, has handled a number of NYPD cases in which it defended police officers charged with crimes ranging from white-collar offenses to murder. The firm has also represented New York politicians, professional athletes, recording artists, and corporate executives, boasting that the attorneys are fluent in handling high-profile cases that get covered by major media, including the *New York Times*.

In other words, Eric had called in the big guns, with a team of four attorneys representing him. He was confident they would get him off.

While MacDonald got up to snuff on the case with Pohlson on the West Coast, Pappalardo continued to defend Eric to the media on the East Coast, including one article that ran in the *Journal News* in Westchester County, New York, right before Eric's twenty-fifth high-school reunion.

"There is no eyewitness. There is no DNA evidence. No forensic evidence," Pappalardo told the reporter. "There's nothing putting him at the scene because he didn't commit the murder. . . . There's no way he could have done what they claimed he did. He certainly didn't kill anybody."

Eric's friends and family set up a website, where they posted his letters from jail, the responses he received, and testimonials from people who had known him for years. Eric was often described as "a healer and a helper, not a killer," as his attorney Richard Portale put it.

*If there was ever a chance for me to practice what I preach to everyone I train, this is it,* Eric wrote. *I fight to remain focused, positive, and determined to complete my goals, to prove my innocence and clear my name.*

The website also spelled out what was needed to get the job done: money.

*Eric needs a strong defense,* the site stated. *That defense is dependent upon monies to support California and NY legal representation in the form of: attorneys, private investigators, recreating [sic] scenarios from 15 years ago, travel, hotels and many other critical legal costs. There is no one else to turn to but Eric's family and friends.*

Eric's mother posted a personal note thanking those who had already donated to her son's cause, and pleading for others to continue to drum up the necessary financial support to bring him home.

*If you have signed onto this website hopefully you have the love, respect and confidence in Eric and know without a doubt that he is innocent of all charges,* Ronnie Naposki wrote. *As many of his friends and associates, coaches and family members have said when they called me, "He's just not that guy."*

Some money was raised at fund-raisers and through the website, but it turned out to be just a fraction of what the case cost to put together.

Pohlson was initially retained by Pappalardo. However, when the money from donations didn't come through as they'd hoped, the New York firm wasn't able to fulfill the agreement with Pohlson. Nonetheless, he agreed to stay on, went to court in California, and got appointed to continue representing Eric. (Pohlson is on a short list of private attorneys who can be paid by the state to represent indigent defendants on death penalty cases. And although this did not end up being a death case, the charges of murder with special-circumstance allegations made Eric eligible for a death sentence, so the court considered it as such.)

In the end, Pohlson said, taxpayers funded perhaps 10 percent of the case because the state paid him only "a very modest fee."

Asked if he worked the rest of the case for free, he said, "It wasn't pro bono. I probably made about ten dollars an hour. . . . Who paid for it was mostly Pappalardo."

"Realistically," Pappalardo agreed, "I funded—we funded—the case."

Given that Pohlson also worked unpaid for a year on the case after the jury verdict, he acknowledged in late 2012 that "this was not a good financial move" for him.

# CHAPTER 34

One of the important tasks for Larry Montgomery and Joe Cartwright was to see if they could prove or disprove whether Eric Naposki really did make that "alibi" phone call at 8:52 P.M., even though Cartwright said he "knew that in my mind's eye that if [Eric] did make this call, he still had time to get over to the house and kill Bill McLaughlin."

In 1995, Eric's then-attorney, Julian Bailey, had written a letter to prosecutor Debbie Lloyd, making reference to the phone records for the call. However, he did not attach them to the letter.

*This was a credit card call, and therefore there is a record of its time and place,* Bailey wrote. *I will make available the names, addresses and phone numbers of persons who can verify my assertions in this letter.*

From the way the letter was carefully worded—"there is a record"—Cartwright suspected that Bailey had not actually *seen* the phone bill for himself. But, knowing that the phone records would "be something that they were going to use as a defense," the detective called Eric's phone company and tried to get a copy of them in June 2009. He was told, however, that they had been purged long ago.

If this phone bill had been *his* alibi, Cartwright joked, "Personally, I'd have it tattooed to my back."

With no records to support Eric's story, Cartwright tried to verify that Eric had talked to the person he'd claimed on that alleged call.

Cartwright listened to Eric's police interview in which he said he was paged by the bar manager, whom he mistakenly recalled as "Teresmo," but the detective saw nothing in the file about police efforts to track this guy down.

Knowing that nightclubs were a magnet for vice activity during the 1990s, Cartwright looked through that unit's old files for a Thunderbird bar manager by that name. He found a couple of employees whose names were close, including a Mike Tuomisto, whom he tried to locate using database searches. He didn't have much luck, although he did find Mike's father in the Southwest. Cartwright called and asked for Mike's number, saying he wanted to interview him for a cold case he was investigating. The father didn't want to give it out, but said he would forward the request to his son.

Mike Tuomisto called Cartwright from Sweden, where he was working as a commercial diver for nuclear power plants.

"Yeah, I was the bar manager. I remember Eric," he told Cartwright, "but I wasn't in charge of security and I wouldn't have any reason to page a security guy."

After the murder, Tuomisto said, he'd flown out of town for Christmas. By the time he got back, the club had let him go. He continued to live a few blocks away for almost a year, but Eric never contacted him.

"That struck me as odd too," Cartwright recalled, noting that if Tuomisto was "Eric's alibi guy," why had Eric never mentioned this to the club owner or contacted Tuomisto personally to say, "Hey, I need you. You're my alibi"?

Later, when Tuomisto talked with Tom Gleim, Pohlson's private investigator, Tuomisto changed his story to say he didn't really remember that period of time very well.

# CHAPTER 35

In addition to the charges of first-degree murder for financial gain, Eric was also charged with discharging a firearm. If found guilty, the expected sentence for him and Nanette was life without the possibility of parole, otherwise known as LWOP.

At her arraignment on May 21, 2009, Nanette mouthed "I love you" to her family as she stood in her navy blue jail-issued jumpsuit to face the charge that she'd conspired to kill Bill McLaughlin.

Billy McNeal and Nanette's now-adult children, Kristofer and Lishele, returned the "I love you," flashed her the "OK" sign, and blew her kisses—all of which prompted a warning from the bailiff not to communicate with the prisoner.

Nanette was being held on no bail, but her attorney, Barry Bernstein, argued that she needed to go home to breast-feed Cruz and take care of Jaycie, who was now in elementary school. He got a bail hearing scheduled for May 26, and he managed to delay her arraignment until June 8.

The bail hearing, held in a Harbor Justice Center court-room that could seat ninety people, was attended by her immediate family and about sixty friends, at least ten of whom said they were willing to cosign loans pledging their savings, retirement accounts, or houses to back her bail bond so she could go home. Nanette had been hanging out with a group of about eight women who had met at the pole-dancing studio, went out partying together, and exchanged Christmas gifts.

Bernstein submitted a motion to set a "fair and reasonable" bail amount for Nanette, arguing that she hadn't committed any violent crimes during the years she'd been free since Bill McLaughlin was murdered. He also underscored that the only crimes she'd ever committed—grand theft and making false financial statements—were now fifteen years old.

Attached to the motion were a half-dozen letters of character reference from neighbors and friends, including the pastor of Legacy Church in Anaheim, a woman who had attended Bible study sessions at the McNeals' home, as well as Cruz and Jaycie's pediatrician.

The packet also included a letter from Nanette's friend Stacy Mallicoat, a criminal justice professor at California State University, Fullerton, who praised Nanette for her church and volunteer school activities, as well as for creating the fashion-design charity, "Jaycie Girl." Mallicoat commended Nanette for donating the proceeds to a good cause, apparently unaware that Nanette had kept the profits for herself.

The professor went on to commend Nanette for helping Lishele raise money to visit Rwanda on a ministry mission, and for helping out Mallicoat with a personal situation in Christmas 2007, when she and her husband had by "unforeseen circumstance" been unable to buy a gift that her twelve-year-old stepson had been eagerly awaiting. They were shocked and pleased to receive a card in the mail a few days later, with enough money to cover the gift.

*This simple generous act made my stepson's holiday,*

Mallicoat wrote. *This demonstrated to me her commitment towards helping others in random acts of kindness that have monumental effects for those around her.*

None of this did any good, however. Judge Karen Robinson pointed out that by law Nanette couldn't be released on bail with capital charges against her.

Outside the courtroom, prosecutor Matt Murphy told reporters that Nanette's supporters were "well-intentioned people, but I can't imagine that they have any clue about what she is really like."

After Nanette was denied bail, Bernstein filed a motion to dismiss the charges, arguing that under the clauses of due process and double jeopardy in the state and federal constitutions, Nanette shouldn't be prosecuted for murder because she'd already completed her sentence for previous charges that were made based on the "same investigation and the same facts."

But the court rejected that argument as well.

Dissatisfied with Bernstein's performance, Billy and Nanette decided she needed a new attorney. Nanette wrote a letter to the court requesting Bernstein's "immediate discharge." First, because she had no more money to pay him, and second, because she had "grievances" against him.

Hiring another criminal defense attorney to represent Nanette would have cost about $1 million, so a PI, who had been working with Billy on Nanette's case, tried to help find a public defender to take the case in early August.

The investigator also suggested that Billy hire an attorney for himself, so Billy spent $5,000 to retain the controversial but successful Newport Beach attorney Allan "Al" Stokke, who made news for expressing insensitive comments about the sixteen-year-old female victim of a gang rape while Stokke was representing one of the alleged perpetrators.

Nanette's case ended up in the hands of Deputy Public Defender Mick Hill, who was well respected in his office, where he had defended—and lost—only one murder case: that client, James Duff, was sentenced to twenty-five years to life for putting his hand over the mouth of an eleven-month-old boy to stop him from crying, thereby suffocating him.

Hill enjoyed going up against the establishment. Born in Cork, Ireland, in 1970, he grew up at a time when many of his countrymen were being released from prison after being wrongly accused of murders and IRA bombings because of corrupt police, prosecutors, and judges. Think Guildford Four and Birmingham Six.

This phenomenon had "a big, big impact on me when I was growing up," he said. As a result, "I was very happy to stand up for the underdog, because I could relate to it."

When Mick was nineteen, his family moved to Los Angeles, where his developer father, Finbar Hill, was transferred for his job. Today, Mick's father is Ireland's honorary consul general in Los Angeles, and he likes to watch his son's court cases.

Mick Hill attended Loyola Marymount University, Bill McLaughlin's alma mater, then graduated from the law school there in 1995, a year after Bill's death, but never heard a thing about the murder. Hill worked at a civil-litigation firm for about a year before he decided the private sector wasn't for him.

"When your life is reduced to billing in six-minute increments, your life is over," he joked.

Hill moved to Orange County in 1997, and has worked for the public defender's office there ever since.

"I absolutely love it. I get up every morning and look

forward to going to work," he said. "Being paid by the government to fight the government is quite heartwarming."

He noted that the irony of working as a public defender was that the better lawyer you were, the tougher the cases you were assigned, and "the more you get promoted in the office, the less chance you have of winning," he said. "We don't have an opportunity to say 'no' to the client to represent them."


In the weeks after Hill got the case, Billy McNeal came to his office several times to defend Nanette and extol her virtues. She was a successful businesswoman in her own right, Billy said. Why would she have been motivated to kill Bill McLaughlin?

"She didn't do it," Billy told Hill, who just sat and listened. "She's a good mom."

When Hill went to visit Nanette in jail for the first time, on August 12, 2009, he thought she seemed nothing like the cold, emotionless predator others perceived her to be when her case finally got to trial nearly three years later.

"She seemed to be a very, very scared, terrified person who didn't understand why she was facing the charges she was facing," he recalled in 2012.

Asked if this could have been an act, Hill replied that, in his view, she'd acted like an innocent person after Bill was murdered. "If you were guilty of this, I wouldn't have stayed living in Southern California. I would have moved somewhere else . . . where people didn't know anything about me." The fact that she didn't, he said, "is not indicative of a guilty person."

He noted that she also seemed to be happily married at the time of her arrest, with a baby at home, "whom she was missing terribly," as well as her nine-year-old daughter, Jaycie.

As he continued to meet with Nanette, he spent eighteen

months going through at least fifty-seven boxes of discovery, and a strategy began to emerge. After reading up on Bill McLaughlin's lawsuits with Jacob Horowitz, he believed that a third-party culpability defense—arguing that Horowitz had killed Bill—was the way to go.

The first few months after Nanette's arrest were a blur for Billy McNeal. Night after night, he lay awake as his mind whirled with the same thoughts that also consumed him during the day: who could help him with this or that, and when was this nightmare going to end?

Exhaustion soon set in as he tried to care for his newborn son alone, while also running his business and trying to understand the unimaginable case against his wife.

*Is this really happening to me? What are the odds?*

"The stress level was just incredible," he said. "It was just survival mode."

As Billy tried to cope with his new role as a single father, he met with a child psychologist to make sure he did right by his infant son, who had essentially lost his mother.

"He absolutely has to bond with another woman in less than twelve months," the psychologist told him. "It's critical."

Knowing what he needed to do, Billy packed up in June, left their big house in Ladera Ranch and moved into his sister's modest home in Winchester, in neighboring Riverside County. He slept in his nephew's bed without even changing the boy's baseball sheets, placing the new crib he'd bought for Cruz at his feet so they almost touched. He wanted his son to sleep as close to him as possible in the tiny ten-foot-by-ten-foot room.

Billy's sister watched Cruz during the day, and Billy took over when he got home from work.

Meanwhile, Nanette, stuck behind bars, wanted him to come see her every day she was allowed to have visitors,

which was Friday, Saturday, and Sunday. But Billy could
barely handle two visits a week. Each trip ate up six hours,
including the drive to Santa Ana and back, and the time
waiting in line to get in, which was tough with a baby.

"Despite my life and our family's life around us being
devastated and destroyed . . . I still felt obligated to let her
see her son," he said.

But that, too, would change.

For the first month, he brought Jaycie with him as well,
until Jaycie went back to live with her father in Long
Beach, after which Billy took her to visit only once a month,
the only weekend he had custody of her.

Taking the baby to jail was never pleasant. In fact, it was
downright stressful for both of them. He had to change Cruz's
diapers on the dirty sidewalk outside, then try to hold the
wiggly six-month-old in one arm while he sat on a metal stool,
talking to his wife on the phone through a pane of glass.

Cruz cried, squirmed, and screamed to get down, but
Billy held on tight because he didn't want his boy crawling
around on the filthy linoleum floor. On the freeway, stuck
in traffic sometimes for three and a half hours on the way
back to his sister's, Cruz wailed some more, wanting to get
out of the car seat, where he was strapped in, feeling like a
captive himself.

But they were in this together, and in the end, Cruz was
the one person who could bring Billy any peace and serenity amid the chaos.

"No matter how bad it was, all I had to do was pick him
up and it just didn't matter."


At first, Billy was convinced that Nanette hadn't killed
anyone, so he focused his energy on ensuring that she had

a strong defense. He tried to be a good husband and give her the benefit of the doubt, encouraging their friends to rally around her.

Meeting with Mick Hill at his office with investigator Jeff McCormack, Billy helped them go over the information the defense team had turned up, and also reviewed information the DA's office had sent over. Everyone was trying to solve the mystery: who was the real Nanette Packard? But mostly what they learned was who she *wasn't*.

One day, they received a document from the DA's office listing dozens of claims that Nanette had made about her personal and professional life. Hill kept asking whether Billy knew more about this or that item, and the answer was almost always "no." By the time they were done, Hill had verified that every single claim was false.

"The only thing that was true on it was her name," Billy recalled.

*It's just an avalanche of lies and mistruths,* Billy thought. *How could it all just be made-up? Is any of our relationship true? How do I even process all of this?*

Billy felt angry and stupid. He just couldn't believe how much Nanette had taken advantage of him. Once he reached this cold, ugly realization, he knew what he needed to do.

*If these stories are true, then anything can be true, so now I've got to go hunting myself, so I know what's true and what's not.*

With a thousand questions, he started at the source: Nanette. But when he tried to confront her with some of the lies he'd discovered, she just shook her head and gave him a blank stare. They both knew the jail was recording their visits.

"It was frustrating," he recalled. "So frustrating."

Billy resorted to going through her personal papers and photos, which is how he confirmed that the face he'd fallen in love with wasn't the one with which she'd been born. When he found the list of cosmetic surgery procedures she'd wanted since 1998, he realized she'd had them all done, with some liposuction too.

It was during this search that he learned John Packard had been sending her $17,500 in support payments each month, not the $6,500 she'd claimed. He cringed as he remembered Nanette's insisting that he pay for all those lavish dinners and nights out. Her level of greed was astonishing, even more so in retrospect. (In September 2009, John Packard asked the court if he could stop the monthly payments to Nanette, given that she was in custody and also that his business had had to file bankruptcy. By that point, he said, he'd already paid Nanette $1.2 million.)

Billy also discovered that she'd been making false claims about her first husband, K. Ross. Just as she'd done with the other men in her life, she'd painted K. Ross to Billy in a negative light, presumably to keep Billy from wanting to talk to him and learning things that would make Nanette look bad.

Nanette had claimed, for example, that while they were still married, K. Ross had pushed her into the closet and forced her to have sex with him—a similar type of story, he would soon learn, that she'd told Eric Naposki about Bill McLaughlin. This incident, she'd told Billy, made her feel paranoid and scared around K. Ross because he was so big.

Billy had thought it was an odd tale at the time, given that K. Ross was her husband. But now he realized that this was Nanette's manipulative way of shaping his perception of her ex-husband for her own benefit.

She'd also told Billy that K. Ross had molested Lishele when their daughter was seven or eight. Nanette had said that she, Lishele, and Kristofer were on a sunset cruise when

Lishele burst out sobbing. Asked what was wrong, Nanette quoted Lishele as saying, "Dad, he touched me."

When Billy talked with Lishele about this story later, the poor girl said Nanette had even tried to convince *her* that this had happened. Over time, however, Lishele had come to realize that it just wasn't true.

# CHAPTER 36

By the time the preliminary hearing started on November 6, 2009, at the Harbor Justice Center in Newport Beach, Billy McNeal believed it was more likely that Nanette would be found guilty than innocent.

On the outside, he pretended to be a supportive, loving husband, but inside, he knew things looked "really, really bad" for his wife as he sat in Judge Robert Gannon's courtroom with Nanette's friends, who rolled their eyes during the proceedings. They still had no idea who she really was.

Nanette had one attorney at the defense table to Eric's three. From where Kim and Jenny McLaughlin were sitting behind Eric, they could see that he'd applied makeup to the back of his neck, apparently to cover all the tribal-design tattoos he'd gotten since the 1990s.

As Detective Tom Voth testified that day, he gave numerous "I don't recall" answers under heated cross-examination by Mick Hill, who flailed his arms as he implied that the NBPD had not done a thorough job. Hill got so worked up that his Irish brogue grew thicker as he spoke faster and faster, prompting the judge to stop him.

"Slow down," Gannon said, adding that Hill also needed to refrain from asking compound questions.

"I get excited," Hill said with his usual mirthful charm.

Voth felt that Hill was obsessing over unimportant details, such as why he hadn't questioned the parents or children at the soccer field, and whether he knew how many parking spaces were in the parking lot.

Sergeant Dave Byington, who couldn't go into the courtroom because he was a witness, asked Sandy Baumgardner during a break in the hallway how it was going inside.

"Did this guy not prepare?" a frustrated Sandy replied, referring to Voth. "It doesn't seem to be going very well. I assume he's had all summer to go through the material."

Byington tried to reassure Sandy and the McLaughlin sisters, who were also concerned, that this was nothing to worry about.

"We knew this was going to happen," he told them.

Later, Voth said he didn't take Hill's questioning personally, knowing that defense attorneys typically attacked a police investigation that led to charges against their clients. To Voth, his job was simply to explain decisions made by "those ultimately responsible," meaning the sergeants, lieutenants, captains, and even the chief, who had directed the investigation.

"I prepared the best I could," Voth recalled, adding that he'd spent many hours reviewing his files, but he didn't know what questions prosecutor Matt Murphy was going to ask him.

No one could change the fact that fifteen years had passed since the murder occurred, memories had faded, details had dissipated, and evidence had disappeared. Which was precisely the point emphasized by both defense teams.

"Mick kicked their butt the first day," Billy recalled recently, adding he didn't believe Murphy did the best job of presenting his witnesses.

Murphy shrugged off the criticism, explaining that he'd

intentionally focused on the technical aspects of the case in a presentation designed specifically for this judge (whom Murphy had met while clerking in the DA's office), not for people watching in the gallery.

"It's not about making a good show. It's about knowing your audience," Murphy said. "Drama at a prelim means nothing. It doesn't get you anywhere. It's unnecessary, and you could actually be damaging your own credibility [with the judge]."

Eric's defense attorneys Gary Pohlson and Angelo MacDonald, who both cross-examined witnesses, saw Voth referring to a binder of extensive handwritten case notes that the defense had never seen before. They demanded to get their own copy.

Things looked better for the prosecution on the second day.

"[Investigator Larry] Montgomery did a great job on the stand, and Mick had a hard time with him because he knew his stuff," Billy said. "He was a rock-solid witness."

That said, it didn't go unnoticed that Montgomery paused for about ten seconds before answering Hill's question about whether Newport Beach police had "adequately" investigated Eric's phone call "alibi" in the 1990s.

"I think that more could have been done," Montgomery finally said. "However, not enough information was available to determine if that was a valid alibi or not."

Hill asked the judge and court reporter to make sure that Montgomery's uncomfortable silence was noted for the record.

\* \* \*

For Billy, Murphy's closing was the turning point, as he outlined how the murder went down, "point by point, minute by minute."

"As soon as Bill McLaughlin realizes that Nanette is stealing from him, I'm going to go out on a limb and bet that their relationship is not going to be healthy," Murphy said. "The evidence is overwhelming that these two people conspired and murdered him."

Voth may not have remembered all the minutiae of the case, Murphy said later, but on the technical areas he'd asked the detective to prepare, "Tom was a rock star." And the bottom line came in the final ruling by the judge, who found enough evidence to bind Eric and Nanette over for trial.

As soon as the ruling was announced, Nanette started shaking, and the back of Eric's shaved head and neck grew red with anger—visible even under the makeup—as his blood pressure rose.

Billy walked out of the courtroom with his feelings confirmed: Nanette was guilty as it gets.

*If I put myself in the shoes of a juror, it all makes sense, and it's very believable,* he thought.

Unlike Billy, however, Eric Naposki's fiancée, Rosie, stood by her man.


Billy had always been able to handle a lot of stress without losing the fight. But this was different. This was a battle like no other he'd seen before, and it seemed like it would never end.

"You can never measure the pain and time and suffering, and all the emotional baggage and damage," he said.

In the couple of months before the prelim, it had become difficult for Billy to keep visiting Nanette. In addition to the

time-consuming and tedious trips to jail with the baby, the
letter-writing on her behalf, and the checks he sent so she
could buy things from the commissary, the dark truths he'd
been learning about her were making it hard for him to hide
his feelings. He couldn't look at her and talk to her the way
he used to, feeling as betrayed as he did.

After the prelim, she noticed that he wasn't telling her
he loved her when they talked on the phone as often as he
once had.

"Are you going to leave me?" she asked. "Are you seeing
somebody?"

"No," he said. "I don't know what you mean."

This was a lie. He had, in fact, started dating someone
but he didn't let on. It wasn't time yet.

After seeing the evidence Murphy had presented against
his wife at the prelim, Billy began to help the prosecution
team any way he could.

"I know she did it," he told his sister and brother-in-law.

By early 2010, he went back to the same child psychologist to discuss what to do next. Not surprisingly, she advised
him to stop taking Cruz to visit Nanette.

"There's no physical contact," she told him. "You're only
going to confuse the child. The only needs that will serve is
the mother's."

Billy had been hanging in for Nanette's kids, so they
didn't feel as though he'd abandoned them too.

"I didn't want it to just disintegrate," he said. All her kids
had left "was me, and they didn't think she did it. No way,
uh-uh."

But he couldn't stand to face Nanette—physically or
psychologically—any longer. He didn't believe anything
she said anymore, and he felt hardened by his anger and
resentment toward her.

Right before Jaycie's birthday on March 20, he decided he was ready to tell Nanette their marriage was over. He went to visit her that day for the last time.

"Are you seeing someone?" Nanette asked him again.

This time, he looked her straight in the eye and said nothing, the same response she'd given him when he'd asked her for answers all those months earlier. The moment had arrived. He was finally ready to confirm her suspicions.

"Yes," he said, "I am seeing somebody else."

Furious, Nanette proceeded to blast him with a stream of expletives.

They had one more conversation by phone when she called his sister's house to talk to him.

"How's the asshole who ruined my family?" she asked.

"I'm sorry, but I'm not the one who's sitting in jail," he said.

When she laid into him again, he told her he didn't want anything from her, and he wasn't going to try to take her house either. He would even help her sell the thing and be done with it.

Bill's next emotionally tough task was to tell Nanette's daughter Lishele and her husband, Shawn, that he was seeing someone. They weren't so much hurt by the news as they were shocked and disappointed that he was leaving Nanette.

He told them he didn't want them to feel alone. "Know I'm here," he said. "I'm just not with your mom."

Billy's father and stepmother continued to take Cruz to visit Nanette, but it wasn't easy.

"My stepmom had a hard time dealing with the immensity and magnitude [of the case]," he said. Being very religious, "they would pray with her and share God's word with her. . . .

Cruz was the first baby [my stepmom had] spent time with
She had this great fear that if Nanette gets out, she's going to
take this child away from all of us, and she didn't want to take
that risk."

It was difficult for Billy to decide what to do about Jaycie.
Although John Packard was her biological father, Billy felt
he was much closer to her than John was.

"She called me 'Papa,'" he said. "I was more her dad
than anyone had ever been in six years."

As he struggled with what to do, he delayed severing
legal ties with Nanette for the children's sake. But on May
24, 2010, he finally filed for divorce, citing "irreconcilable differences," an understatement given that she was
behind bars. Even though she'd been in jail since May 2009,
Billy told the court that they hadn't officially separated until
March 20, 2010.

Noting in court papers that he and Cruz were living with
his sister's family in Winchester, he wrote, *I request that I
have sole legal and sole physical custody with no visitation to respondent until further order of the court.*

Nanette responded a month later, saying she didn't consent to his terms. Although she acknowledged that she was
incarcerated, she wrote, *Once released I want custody of my
child back in full.* She said the extent of separate property
and debts of each party was unknown at that time, so she reserved the right to address those issues later.

But in the meantime, she wrote—with a shocking level
of narcissism and arrogance—that she wanted legal and
physical custody and was "willing" to grant visitation to
Billy. She also said she wanted him to pay her spousal support and "such other and further relief" as the court "deems
just and proper."

Billy countered with a filing that said there was "no possibility of reconciliation," and that no delay in ending their
marriage would help resolve the issues between them.

*There is only one piece of community property to divide, painting purchased on our honeymoon,* he wrote, referencing a Greek painting valued at $3,500. All other property had been deemed separate under an agreement they signed on April 26, 2007, eight months after they were married.

The last time Billy's parents took Cruz to see Nanette was in June 2010. They got a flat tire on the way and Cruz had a meltdown. Billy finally put his foot down and said he wouldn't allow them to take Cruz to visit Nanette anymore, and they conceded that that was the right decision.

Not surprisingly, Judge Michael Naughton awarded sole legal and physical custody to Billy that July. The divorce was granted on May 24, 2011.

# CHAPTER 37

In July and August 2010, prosecutor Matt Murphy an
DA Investigator Larry Montgomery spoke with Nanette
first ex-husband, K. Ross Johnston, who was going to testif
for the prosecution, and his wife, Julia. The couple offere
some interesting details that they hadn't previously tol
police.

For one, before Nanette got out of jail in December 199
Julia said Eric had called her to complain that Nanette re
fused to let him come back to California to see her until sl
had a chance to get back on her feet for a couple of month
Julia also said that Nanette told her she was going to be sta}
ing at the Ritz-Carlton when she was released, because Er
had some contacts there. As it turned out, Nanette ended u
at a Motel 6.

Another tidbit: K. Ross said Nanette had taken out
$250,000 life insurance policy on *him* before Bill wa
murdered. After the shooting, K. Ross asked her—an
she refused—to cancel the policy. K. Ross had to force th
matter by starting legal proceedings against her. Whe
she finally said she'd canceled it, he called to confirm an
discovered that she was lying. He confronted her, whic
made Nanette so angry at his distrustful behavior that sh

threatened not to cancel the policy after all. Ultimately she conceded.


Early on in the case, Eric's defense attorneys Angelo MacDonald and John Pappalardo came out from New York for a court appearance and engaged in their ongoing "plea bargain dance" with prosecutor Matt Murphy, informally discussing the case to explore various resolutions.

Murphy took them to a restaurant and then to a bar in Manhattan Beach. Along the way, MacDonald said that as a former prosecutor, he would have tried the case back in 1995.

On October 22, 2010, the Orange County District Attorney's Office announced it wouldn't be seeking the death penalty. This came as no surprise to the defense teams, however, because they were already aware of this.

Murphy, who was on the committee that decides on which cases the DA will choose to seek the death penalty, explained later that this case didn't meet the criteria, partly because of the case's age and the anticipated problems with witnesses' memories. But, he added, as "diabolical" as it was, this was "essentially a domestic violence case for murder," and the DA rarely sought death on such cases.

"Death penalties are reserved for the most heinous of heinous," he said.


In January 2011, the prosecution team decided to run a new slate of ballistics tests on the nine-millimeter bullets that had killed Bill McLaughlin. This proved to be a winning idea.

When the results came back, they saw that the more modern analysis had dramatically narrowed the field of guns that could have fired the bullets to just one: The murder weapon was, in fact, a Beretta 92F, the same type of gun that Naposki had purchased, lied to police about, and had claimed was lost or stolen.

Investigator Larry Montgomery conducted a new series of driving-time trials to test Eric's "alibi," to see if his story made sense, and to determine if it was even possible to do what he'd claimed: to drive from the soccer field in Diamond Bar, stop at his apartment, go by Leonard Jomsky's house, then make the call at Denny's by 8:52 P.M. The answer was no.

"Skedaddling" away from the field at 8:20 P.M.—as K. Ross described it—took Montgomery three minutes to walk to the parking lot. He left the lot at 8:23 P.M., but made it only as far as Eric's apartment before he ran out of time.

"The result was, driving as fast as I could, without getting into an accident, I was able to get to his apartment about a minute before eight fifty-two," he testified later. "I couldn't fathom" that he could get to Denny's in time to make a call by that time, he said, let alone stop at Leonard Jomsky's beforehand. It took the investigator six minutes to drive from Eric's apartment to Jomsky's.

Montgomery also tested whether Eric, even if he had made the 8:52 call at Denny's, could still get from there to Balboa Coves in time to shoot Bill by 9:10 P.M.—stopping at the bridge near the stairs, running down them to the bike path, going through the pedestrian-access gate and across the street to Bill's house—and the answer was yes.

Leaving the Denny's parking lot at 8:55, he arrived at the bridge at 9:08 P.M. and eight seconds, leaving a slim window of about two minutes—but a window, nonetheless—to commit the murder.

Comparing his drive times with those the police had done in 1995, he found that they had taken even less time to get from the soccer field to the bridge—only thirty-five minutes as compared to his thirty-seven and a half minutes.

And because the prosecution team didn't believe Eric had truly stopped to make that call, they determined that he had plenty of time to leave the soccer field at 8:23 and get to Balboa Coves in time to commit the murder before Kevin called 911 at 9:11 P.M.

Nanette's attorney was moving forward with his third-party culpability defense until he saw a copy of the new ballistics report. All this time, Mick Hill had thought that Eric Naposki had had nothing to do with killing Bill, but with a single report, everything changed.

*Oh, my God, he* did *have something to do with it.*

From that point on, Hill switched his strategy to proving that Eric was the shooter. He also sought to prove that Nanette was a good, loving mother who was also a liar, a cheat, and a thief, but not a killer. His goal was to persuade the jurors that they shouldn't let their distaste for her bad sexual and moral behavior affect their judgment on the murder charge against her.

There was one nagging problem, however. In 2010, Nanette wrote a letter to Eric, her ex-boyfriend and now co-defendant, from one Orange County jail inmate to another, expressing condolences about his mother's death and saying she was devastated—spelled "devasted"—to hear about it.

*You are strong, you're a warrior and we <u>will</u> make [it] through this nightmare with a testimony and a story that needs telling,* she wrote. *Your mom loved you and I know that she is watching over you right this very moment.* Nanette closed by saying that she was praying for him, and predicted that they soon would be "celebrating our victory."

Hill knew he needed to keep that letter out of the jury's hands, and he ultimately succeeded.

His best course of action, Hill decided, was to show how proficient Nanette was at spinning her lies, "different sets of lies to different people, depending on the circumstances. . . . She's really, really good at being a con woman. She completely had McLaughlin fooled, so why was she going to kill him?"

And so evolved Hill's "golden goose" argument: why would Nanette kill her wealthy fiancé, Bill McLaughlin, to be with a penniless loser like Eric Naposki, when she had much more to gain from Bill if he were alive?

In late July 2010, Eric's defense team filed a motion to dismiss the case, claiming that his state and federal rights to due process and a fair trial had been violated. The gist of the motion was that the NBPD had conducted "a grossly negligent investigation" in the mid-1990s, an injury compounded by the DA's delaying prosecution of the case for so long that Eric couldn't get a fair trial because of the lost records, witnesses, and memories.

Within a month, documents suddenly surfaced from Eric's original defense effort, including several memos that summarized the investigative work of James W. Box, a former police officer who had worked for the DA's office before becoming a private investigator, and had worked on Eric's case when Julian Bailey was his attorney.

Pohlson wrote Pappalardo that the records were recently discovered in an old storage box. The file, Pohlson later explained, was found by Bailey's former partner, Jim Brott when he was moving offices.

In March 2011, before Eric's trial, the defense filed a supplemental brief that included the meat of these newfound documents, claiming that its case for dismissal was even stronger.

The documents included the letter from Bailey to prosecutor Debbie Lloyd, discussing Eric's phone call alibi and the fact that the credit card bill existed.

They also included a memo from Box to Bailey, dated February 18, 1995, summarizing Box's interview with Mike Tuomisto, in which the bar manager said he observed heavy traffic coming into Newport Beach on the night of the murder, and assumed it was related to the boat parade.

*Shortly before 9:00 P.M. he paged Eric Naposki to inform him that he probably should try and leave a little earlier because of the heavy traffic,* Box wrote. *Within a few minutes Eric Naposki returned his page and told him that he was on his way to work. . . . Sometime between 9:30 and 10:00 P.M. he went into the club portion of the nightclub and saw Eric Naposki working as security and noticed nothing unusual about his demeanor, appearance or attire.*

One memo chronicled a driving-time trial by Box from Denny's to Balboa Coves that took twenty-one minutes and forty-seven seconds to go 12.5 miles. The defense argued that it was thus "impossible" for Eric to have committed the crime by 9:10 after making the 8:52 P.M. phone call.

Another memo described Box's interview of Tustin hardware manager David Vandaveer, in which the defense claimed that Vandaveer made statements that were arguably different from what he told police and/or different from how police characterized his remarks in their search warrant affidavit, constituting "at best, misleading information," and "at worst, complete fabrication," which therefore challenged the prosecution's credibility.

The original affidavit stated, *Vandaveer advised Detective Voth that there was no way to be positive that those were the exact key copies he had made, but stated his hardware store used the same type of key blanks to make their duplicates.* According to the Box memo, Vandaveer had said the silver key could have been cut at his store or several other Ace Hardware stores, but that the gold key "was not cut at his store." He also said he was certain the keys made for Eric at his store were not stamped "do not duplicate."

When Detective Tom Voth saw these memos, he had a funny feeling in his gut about the convenient timing of their discovery after they'd supposedly been lost, with the paper file thrown away and the electronic file destroyed when Box's hard drive crashed in 2000.

The more he looked at the documents, the more he questioned their authenticity. To him, it looked as if they had different fonts and phone numbers on copies of the same memo, and that the newly discovered memos listed different phone numbers than were on the memos the NBPD had received in the 1990s.

Voth presented his concerns to Murphy, who agreed something seemed off. After looking further into it, Murphy realized that certain portions of early versions of the same memos had been reworded or deleted in later versions.

"It's about him writing and then rewriting [the memos]," Murphy said in 2012, referring to a practice to which Box admitted during the trial. "It looks shady because it is shady. Police don't write multiple reports . . . with different information in different versions."

After doing some research, Voth and Montgomery learned that the boat parade didn't even start until December 17 in 1994—two days after the murder—so Tuomisto's claims about traffic in the Box memo didn't even make sense.

The defense motion also made the case that Kevin McLaughlin could have killed his father, with the help of his friend Daniel Ziese: *[Ziese] was very likely Kevin's accomplice in the murder of Bill McLaughlin.*

Kevin had motive, the defense argued, because he and Bill were at war over his drug use, evidenced by the drug test kits that Bill kept in the refrigerator. Ziese, the defense said, had motive because Bill had denied his request for a $20,000 loan, because he thought Ziese's business plan was "deficient to the point of being humorous."

The defense bolstered the accusation against Kevin with

tatements in a Box interview of Rosemary Luxton, a neighbor who said she hadn't seen anyone leaving the McLaughlin house. The defense argued, *[This] strongly suggests that the person who committed the crime never left the home.* Furthermore, because Luxton and Kevin were both dead, neither could be called to the stand to testify or be cross-examined. *As such, Mr. Naposki has been robbed of yet another witness critical in establishing his alibi and third party culpability defenses.*

Not surprisingly, this last accusation particularly enraged the McLaughlin sisters and Kevin's former girlfriend, Sandy Baumgardner. As if losing Bill wasn't enough, Kevin wasn't even alive to defend himself against what they saw as a ridiculous allegation.

In March 2011, Judge William R. Froeberg held a hearing on the motion, during which defense attorney Gary Pohlson argued that his client had "suffered acute prejudice" because of the undue length of time between the crime and the trial. At this point, neither defense team appeared to be blaming the other defendant for the crime.

If Eric had an alibi, then Nanette was also not guilty by association, said Deputy Public Defender Denise Gragg, who accused prosecutors of unethical conduct and the NBPD of incompetence for purposely letting the "evidence disappear."

"There was an alibi that we can't put in front of a jury anymore," Gragg said. "That's prejudice."

Keith Bogardus, a deputy district attorney working with Murphy, responded that the defense attorneys were "little more than paper tigers," and that the prosecution didn't believe the phone call was ever made. To believe otherwise, Bogardus said, was just "notoriously riddled speculation."

Judge Froeberg denied the motion, but said the defense could raise the issues again after the trial, once he saw how things had played out.

In what the *Orange County Register* billed to be "the most anticipated trial of the year," Nanette Packard and Eric Naposki were set to be tried together in front of the rather easygoing Judge Froeberg, who had served longer on the local bench than most.

After graduating with a bachelor's degree in political science from the University of California, Riverside, Froeberg earned his law degree from Pacific McGeorge School of Law in Sacramento and passed the bar in 1974. His wife, Roseanne, headed up the DA's Sexual Assault Unit.

First appointed to the bench in 1986 by Republican Governor George Deukmejian, Froeberg was subsequently elected unopposed.

"Generally his reputation is he's a very fair judge to try your case," Pohlson said. "He's probably considered prosecution oriented by some, but I think he's a really good judge. He's really easy to try a case in front of. I'm always pleased when I'm assigned there."

On the eve of the trial, slated to begin on Monday, June 13, 2011, Eric's and Nanette's trials were severed, which was the prosecutor's choice. Eric's case was set to go first, and that's when the finger-pointing between defendants began.

Jury selection began on June 15, resulting in eight women and four men being chosen to serve on the panel.

To counter Pohlson's comments that this was a "totally circumstantial case," Murphy pointed out that "the idea that circumstantial evidence is somehow bad evidence is a very commonly believed myth. But it is a myth. The law is crystal clear on that."

\* \* \*

After the successful and high-profile prosecution of killer Skylar Deleon, prosecutor Matt Murphy was ready for round two with his now-familiar rival, Gary Pohlson.

Murphy and Pohlson had completely different courtroom styles. Murphy could be as sarcastic as they come, while Pohlson had more of the friendly-uncle approach. But the two men respected each other's capabilities.

"Everybody likes Gary," Murphy said. "Gary Pohlson has one of the very best reputations in the Orange County legal community. . . . Even though he appears doddering sometimes, it's part of his schtick. . . . He's extremely effective with juries. . . . He's such a good, sincere person, he doesn't have to act because that's actually who he is."

Of Murphy's reputation, Pohlson said, "He's supposed to be really good. Got a great courtroom presence. He's got that flair for the dramatic, you know. I've never heard anything negative about him."

But in this East Coast versus West Coast legal cage match, Murphy had the home court advantage over Angelo MacDonald, which the defense would later accuse Murphy of using to try to win points with the jury. This was especially evident when MacDonald tried to question the effectiveness of the police detectives' investigation techniques, a tactic that historically hasn't played well in Orange County.

As Murphy prepared for Eric Naposki's trial, he planned to use some of the same strategies and present some of the same types of evidence that had helped him win the largely circumstantial conspiracy-to-murder case for financial gain against Skylar and Jennifer Deleon.

Like that case, this one also involved cross-checking the conspirators' phone and bank records to form a timeline of the conspiracy, the murder, and the financial benefit that

followed. Ironically, the four-minute call to Nanette's ca
phone after Eric finished his shift at the Thunderbird th
night of the murder pinged off the same cell phone tower i
Newport Beach as the call that was made by the Deleons' co
conspirator, John F. Kennedy, as they were sailing into th
harbor on their victims' yacht after killing them offshore.

With Investigator Larry Montgomery's help, Murphy
spent two years putting together twenty-two pages of ques
tions to ask Eric on cross-examination. Because Eric ha
displayed so much bravado and arrogance, Murphy wa
pretty confident that he wouldn't be able to resist testifying

The prosecutor prepared for trial by listening repeatedly—
at the gym, over holiday breaks, any chance he got—t
every tape of the police interviews with Eric, as well as hi
call with Jenny McLaughlin, until he knew them backwar
and forward and was ready to catch Eric in a contradictio
or error on the stand. Murphy also practiced his deliver
of confrontational questions, hoping to make the hothead s
angry that he exploded in the witness chair.

"You have to know that she murdered him and yet yo
move into the beach house?" Murphy planned to say. An
when Eric was staying at the beach house, Nanette was i
jail and Kevin came back to change the locks, "Tell us abou
Kevin's expression when you opened the door!"

At a hearing before opening statements and outside th
jury's presence on June 20, the defense argued its "402
motion to introduce verbal evidence of Eric's "missing
credit card bill in an effort to prove he made the pay phon
call from Denny's at 8:52 P.M.

Eric's original attorney, Julian Bailey, who had know
Pohlson and Judge Froeberg for forty years, testified tha

he had personally seen the phone bill. At least he thought
he had.

Before taking on Eric's case, whom, he said, he didn't
recognize now, Bailey explained that he'd worked as a prosecutor, and had then handled more than thirty homicide
trials as a criminal defense attorney. He went on to work as
a "referee" in the juvenile and superior courts.

When he was a defense attorney, Bailey said, James Box
was "pretty much" the only investigator he'd used. They'd
worked together ever since Box was a police officer in
Garden Grove, before he was an investigator in the DA's
office, and before he'd gone into private practice.

"Why's that?" Pohlson asked.

"I found him to be competent and honest, hardworking,
smart."

Pohlson showed Bailey the letter he'd written to then-
prosecutor Debbie Lloyd in 1995, mentioning Eric's phone
call—"there is a record of its time and place"—and asked
Bailey what he remembered about it.

"I don't remember anything about it," Bailey said, but he
added, "It's my belief that I saw a bill and that that's the
reason I specifically stated that. It's also my belief that I
gave that bill to James Box."

Bailey said he'd gone through some files recently in his
cellar, his home, his storage unit, and his work office building from that time, but he'd found nothing. When his former
partner finally located Eric's file, he acknowledged, "it did
not contain a phone bill."

"Would you have written a letter to the district attorney,
providing an alibi for a client just based on the word of the
client, or would you have to have more proof?" Pohlson
asked.

Bailey said he wouldn't have just taken a client's word.
"That would be fraught with danger, and . . . it's just not the

way I practice law," he said. "That's why I believe I saw the phone bill."

On cross-examination, Murphy, who also had known Bailey for years and had even worked on his election campaign for a superior court judgeship, felt awkward about having to question a judicial officer about the "interesting language" he'd used in his letter to Lloyd. Still, he pressed on and asked why Bailey hadn't attached a copy of the bill.

"It seems like you could have ended this whole issue by stapling a copy of it, sending it to Debbie," Murphy said.

"You're absolutely right," Bailey said. However, he added, he wasn't happy that the media had been publishing the DA's version of the case, or that the search warrants had been leaked to the media but not to him, so he decided he should keep "what few cards we had close to the vest."

Box got up to testify next, sounding very sure of himself.

"Do you have any doubt as you're sitting there right now that you saw that phone bill or that it was communicated to you that on the phone bill there was an eight fifty-two time?" Pohlson asked.

"I have no doubt," Box said.

On cross, Murphy pointed out that Box seemed "tentative on exactly what you saw versus what you were told. Is that fair to say?"

Box began to hem and haw. "Well, I did see something, and I'm assuming it was the bill. I mean, if it wasn't the bill, I'm sure I would have asked, 'Where's the bill?'"

"Why don't you remember the phone bill?" Murphy pressed. "You see a document that exonerates somebody for a murder. I'm just trying to understand. It seems like that's not an everyday sort of thing."

Murphy asked if Bailey had a copy machine in his office, which Box could have used, again noting the absence of the phone bill in the file. "It didn't occur to you to make a copy of the phone bill?"

As Box answered a series of related questions, Murphy diced his credibility, his memory, and his professionalism into slivers. Box couldn't definitively tell Murphy that he remembered seeing Eric's phone bill, or what it looked like. At one point, he was so tentative that he said, "I was told it was discovered he made a phone call."

Under further questioning by Pohlson, Box said that to the best of his recollection, he was sure he'd seen the bill. However, he subsequently told the judge that he couldn't be absolutely sure.

For the moment, the bottom line of the hearing was this: After the attorneys stipulated that the calling-card bill could not be found, the judge decided that Bailey and Box could testify that they'd seen the bill, which meant that someone—not the defendant in particular—used a calling card to make the 8:52 P.M. phone call. But only Eric himself could say he made the call, and to do that he would have to take the stand.

Although the defense essentially won its motion, this hearing did more to expose these witnesses' weaknesses to Murphy, which would only help him shred Box on cross-examination in front of the jury. By this point, Murphy had all the ammunition he needed to make the jury doubt there ever was a phone call, let alone a phone bill, or it surely would have been in the attorney's file.

# CHAPTER 38

The seats in Judge Froeberg's courtroom quickly filled before opening statements began after lunch that day. As word spread throughout the courthouse, defense attorneys and prosecutors filtered in to watch the start of the high-profile trial, and Murphy's performance in particular.

In addition to the McLaughlin family members and friends, who had been waiting nearly two decades for this trial, the proceedings also drew well-heeled Orange County looky-loos who had heard about the case in the news. The media was there in force as well, taking up several rows of seats near the crowded power outlets.

During Murphy's two-hour presentation, he gave the jury a case overview with a timeline for the murder and a rundown of the relationships between the key players. The defense team decided to delay its opening until after the prosecution had rested.

Anticipating the defense's case based on points raised during the preliminary hearing and in the due process motion, the prosecutor deftly laid out the most damning evidence that implicated Nanette Packard in a conspiracy with Eric Naposki to shoot Bill McLaughlin for financial gain.

Characterizing Nanette as a greedy, unfeeling woman

out for Bill's money, Murphy said, "Nanette asks very few questions of the officers at the scene. You're going to listen to this [interview] tape. She didn't ask to see Bill and she didn't cry."

Murphy said the evidence would show that Eric not only stood to gain from Bill's death, but that the penniless football player had purchased a nine-millimeter Beretta 92F in August 1994—the same type of firearm that had killed Bill McLaughlin.

Noting that such guns cost about $700, Murphy said, "This gun is a beautiful gun in the gun world. It's Italian made. It's very popular," adding that it was the same model used by heroes in movies such as *Die Hard* and *The Terminator*.

Murphy described the layout around the McLaughlin house in Balboa Coves, including the locked gates and the barbwire fence that surrounded the community, which made it "a tough place to get in or out of," he said.

Kevin McLaughlin didn't need a key, he pointed out, "because he was already in the house," and he also tested negative for gunshot residue. Nanette, however, who was "an active Rollerblader," was missing her key to the pedestrian-access gate.

As he flashed a series of crime scene photos on the overhead screen, featuring Bill's body on the white tile floor, with blood smears and scattered bullet casings around him, Kim McLaughlin covered her eyes.

"Three of the bullets remained in his body and three passed through his body," Murphy explained, referring to the evidence that, in addition to the two keys, the killer left behind. "We know the killer escaped, which means he got to a car or he had someplace to run to."

"Now, Nanette, . . . of course, she had keys to the house, but, in addition to keys, Nanette had a very big secret. And Nanette's secret was Eric Naposki," he said, showing photos of the "happy couple."

As Murphy described Eric and his history, the defendant sat at the defense table, his shaved head reflecting the fluorescent light and his bulky torso straining his blue dress shirt. But unlike Nanette, who remained expressionless when she got to trial, Eric made no effort to hide his cocky smirk and swagger as he chortled and whispered to his attorneys throughout Murphy's presentation, exhibiting a flagrant disrespect for the proceedings.

Murphy painted Eric as a penniless, deadbeat dad whose various setbacks included the loss of several jobs because of his temper and aggressive attitude. Meanwhile, he said, Eric's relationship with Nanette "was progressing nicely," as she paid his rent, bought him clothes, dinners, and expensive gym memberships and took him on vacations.

"On that same trip after Chicago, they went to Jamaica, all paid for, of course, by Bill, unbeknownst to Bill," he said, adding that Nanette also bought Eric a pair of size-twelve alligator boots the day of Bill's murder—with Bill's credit card.

Neither Eric nor Nanette had money of his or her own, and yet the two of them were shopping for $900,000 homes in July 1994. And while Nanette was discussing a possible $200,000 investment with Robert Cottrill, she also "told him she planned on marrying Eric."

Murphy then ran through Eric's incriminating remarks to Suzanne Cogar, noting that he had keys and a phony silencer made to fit his nine-millimeter at Tustin Hardware in November and December. He also noted that Eric and Nanette were seen at a shooting range during that same period, before they went back east for Thanksgiving and her sister's wedding.

Putting up the photo of Eric slipping the garter belt up Nanette's thigh in front of all the wedding guests, Murphy brought the juxtaposition home for the jury. "This is our happy couple again. . . . This is just a couple of weeks before Bill is brutally murdered in his kitchen."

During this time, he said, the couple's public displays of affection "kick[ed] into overdrive," even in Newport Beach, where Bill lived and knew people, as the amount of money Nanette was stealing from him increased exponentially.

"I'm not even going to try to get into all the various different kinds of thefts she was doing but the bank account forgeries by themselves," he said, "because they're nice and clean." He noted that the $250,000 check she wrote to herself on Bill's account the day before the murder "went into the bank on Saturday morning," two days after the murder.

Laying out a timeline for the crime with his PowerPoint presentation, Murphy said, "Around nine minutes after nine, the killer used the original pedestrian-access key to enter Balboa Coves. At nine-ten, the killer used an Ace Hardware key to enter the gate—in the front door. We know the key got stuck. The evidence is going to show that he dropped the pedestrian-access key, nine-ten murdered McLaughlin. . . . At nine-ten and one second, right after Bill McLaughlin's heart stopped beating, Nanette Johnston became a millionaire, at least on paper. At nine-eleven, Kevin dialed 911. Every police car in Newport sped to the scene."

"The evidence, ladies and gentlemen, is going to be crystal clear that during the time of the murder, nobody at the Thunderbird nightclub is going to say Eric Naposki is there."

When Nanette showed up at the house, he said, she didn't mention Eric. In fact, she gave detectives the impression that she'd gone to the game and went shopping by herself. Later, after being dropped at the beach house, even though "there's an active landline [there] . . . what does Nanette do? The evidence shows that Nanette goes back down to her car and checks her messages on her cell phone."

At 1:36 A.M., "she paged Eric Naposki," then received a

"four-minute incoming call immediately thereafter," the same amount of time it took to drive to the Thunderbird, he said, displaying the route on a map.

In the aftermath of Bill's murder, when his daughters were distraught as they tried to figure out how to meet Bill's financial obligations and take care of Kevin, Eric and Nanette's experience "was entirely different. The aftermath for them involved a lot of shopping."

Nanette didn't cry at the funeral, he said, after which she immediately paged Eric, used Bill's credit card to pay for three motorcycles, and cashed a check for several thousand dollars at her bank, while Eric moved into a hotel.

"Then there was more shopping," Murphy said, noting that with less than $1,000 in his bank account, Eric bought Nanette a $600 Movado watch for Christmas.

As Murphy went through the most telling and deceptive highlights of Eric's first interview with police, he said the linebacker was "very, very convincing" as he described Bill as simply a mentor to Nanette, "almost a father-daughter–type thing," and downplayed the closeness of his own relationship with the woman he'd been dating seriously for the past year.

"Naposki planned to propose on New Year's Eve," Murphy said. "That's something I hadn't told you yet. He's ring shopping. He plans on proposing seven days after this interview."

And then Eric lied again, telling police he had only one gun, Murphy said, a .380 he'd bought in Dallas and had given to his dad. Although twenty-eight types of guns were originally thought to be possible murder weapons, Murphy said, Thomas Matsudaira from the crime lab would testify that "there's one gun, not twenty-eight, that could have ejected these shell casings, and that gun is a Beretta 92F."

Yet, when the police searched Eric's apartment in January 1995, they found none of the accoutrements that most gun owners kept around. "They don't find any ammo. They don't find any gun-cleaning equipment, holsters, storage boxes, or anything relating to gun ownership." To police, he said, that was like a hot dog without a bun.

By now, Murphy said, reading aloud excerpts from Eric's second interview with police, the defendant had become "hostile and confrontational." He wouldn't even talk about where his 9mm gun was, and he also changed his story about his route to work the night of the murder.

And although Eric offered to produce his phone bill to prove he'd made the 8:52 P.M. call from Denny's—and Detective Voth agreed it would be helpful if he did—Eric never came through.

Curiously, the prosecutor noted, Eric never complained when the police searched his apartment, his car, or his hotel—only his notebook, where he'd scribbled Bill McLaughlin's license plate number, and then accused the police of "illegal search and seizure."

After Bill's children returned from Hawaii, Murphy said, they found his office had been cleaned out, and "Nanette is giving them the runaround. Then Kim and Jenny learn the horrible truth. They get in there, and the bank account that should have seven hundred thousand dollars in it, that they're relying on to take care of all these financial matters in the short term, has eleven thousand dollars—actually less. It's like ten thousand five hundred, okay? Leaves them high and dry."

After the McLaughlins' friend Jason Gendron repossessed the Cadillac, Murphy said, "he starts getting all these angry phone messages from Eric Naposki, with Nanette screaming in the background. . . . The guy ended up so scared, he wound up changing his phone number."

Police arrested Nanette on grand theft and forgery charges, Murphy said, showing the jury a photo of her "peeking out of the custody tank, and, in tow, dutiful boyfriend Eric Naposki shows up in court."

When the family tried to regain custody of the beach house, Eric tried to stop them. He also called Jenny, trying to get back the Infiniti, and complaining about the police investigation, saying Nanette didn't deserve to be in jail for such "bull-dinky stuff."

After Nanette got out, she used the $220,000 settlement in the palimony lawsuit to rent a house, where "police saw Mr. Naposki's Pathfinder in the garage" eight months after the murder.

"Our indications are this relationship lasts for about a year afterward. We don't have a real set time/date," he said. "They're living together on Foxhollow. They start a movie production company called Midnight Moon Productions . . . where Naposki is listed as a producer."

Summing up, Murphy connected the dots for the jury with precision. "The killer wanted to kill Bill. Mr. Naposki said he wanted to kill Bill. . . . The evidence will certainly show he is thinking in the month of October about ways to silence that [nine-millimeter] gun. The killer knew how to shoot. The evidence will show Naposki knew how to shoot."

The killer used the same ammunition that Eric kept in his Jennings .380, Murphy said. "Nanette tried to hide Mr. Naposki's identity from the police," and Eric had Bill's license plate in his notebook. Eric also "lied about his relationship with Nanette. He lied about where he was that night, or at least he changed his story dramatically from the first interview to the second . . . and, of course, he lied about his nine-millimeter."

Murphy pointed out that the interview during which Eric lied about that gun took place on December 23, 1994—before the crime lab had even received the bullet casings to process, and at a time when only the killer and a half-dozen detectives knew that the murder weapon was a nine-millimeter.

By the end of the trial, he said, "if you're the group I

think you are, you are going to hold this guy accountable for what he did. I guarantee it. Every one of you is going to be convinced to an abiding conviction beyond a reasonable doubt."

After a brief recess, Murphy started off his seven days of calling two dozen witnesses, beginning with Kim McLaughlin Bayless. Kim, who continued her testimony the next morning, spent much of the trial wearing her emotional pain on her face and conveying it in her body language. She covered her ears, closed her eyes, leaned over in her seat, and curled into a ball. Other times, the sensitive schoolteacher walked out of the courtroom when the testimony was too hard to hear.

Murphy used Kim to show that Bill and his son, Kevin, had a very close relationship, to proactively debunk the defense's implication that Kevin was a suspect in his father's murder.

Even though Bill was hurt by Kevin's pot-smoking habit, Kim said, "My dad loved his own son unconditionally."

After the murder, she said, Newport Beach detectives asked her to time how long it took Kevin to get down the two flights of stairs from his room, so she timed him "going as fast as he could." It took him fifty-two seconds.

On day two, Murphy called Bill's accountant, Brian Ringler, to explain Nanette's access to Bill's various accounts. He also called Sharon Hedberg, the Turtle Rock real estate agent who showed the $900,000 homes to Eric and Nanette in the summer of 1994, when they said they wouldn't move in until the spring. Robert Cottrill, the software developer who met with Nanette in November 1994 to discuss an investment in his start-up, was also called.

Eric's attorneys had counseled him about his courtroom behavior, yet he continued to act cocky and sure of himself, smirking and laughing at the counsel table. He even turned around and winked at Rosie, who sat in the gallery with John Pappalardo.

"I told Eric that if he didn't stop acting like he was, he might as well plead guilty," Pohlson said later.

Eric told his attorneys that he understood how his behavior came off, and by the third day of his trial, his persistent and open challenging of Murphy had eased off. When the prosecutor played Kevin McLaughlin's almost incoherent 911 tape, it was no laughing matter. For anyone.

The tape was absolutely wrenching to listen to, even for those who had never met the twenty-four-year-old. It was so hellish for his family that Kim McLaughlin put her fingers in her ears while the tape played.

But it wasn't long before Eric started acting out again.

"Pro athletes, they tend to believe that they're invincible and they know what they're doing," Pohlson said later. "They [believe you] have to attack, or you have to do it your way. He was convinced that his way was the best way, and he didn't want to take any guff from Murphy."

Suzanne Cogar, one of the prosecution's most important witnesses, testified for about seventy-five minutes that day, relating Eric's comments about wanting to have Bill's plane blown up because he was angry that Bill "had been making sexual advances" toward Nanette.

Pohlson objected to the answer as hearsay. After a sidebar with the judge, he said he wanted to register a continuing objection to all of Cogar's testimony about her conversations with Eric, which Froeberg overruled.

Cogar said she ended the first conversation with Eric "freaked out over that statement because he seemed so serious. . . . I didn't like what I was hearing, and I just didn't want to hang out with somebody who would talk like that."

On cross-examination, Pohlson tried to diminish Cogar's credibility. "Eric Naposki never threatened you, did he?"

"No," she said.

"You used the word 'paranoid,'" a point about which Pohlson reminded her—and the jury—several times throughout her testimony. "Are you normally paranoid?"

"No."

"Did he tell you when he's doing this 'blown away' conversation that Nanette wanted Bill McLaughlin killed?"

Cogar said no, not that she recalled.

"Were you jealous of her?"

"No."

After Cogar admitted that she'd seen Nanette going into Eric's apartment a dozen times, Pohlson said, "Kinda sounds like spying, doesn't it?"

"No," she said. "I saw everyone who walked by."

Once he'd established that Cogar knew Bill McLaughlin lived in Newport, he asked, "You thought Eric Naposki was serious about having him blown away. You, of course, called McLaughlin to warn him, right?"

"I did not," she said, acknowledging that she didn't call the police either.

"Because you didn't think Eric Naposki was going to kill him, did you?"

"It was hard to believe," she said, acknowledging that for the most part she'd seen Eric be nice to people around the apartment complex.

Asked if Eric mentioned how he planned to blow up

Bill's plane, Cogar quoted him as saying, "I know how to have that done."

"Do you ever remember him saying to you . . . he was going to be wealthy, or he was going to make money, or he was going to have more money?"

No, she said, she didn't.

On redirect, Murphy got Cogar to say that she believed Nanette had been dating both men, even if Eric didn't realize it.

"That wasn't anything Mr. Naposki told you?"

"That was my own thoughts on the situation."

Pohlson came back with more innuendo, implying that Cogar showed up at Eric's apartment late at night in a bikini for a Jacuzzi because she was romantically interested in him.

"Did that indicate that you wanted to have more of a relationship, kind of move to the next level, you might say?"

"To me, it didn't."

On cross, Murphy asked if she did what she "told him Nanette should just do if something inappropriate is going on," which, in Cogar's case, was when the naked linebacker started kissing her.

"That's right," Cogar said. "Just leave."

"I have nothing further," Murphy said.


On day four, Murphy called Gary Rorden, a baseball team coach whose kids played with Nanette's son Kristofer, to show that Eric and Nanette were increasingly brazen and open with their relationship, even among people in Newport Beach who knew Bill personally.

Judge Froeberg was not easily ruffled. Once the attorneys had finished asking their questions, he often stepped in to ask a witness, including Rorden, to clarify or elaborate on certain answers.

Rorden's testimony was a bit surprising in that he admitted

to liking the defendant, an accused killer, more than Bill McLaughlin, the murder victim. He said he didn't care much for Bill personally, although he explained to the judge that he was admittedly "in awe" of the man for showing up at the baseball field with Nanette, who was so attractive and so much younger than Bill.

Rorden described Eric as "a very nice gentleman" who had helped him out with batting practice one afternoon in Newport Beach. However, Rorden admitted he also thought "hmm" when he saw the professional athlete showing up at games with Nanette, and being "friendly—very friendly"— because Rorden knew she was living with Bill. He acknowledged during cross-examination that Eric and Bill were never at the field at the same time.

"We knew the McLaughlin family, so it was just kind of awkward," he said, adding that he didn't think Nanette was aware of that knowledge. "In my mind, it was clear something was going on . . . and [Nanette and Eric] weren't trying to hide it."

Murphy called Detective Tom Voth to the stand and introduced the tape of Nanette's first interview with police the night of the murder. This allowed the jurors to hear the low, scratchy, and monotone voice of the "black widow" who stole from Bill and cheated on him with the defendant, leaving them to wonder if she sounded that way because she'd been screaming at her son's soccer game, or if she was simply unemotional about Bill's death.

Although she was not in the courtroom, this tape was just one brick in the wall that both sides were building to convince the jury that Nanette was one of the world's most evil, greedy, and manipulative women.

Murphy also played the tape of Eric Naposki's first police interview, in which he jocularly described his football career, so jurors could hear for themselves Eric's attempts to hide his deep feelings for Nanette. Then, in his second interview, they heard his increasingly confrontational exchanges with the detectives as they confronted him with his conflicting statements.

The prosecutor asked Voth to reiterate whether anyone knew early on that a 9mm gun had been used in the murder.

"Outside the police department, not that I'm aware of," Voth said, acknowledging that gunshot residue could be washed off or go undetected if a killer wore gloves. He added that the murder weapon being a nine-millimeter didn't come out publicly until early February, when the media wrote about the search warrant affidavits.

"Now, in the seventeen years since this murder, has Mr. Naposki's Beretta nine-millimeter ever turned up?"

"No, sir."

Matt Murphy spent a good portion of the trial going over the numerous driving-time tests that the detectives conducted during the 1990s and again in recent years to prove that Eric had plenty of time to kill Bill McLaughlin before the 911 call was made.

Murphy showed the jury a videotaped drive, maps of the possible routes from the soccer field to Eric's apartment and on to Balboa Coves, and had several witnesses discuss these trips. It was tedious, but, as it turned out, important to the jury.

The defense came back with many questions for these witnesses, asking about changes in traffic patterns and challenging the thoroughness of NBPD's investigation, with the hope of showing that the passage of time had dramatically reduced Eric's ability to get a fair trial.

When Murphy asked a question that implied Eric had

enough time to commit the murder, Angelo MacDonald objected, saying the question was "conclusionary." Froeberg sustained the objection.

Nonetheless, the prosecutor remained collegial with the two defense attorneys. At the end of the day, as the three of them headed back to the judge's chambers to discuss a few issues, MacDonald touched Murphy's back as he walked behind him—the same way male athletes pat each other during a game.

But that collegiality would soon turn to contentiousness.

As many experienced attorneys do, Murphy, Pohlson, and MacDonald had forged a pretrial agreement not to launch unnecessary objections, believing they were disrespectful to the judge, slowed things down, and sometimes served no purpose except to make the lawyers look bad to the jury.

Murphy was prepared for MacDonald to be more aggressive than his usual Orange County opponents might be, because the defense attorney had nothing to lose. Being from New York, MacDonald wouldn't have to appear before this judge again. Murphy also figured that MacDonald would likely try to slip in a mention of Jacob Horowitz, which Murphy believed was inappropriate.

Under the rules governing a third-party culpability defense in California, Murphy explained later, an attorney has to have "actual evidence that somebody did it, you can't just point your finger at somebody."

The attorneys had agreed to let some evidence come in for purposes of streamlining the case. However, when MacDonald slipped into a question that Horowitz had just lost his lawsuit with Bill, implying that Horowitz had a strong motive for murder, Murphy dealt with the issue by talking to defense attorneys privately rather than object in front of the jury. Then he "cleaned it up" in open court with a slide he'd prepared for this explicit purpose.

"I wasn't upset about it," he explained later. "I fully anticipated that they were going to do that."

But as a result of this type of courtroom sparring, the pretrial agreement broke down, prompting Murphy to repeatedly object to certain defense questions—no matter how they were asked—until he was effectively able to block them.

Tit for tat, the defense also started lodging objections, and even the judge agreed that Murphy hadn't laid enough foundation for a certain question. As Murphy grew visibly and audibly irritated, his voice dripped with sarcasm as he asked questions in such a way that the jury knew he was upset: "Are you familiar with this thing we have in the United States called 'states'?" he asked.

By this time, even the judge had noticed the friction that had developed between the attorneys.

"My, the mood has changed," Froeberg said.

On cross-examination, MacDonald grilled Detective Voth about nitpicky details, implying that the investigation had wrongly overlooked them, such as why police never interviewed the soccer players' families, the referee, grounds crew, or record keeper from the game on the night of the murder. Why he didn't look for pieces of torn clothing caught on the barbed wire around Balboa Coves, or follow up on getting Eric's phone records?

Then came a surprise for the prosecution team. MacDonald flashed a page from Nanette's check register on the overhead screen, showing that she'd written a check to Frankie's Lock and Key in November, the same time frame that the prosecution had claimed that Eric was getting keys copied.

Seeing this unexpected piece of evidence, Murphy's heart started to race.

*Oh, my God,* Murphy panicked. *We just lost the trial. ow did we miss the fact that, days before the murder, she's ot a record of getting keys made?*

It was right before noon. As soon as they broke for lunch, urphy, Larry Montgomery, and Detective Joe Cartwright rushed out to start Googling and digging through boxes of evidence. To their relief, they discovered that Frankie's was actually a key shop in Arizona, where some of Nanette's family lived. And once they reviewed the check register, they realized that the Frankie's key shop transaction actually occurred in November *1993*—more than a year before the murder.

Heaving a collective sigh of relief, Murphy and his team were able to come back to court to present the full picture, which also allowed the prosecutor "to take some shots" at the defense in front of the jury.

"It's part of the duel," Murphy said later. "It's nothing slimy."

Even so, he believed that the defense took a credibility hit from the exchange.

On June 29, Murphy went quickly through the forensic evidence from the autopsy with Dr. Anthony Juguilon, the county's chief pathologist, subtly hinting to the jurors that he didn't want to waste anyone's time by going into more detail than necessary about the victim's bullet wounds.

"Every one was potentially fatal, independently," Juguilon said, and each one would have killed Bill McLaughlin quickly.

Asked which was the fatal shot, the pathologist said, "If

you're asking me what the most serious one would be, it would be the one that passed through the aorta," explaining that bullets also tore through the abdominal cavity and lacerated the intestines, pancreas, liver, and vena cava.

When ballistics expert Thomas Matsudaira testified, Angelo MacDonald tried to poke holes in the analysis that the Hydra-Shok bullets could have been fired by only one type of gun, a Beretta 92F like Eric Naposki's.

"Pretty much anyone can commonly get Hydra-Shok bullets, right? Any Tom, Dick, Harry, or Nanette can get it, right?" MacDonald asked.

Murphy objected, and the judge sustained the objection—twice.

On redirect, Murphy came back with his own form of the question, focusing on the gun itself.

"Am I wrong saying it's popular?"

"Oh, no, it's popular," Matsudaira said.

"It's available to you, me, Tom, Dick, Harry, or Eric?"

When the defense objected to Murphy's question, Froeberg overruled the objection.

"That's based on what's good for the goose is good for the gander," the judge said.

Murphy typically started off a trial with a laid-back speaking approach, often talking so low and soft that his voice couldn't be heard in the gallery. His aim was to make things as simple, fast, and easy as possible for the jury to understand, growing more aggressive when he wanted to make a point or show he was "fired up" on cross-examination. Only then did his tone grow sharper and his questions more

cerbic, signaling jurors that he thought a witness was not
redible or was being uncooperative.

Murphy usually kept his cool, shaking his head, or star-
ng down at his yellow legal pad as he pondered the next
harp comeback to dispel whatever questions the defense
night have raised with the jury. But sometimes his enthusi-
sm was palpable as he jumped out of his seat to get in a
ouple last pithy questions to bring his points home. And he
lmost always got the last word.

After facing Pohlson in the Skylar Deleon trial, Murphy
ad feared going up against him again, "because he's so
riggin' likeable." But Murphy was even more scared that
he combination of Pohlson and his co-counsel Angelo
MacDonald—"the perfect New York lawyer and the home-
own loveable guy"—could be deadly.

"I feared that before the trial and my worst fears came
ue," he said, referring to the hammering, staccato style of
ross-examination MacDonald had mastered, which made
im a "tremendous trial attorney."

A sharp contrast to Murphy's tall, lean, and athletic con-
idence during his direct questioning, Pohlson came across
nore as a humble, stocky Joe Everyman during his brief
tints of cross-examination. While Murphy often used
iting wit, Pohlson related to the jury by speaking in even
nore simple language, making self-deprecating jokes about
ot knowing how to turn off his own cell phone, teasing
vitnesses—even the judge—to let the jury know that he'd
een around awhile. Rarely confrontational, he tended to
sk short bursts of questions, not wanting to tax the jury's
ttention span.

But both of these attorneys marked a stark contrast to
MacDonald, whose more theatrical, New York style was to
sk about minute details and to repeat questions to under-
core certain points. A man in motion, MacDonald was very

animated, pacing around the courtroom, leaning on th
defense table, grabbing his lip, and taking his glasses o
and off. However, at one point, he asked so many simila
questions that Judge Froeberg told him during a sidebar t
cut down on the unnecessary and irrelevant ones.

"A lot of questions are being asked of these witnesse
and they're not the right witnesses, and it's just . . . it's ge
ting very tedious," the judge said.

"Are you telling me that I need to object more?" Murph
asked. "That might be the first I've heard that."

Froeberg said that from his viewpoint, 90 percent o
MacDonald's questions were objectionable, saying h
would step in if Murphy didn't. The judge also scolde
MacDonald for putting his hand on the railing separatin
him from the jury.

After his very detailed cross-examination of Juguilo
and Matsudaira, MacDonald explained in the hallway tha
he was simply trying to educate the jury about guns, bullet
and forensics. This tactic could just as easily be viewec
however, as an effort to show the jury that he was know
edgeable and experienced as he questioned the witnes
Either way, he came off as smart and likeable, albeit a littl
long-winded.

Pohlson continued to score points with the jury fc
humor, which helped break the tension in the courtroon
After Murphy questioned Lieutenant Craig Frizzell, no
retired, about his surveillance of Eric Naposki and Eric
countersurveillance tactics, such as switching cars wit
Leonard Jomsky to try to trick police, Pohlson said lightl
"It sounds like neither you nor Mr. Naposki was very goo
at what you were doing."

"What do you mean by that?" Frizzell countered dryly i
an exchange that evoked some chuckling from the gallery

\* \* \*

Detective Voth, who spent something like nine hours on the stand, was recalled again toward the end of the prosecution's case, on July 7.

"Did Eric Naposki ever approach you and ask you any questions like, 'Can we get extra patrols? I'm concerned about my girlfriend. There's a killer on the loose.' Anything like that?" Murphy asked.

"No, sir."

Murphy then had Voth talk about two mailers for credit cards, which were addressed to Eric at the Seashore Drive house, which proved that Eric was, in fact, "living" there, a fact that he has denied to this day.

On cross-examination by Pohlson, Voth testified that he looked through forty or fifty different sets of phone bills for Nanette, and he also asked a manager at the Thunderbird for the nightclub's phone records. But he acknowledged that he never got Eric's.

"We asked him a couple of times and didn't receive them," Voth said, acknowledging that he never obtained a search warrant to get the records.

"Isn't that something that you normally, in the course of an investigation of a murder case, would have obtained?" Pohlson asked, following up with a series of questions about other items for which the police had obtained warrants.

"Maybe, maybe not," Voth said, refusing to give Pohlson what he wanted, which was an admission that it was, essentially, the police department's responsibility to prove Eric's alibi for him. "We didn't put that effort into that particular thing at that time. No, sir."

During a sidebar with the judge, Pohlson said he wanted to use a page in Eric's notebook to counter the prosecution's characterization of Eric as "a money-grubber."

Murphy disputed that he was trying to characterize Eric

that way, contending that the defense was trying to use the journal as "self-promoted character evidence," such as the defendant's goal of developing a better relationship with his children.

Trying to block the defense's move, Murphy said, "I got bad stuff on him for character. We have information he's worked as a collection agent for a loan shark in New York and was actually arrested for that."

As far as illustrating Eric's state of mind or the truth of what he was saying, the judge said he didn't think the journal was relevant.

Jenny McLaughlin was the last prosecution witness, whom Murphy used to show, once and for all, that the defense's attempts to raise doubts about Eric being the shooter by casting a shadow over the late Kevin McLaughlin were fruitless and wrong.

"Ever hear your brother say, 'I'm going to kill Dad'?" Murphy asked.

"No," she said.

Asked about Kevin's reaction to his father's murder, she said, "He was very upset."

"We've heard it a number of times throughout the trial. Did Kevin McLaughlin kill your father?"

"No."

During his cross-examination, Pohlson tried to put the focus back on Nanette, reiterating that she was the one to steal from the McLaughlin family, not Eric.

"She even took your father's Babe Ruth baseball, right?"

"She very well may have," Jenny said.

"Did you ever meet Mr. Naposki?"

"No."

Then Pohlson switched tactics, asking questions that suggested Jenny had been a pawn used by police to entrap

Eric into saying something incriminating, by pretending to be on his side.

Did the police ever ask you to "induce admissions or anything like that?" he asked.

"No," she said.

When Jenny mentioned that it seemed that Eric got scammed by Nanette, Pohlson asked, "did you mean that or were you just saying that?"

"I was trying to listen to what he had to say. Interpret it."

Pohlson also tried to show that Eric didn't actually benefit from Nanette's financial shenanigans, one of the requirements needed for the jury to find the "special circumstances" allegation to be true.

"Your family or estate never paid any money to Mr. Naposki, correct?"

"Correct."

Murphy jumped back in to show that the opposite was, in fact, true, and that Eric had thrown veiled legal threats at Jenny over the phone while Nanette was in jail.

"Remember that whole litany?"

"Yes."

Did Naposki ever call and say, "I'm terribly sorry about your father's death, or I have a security company, I can offer you guys protection?"

"No."

Asked if she remembered any times when Nanette went shooting with Bill, Jenny said no.

And with that, the prosecution rested its case.

# CHAPTER 39

The day before the defense was ready to start its case Gary Pohlson and Angelo MacDonald spent that entire Sunday afternoon at the jail with Eric, discussing the pro and cons of him testifying. Murphy, they said, was a very tough cross-examiner. Just look at what he had done during the motion hearing to one of their witnesses, private investigator James Box.

They had debated this question throughout the trial, Pohlson said, "on an almost nonstop basis." Some days Eric wanted to testify; other days, he realized he shouldn't.

While Murphy had tried to show that Nanette had made a patsy out of Eric, who then killed for her, the defense was now going to try to show that Eric had a real alibi and that Nanette was a more likely killer than he was. The defense had about eight witnesses lined up, some of whom would be asked to provide testimony that proved it would have been impossible for Eric to commit the murder.

Over Murphy's repeated objections, Judge Froeberg granted the defense's motion to allow Box to testify about his knowledge of the telephone call Eric made the day of the crime. Although the judge acknowledged it was hearsay evidence, he said this was a remedy "to somewhat rectify the delay in prosecution," which he believed was "the fair thing to do."

That said, Froeberg denied the defense's request to take the jury on a field trip to view the soccer fields in Walnut Ranch Park. There was no need for the jury to get a feel for the distance between the field and the parking lot, he said, because they already had a phone record in evidence showing a call was made on Nanette's car phone at 8:24 P.M., immediately after she and Eric skedaddled off the field.


After lunch, Angelo MacDonald gave a sixty-four-minute opening statement, lending a whole new meaning to the words "timeline" and "patsy."

MacDonald said the defense intended to prove that Eric was innocent, "because he was somewhere else at the time of the murder. He has an alibi that proves he could not—and did not—commit this crime."

"If you find that Mr. Naposki had an alibi—you must find him not guilty," he said. "It is an absolute."

The defense will prove, he said, that Eric and Nanette drove twenty-six minutes from the soccer field parking lot to his apartment in Tustin, where Nanette dropped him off.

"It's now eight-fifty in the evening," MacDonald said, "and she's off, lickety-split."

After Eric changed clothes, he set off in "his lumbering Nissan Pathfinder" and drove by his friend Leonard Jomsky's house, heading toward the southbound 55 Freeway. He was about to get on the highway when he got paged, so he pulled into Denny's on Seventeenth Street, went inside, and called the bar manager on one of the pay phones.

"The defense will show there was a call placed at eight fifty-two P.M.," he said.

In his dramatic, theatrical presentation, punctuated by gesturing and verbal exclamation points to hold the jury's attention, MacDonald presented a timeline incorporating Eric's varying claims. But with all the numbers of minutes and time trials being tossed around by the prosecution and now the defense, it may not have sunk in right away for the jury that this timeline lacked credibility. And when jurors applied common sense and basic mathematics to this scenario they decided that it was physically impossible, as the prosecution—and even the judge—would later proclaim.

MacDonald didn't take into account the time it would have taken Eric to get changed and get in his car before he even started to drive to Jomsky's house. But MacDonald was a great storyteller, just like Eric.

Eric was the "popular suspect, the patsy," he said, but you "can't convict someone on innuendo."

Eric was, in fact, late for a meeting that evening, the defense attorney said, an eight o'clock session with city officials about parking outside the Thunderbird. (MacDonald didn't mention that Eric originally had told police that he didn't have a meeting that night; it was the *next* night.)

After Eric returned the page from bar manager Mike Tuomisto, MacDonald said, Eric got back on the road around 8:54 or 8:55 P.M. And by then, he said, it would have been impossible to make it to Newport in just thirteen or fourteen minutes, in time to kill Bill McLaughlin.

"I'll tell you why that particular night, that night of all nights" it was impossible, MacDonald said. "It was a Thursday night. It was a big night . . . the first night of the boat parade," which translated into heavy traffic congestion.

Giving Eric fifteen minutes to get to the Thunderbird, he said, "gets us to nine after nine, nine-ten." He added that Eric would have to be "superhuman" to park at the club, cross the bridge, go down the steps to the pedestrian-access gate, which was shrouded in trees and had no lighting, use the key to get in the gate, enter the house, leave the key in the door, drop one on the mat, go into the house, and then shoot Bill, all by 9:10 P.M., when Kevin heard the shots.

Because, by then, the defense will show that "the crime is already done. Someone else had already killed Mr. McLaughlin," and that Eric had a "solid, simple, logical, reasonable, and compelling alibi," he said. "He simply could not have done it."

Nanette Johnston was the real culprit, he said, "an accomplished liar, cheat, thief, manipulator, con woman, and selfish, promiscuous gold digger. . . . When you combine those qualities with pretty, good-looking, in great shape, young, literally with the ability to charm the pants off the man she wants, extremely successful at fooling people, cheating people, taking advantage of people . . . Ladies and gentlemen, the defense will prove that Eric Naposki was just one of the many men she took advantage of. One of the litany of names we heard. One of the gym guys."

Nanette was the one who "plotted and schemed . . . and she planned the killing of William McLaughlin. . . . She is the only person in this world who had the motive, the means, the opportunity, the knowledge, the wherewithal, the callousness, the dispassionateness, to pull this off."

Only she knew when Bill was coming home, the extent of Kevin's disability, and how far away his bedroom was. The dog knew her and wouldn't attack her. Eric was getting too serious in the relationship, MacDonald said, and "only she knew that he could never keep her in the life that she was accustomed to."

"The defense will show she had plenty of time to do this," the defense attorney said.

The crime scene photos of the dining-room table and chairs show that Bill's papers are not askew, the table has not shifted, he said. "It's telling us that Mr. McLaughlin got out of his chair to greet someone he knew."

As MacDonald described Kevin dialing 911, Kim McLaughlin put her fingers in her ears. Once he finished the violent portion of the story arc, Kim returned to doodling with colored pens.

Eric's alibi and the overwhelming evidence that Nanette "independently and exclusively committed this crime" created reasonable doubt, MacDonald said. The defense will prove that Eric is not guilty, he continued, but it did not have to prove that Nanette committed this crime.

"That's the government's job," he said. But if the jury thought it was possible that she did it, "then that's a reasonable doubt."

The government has a lot of power and manpower, MacDonald said. "The question for you is, did they exercise enough responsibility? Because at the end of this case, we're going to argue that they did not."


As soon as the defense's first witness, PI James Box, started to testify, its case began to take a slow and painful tumble.

Box sounded just as sure of himself on the stand as he had during the first part of the "402" hearing, telling Gary Pohlson definitively that he'd seen the infamous "alibi" phone bill, with the 8:52 P.M. call.

Box said his boss, Julian Bailey, asked him to verify that there was a pay phone with that number at the Denny's in Tustin, and also to verify the Thunderbird's number, both of which he did.

Box described his drive from Denny's to the main entrance of Balboa Coves on February 15, 1995, a "driving-experience experiment," which had taken him twenty-one

inutes and forty-seven seconds. This showed him that Eric
vould have arrived too late to commit the murder.

A major liability for the defense, Box voluntarily fed the
rosecution some juicy details. He explained, for example,
1at the pattern of shots described by Bill's neighbor, Rose-
1ary Luxton, fit the "double-tap" technique, in which Eric
1d been trained with the SWAT team.

In the interview with Luxton, Box said, she described
1at "the popping sound or gunfire was kind of in a uniform
1ttern," which she thought was "odd."

Asked to elaborate, Box said Luxton recalled hearing
ve shots around 9:10 P.M., but "it wasn't random, like they
ere scattered about. It was there were two shots, and then
period of time went by, and there were two shots, and the
ots' sequence just seemed to be uniform."

Pohlson then asked him to talk about his interview with
like Tuomisto, the Thunderbird bar manager who noticed
1ere was "a lot of traffic, more than normal traffic," which
e attributed to "the first night of the boat parade. . . . He
ld our client that he ought to leave a little bit early, be-
ause there was heavy traffic and he may need some extra
me."

"Did he tell you at what time he paged Mr. Naposki?"

"Probably did. I don't recall off the top of my head."
fter Pohlson showed Box his own report, Box remem-
ered. "Shortly before nine P.M."

Finally, Box talked about his interview with the manager
f the Tustin Hardware store, who "told the officers that the
ilver key could have been made at his store or another
ne of several Ace stores, either in Orange County or in
1e nation."

Matt Murphy, a master of cross-examination, could slide
1e proverbial knife into witnesses before they even knew

it, and get them to look like incompetent idiots or, even worse, liars. As he walked Box through his driving-time route, Murphy was able to show that Box took a completely roundabout way to get to Balboa Coves, insinuating that he did it on purpose to help his client.

"You drove that in twenty-two, sorry, twenty-one minutes, forty-seven seconds. Would it shock you to learn that we've driven it eight times and it takes an average of about thirteen minutes?"

"Objection, Your Honor," Pohlson said. "Mr. Murphy's testifying."

They broke for the day, but Murphy was in his element and it would only get worse when they returned after the Fourth of July holiday.

On July 5, in open court but out of the jury's presence, Pohlson raised some objections to Murphy's line of questioning of Box, which prompted the prosecutor to issue a counterwarning, implying that he could make things even worse for the defense's key witness.

"Jim Box has a horrible reputation," Murphy said. "His reputation for veracity is bad. If Julian's going to testify [Box is] an honest guy, I can line this hallway with people that are going to come in and say he is not an honest guy, investigators that work with him, people in the DA's office."

Enough said.


By the time Murphy had finished cross-examining Box in front of the jury, he'd filleted the defense's "facts" of the case, along with Box's memory, his professional standards, ethics, methodology, and overall credibility by implying that the investigator was not only unprofessional but untruthful.

"Was there anything bizarre about the time-space continuum when you drove from Mr. Naposki's apartment to the Denny's pay phone?" Murphy asked with his classic sarcasm. "Like Bermuda Triangle stuff, lights in the air, anything like that?"

"No, there was nothing like that," Box replied.

Murphy took Box through the same exercise as he had at the "402" hearing—"Do you remember whether you actually saw the bill, or if you were just told about the bill?"—as he reminded Box of his previous testimony from just a week earlier, which the investigator said he couldn't remember.

By his own admission, Box said he sometimes omitted facts from his reports to his boss, and also rewrote them. When Murphy asked if this was because Box knew he was legally bound to give these reports to the prosecution as discovery, Box said no, but his credibility was tainted nonetheless.

Even when Pohlson questioned Box, he couldn't do much to dispel Murphy's implications that Box had specifically chosen a longer route in an effort to prove that Eric couldn't have murdered Bill McLaughlin.

"Would the reason you drove down Superior have been so you could have an inflated number in terms of how long it took you?" Pohlson asked.

"Not really."

"Was it even some part of 'really'?"

On recross, Murphy had Box firmly and repeatedly confirm that he was sure the night of the murder was the first night of the boat parade. Pohlson had tried to hint in his questioning that Box had the wrong night, but the judge sustained Murphy's objection before Box could answer.

After Murphy had solidly made his point, he triumphantly pulled out an official record from the Newport Beach Chamber of Commerce, showing the jury that the boat parade had not actually started until December 17, two days *after* the murder. He then got Box to admit that if he wasn't being untruthful, then he was inaccurate—neither one of which was good for the defense. (Murphy subsequently called Raymond Luehrs, a chamber of commerce official, who undermined Box's credibility even more.)

Murphy also got Box to admit that if Mike Tuomisto said he only had one conversation with Eric, and it was about heavy traffic from the boat parade, then "that conversation didn't take place on the fifteenth, right?"

"If this document's accurate, that's right," Box said, referring to the chamber record and essentially admitting that if Eric had been paged at all, it must have been two nights after the murder.

In addition, Murphy forced Box to reluctantly admit that although he'd previously testified that he'd worked only for Bailey on this case, he'd actually fed information in conference calls to Nanette's attorney as well.

"You even wrote a memo to Barry Bernstein, saying 'She still owes me nineteen hundred dollars.' Do you remember that?" Murphy asked.

"No."

"Are there ethical problems, sir, when you're working for two different people at the same time that might have conflicting defenses?"

"If the attorneys have worked out a conflict of interest, no."

"It just seems to me, sir—and correct me if I'm wrong—you seem to be very sure about things when Mr. Pohlson's asking you questions and not so sure when I'm asking you questions. Is there any reason for that?"

Murphy's cross-examination of Box had decimated this witness, and Julian Bailey's subsequent testimony didn't help the defense recover all that much.

When the defense submitted a motion for a new trial a year later, it described Murphy's treatment of Box as follows: *Mr. Murphy savagely, unfairly and often sarcastically*

*questioned Mr. Box to the point that would have been a*
*rock-solid claim to an 8:52 phone call in 1995 . . . was now*
*reduced to little more than a punch line. . . . As a result,*
*every single item that Mr. Box testified on was tainted by*
*this cross-examination and further prejudiced Mr. Naposki.*

The same day that Box and Bailey testified, the Casey Anthony verdict of "not guilty" came down in Florida and shocked the nation. A couple of the Florida jurors said in posttrial interviews that they weren't persuaded by the prosecution's case of circumstantial evidence, as if it didn't count.

"Everyone was shitting bricks," Sandy Baumgardner said, recalling that Murphy had stated that prosecutors couldn't get a win for months after the "not guilty" verdict in OJ Simpson's criminal trial came down.

Much of the defense's questioning of Eric's friends was geared primarily toward portraying Nanette as a lying manipulator who knew how to fire a gun.

Defense attorney MacDonald called Abbey Shilleh, the head valet at the Thunderbird, who routinely parked Eric's truck. Shilleh testified that he didn't remember whether he parked Eric's vehicle the night of the murder, but said Eric was "later than usual" when he got to work that night. He also said that Eric was considered a manager in charge of security and parking, so it made sense for him to attend the meeting between city and club officials about parking issues at eight o'clock that night, but Eric didn't make it.

Murphy proceeded to shred Shilleh's credibility, however, by forcing the valet to admit that he'd recently been convicted of paying a $50,000 bribe to the chief of an Indian reservation and that he'd started his home confinement just a month earlier.

After Shilleh left the witness stand, Murphy hammered the nail home. "Your Honor," he said, "can I just put on the record, as the witness was leaving, he wished Mr. Naposki 'good luck.'"

Leonard Jomsky, Eric's friend and off-and-on roommate, took the stand to recount a trip to the shooting range during which he, Eric, and Nanette shot at targets for an hour, after which Nanette teased him about being a better shot.

After defense witness Rob Frias was called, Murphy used him to poke holes in Eric's claim that he never moved in with Nanette after the murder, because he wanted nothing to do with her. When Frias claimed that he didn't know whether Eric was really "living" at Nanette's house on Foxhollow in Dove Canyon (a neighboring community to Coto de Caza), Murphy reminded the witness of statements he'd made in an interview two years earlier.

"After the murder, Naposki moved into Nanette's residence in Coto de Caza, and you recall visiting their house for a barbecue, and that they, in fact, lived together . . . and that when you visited them, they appeared to get along well. Remember making those statements?"

Confronted with his own words, Frias had to agree. "That sounds pretty accurate."

"Wasn't Mr. Naposki living with her at the beach house for a time too?"

"He might have," Frias said. "I might have heard that."

Some of the prosecution's rebuttal witnesses testified out of order, before the defense had rested, which was a little confusing. These included Larry Montgomery, Tom Matsudaira, who talked about the ballistics testing, and Detective Scott Smith, who was unable to answer certain questions as MacDonald repeatedly tried to poke holes in the NBPD investigation.

But over the weekend, Smith took the initiative to do some research on his own so he could answer those questions when he retook the stand on Monday, which seemed to take MacDonald by surprise.

One nagging debate between the two sides was whether the traffic patterns for Tustin, Costa Mesa, and Newport Beach had changed significantly since 1995, as the defense tried to nullify or at least challenge the relevancy of the prosecution's recent time trials.

By presenting its contrasting time trials and cross-examining the prosecution witnesses, the defense tried to persuade the jury that the prosecution had left out important details that would have added precious minutes to that timeline.

"They'd never even looked at the phones," Pohlson said later. "They'd never even checked this stuff. They didn't check records." He added that the defense also highlighted the failures in the NBPD's original investigation, such as the failure to interview Mike Tuomisto, which wasn't done until 2009.

"[Eric] also mentioned 'Teresmo?'" Pohlson asked Voth during cross-examination. "We now know it's Mr. Tuomisto. Your whole team never contacted him in 1994 to 1995, correct?"

"I think I left a message on his phone and didn't get a return call," Voth said.

In an odd move, given that the defense had apparently scored on that point, Murphy and the defense attorneys entered into a stipulation that if Tuomisto was called as a witness, he would testify that he had no recollection of paging Eric the night of the murder, or any other night, and didn't know why he would have, because he was the alcohol manager and Eric was the security manager. Tuomisto would also say that he didn't recall speaking to Eric on the phone, or having any conversation with him before or after December 15, 1995, and that the club wasn't busy at 9:00 P.M. The club had just opened that October, so he and Eric had worked together only a short time by then.

On July 7, out of the jury's presence, the defense lost a motion objecting to three areas of prosecution evidence: Joseph Stoltman Jr.'s testimony that Eric had been trained in the "double-tap" shooting method; testimony that Eric was present at all of Nanette's court hearings related to her 1995 forgery case (meaning that he had to be aware of all the charges against her); and the testimony of Investigator Larry Montgomery, for whom Pohlson coined the nickname "Saint Larry" for his role in resurrecting the cold case.

The defense asked for a recess around 2:45 P.M., which lasted about thirty minutes, during which Eric and his attorneys debated once more whether it was in the defendant's best interest to testify.

"It was just a question of what was a better strategy," Pohlson said later. "We left it up to him. It was completely his call. We did tell him the pros and cons and everything in detail."

By the time they emerged from the cell with Eric, the matter had been settled. He was not going to testify, and the defense rested.

Murphy figured that Eric must have realized that testifying would only hurt him. "There was too much he couldn' answer," the prosecutor said, looking back later, adding almost remorsefully that he'd lost the opportunity to ask his twenty-two pages of questions. "It would have been fun to do."

Instead, the prosecutor worked on incorporating those points into his closing argument.


Murphy immediately called rebuttal witness Joseph Stoltman Jr., who testified in detail about teaching the double-tap technique the day Eric was in training, which dovetailed with Box's recent testimony about the pattern of shots that Rosemary Luxton had heard the night of the murder.

Stoltman also testified that as part of the training, the SWAT members were taught to shoot to kill and to aim down toward a target's chest, not his head, so as not to block the shooter's view of the target's hands.

"Approximately how long before that was it that you had this session with Eric Naposki that you taught him about double taps?" Murphy asked.

"I would say probably about three to four months earlier," said Stoltman, who had originally told police that the session occurred in late 1992, when Eric still worked at Metropolis.

On cross-examination, Pohlson tried to get Stoltman to say that he trained SWAT team members to duck back and pause when someone was shooting back at them, but Stoltman said that was not necessarily the case.

"Do you know what 'stippling' is?" Pohlson asked.

"'Stippling'? No, I do not," Stoltman replied.

"You didn't train anybody in how you cause stippling, then?"

"No, I did not."

Responding to Stoltman's testimony about training to

shoot targets in the chest, Pohlson asked, "The ideal place, if you're going to shoot somebody trying to kill them, would be to shoot them in the head, right?"

"That's correct."

But in the end, nothing could undue the damage caused by the testimony about Eric's training in the "double-tap" technique.

# CHAPTER 40

Matt Murphy started his four-hour closing argument on the afternoon of July 11, and finished the next morning, using a pointillistic painting as a metaphor for connecting the dots of the largely circumstantial case to form the conclusion that Eric was guilty.

Murphy spent much of his time picking apart individual aspects of the defense's case, and asking the jury to consider why, if Eric were truly innocent, would he make questionable claims and commit incriminating acts? And why would witnesses, such as Suzanne Cogar, lie?

"There's no mind-f'ing the police when you're innocent in a murder investigation," he said, referring to Eric's admission that he "mind-fucked" the police when he lied about loaning his 9mm Beretta to Joe David Jimenez.

Eric's motive for murder, he said, was greed—to share in Bill's money—as well as jealousy, so he could have Nanette all to himself. The killing was carried out in the couple's "evolving plan."

But Nanette was still at the heart of this case for both the prosecution and the defense—a woman, Murphy said, who had a "motive on steroids" to kill Bill McLaughlin before he found out she was cheating on and stealing from him.

"She's got one gift. She's better at this than anyone I've eve seen," he said. "She's good at the manipulation of men . . at wrapping men around her little finger and getting them to do what she wants."

If Eric did any one of the things that the witnesses claimed—told Cogar he wanted to kill Bill, made copies o the keys, or wrote down the license plate number for Bill' car before the murder—and "if any of these are related to the murder, he's good for it. I don't have to prove all of them In fact, I don't have to prove any of them."

Why was Eric so upset that the detectives had seized his notebook, which was just a bunch of lists and "gibberish"; he asked rhetorically. "Page three," he said, using the laser pointer to circle the handwritten license plate number on the overhead screen for the jury. "This, ladies and gentlemen is what he's so upset about."

In comments that raised the ire of the defense team so much that they objected in a motion filed a year later. Murphy made a dismissive reference to MacDonald's out-of-town style and Pohlson's jovial courtroom presence as the prosecutor tried to win another round of gamesmanship in front of the jury.

MacDonald, he said, had the suit, the hair, the watch, the shoes, and the New York accent: "How could you not check that out?" he said. "Maybe that works in New York." And Pohlson, he said, was a jokester, who made everyone laugh.

"Each one of them is a master at his own style, but it's a tactic," Murphy said.

The prosecutor countered the defense's accusations that the NBPD had done a shoddy investigation by noting that the detectives had enough "heads-up" to copy the pages of the notebook, calling it "good police work." He did acknowledge, however, that this wasn't "a perfect investigation, no investigation is," and that the police made some mistakes.

"The big question is, so what? Is there an expiration date

on evidence? . . . Naposki got the best benefit—he got fifteen years [out of prison] he didn't deserve."

Even if Eric's license plate notation was the only piece of evidence, Murphy told the jurors just before they broke for the day, so they could ponder his points overnight, "you'll hold him accountable for what he did."

The next morning, Murphy took up where he left off.

Given that the defense started its case claiming that Nanette was the actual shooter, Murphy reinforced his "aiding and abetting" conspiracy theory—that Eric was guilty of murder even if he'd just "helped" Nanette kill Bill.

"Is it Nanette who killed him or did *they* kill him?" he said. "Legally, under 'aiding and abetting,' help is all it takes."

Eric was either dropped off at his apartment or he rode with Nanette all the way to Newport, he said, where she left him within walking distance of Balboa Coves.

"I don't have to prove it. You don't have to figure it out. Either one is an option," he said. "I think she dropped him off, because they were in it together."

Eric's so-called "alibi" didn't even meet the definition of the word, he said, because the investigators had proved in numerous time trials that he still had time to commit the murder.

If Nanette was the shooter, as the defense suggested, then why would she make a copy of her own key?

"How do you plan to get a key stuck?" he asked. "Why take her pedestrian key off her key ring if it's not to give to somebody else? . . . All the evidence at the scene, none of it points to Nanette as being the shooter."

Murphy stood with his arms crossed like a soldier, his voice rising from the soft, low tones with which he'd started to emphasize his disgust with the defendant's threatening call to Jenny McLaughlin.

"Not a single word of condolence, not a single word to her about the investigation, doesn't offer help of any kind. He wants the Infiniti. . . . It's all about him, the stuff that he wants," he said, underscoring the evidence to support the special circumstance of "financial gain."

"Him, him, him, him . . . the bully that is Eric Naposki. That is outrageous, and I submit to you totally inconsistent with an innocent man."

After the murder, Murphy said, Eric moved in to the beach house, forcing the McLaughlins to evict him. Then he moved in with Nanette in Dove Canyon and started a movie production business with her.

"The money for this house is the direct result of the murder of Bill McLaughlin, and [Eric] has no problem with that," he said.

But Murphy didn't just throw Eric into the liar's circle. He included his private investigator, James Box, as well.

"How dumb does Mr. Box think you folks are?" he asked. "It's rare when you see an investigator turn to the jury and lie to them, and that's what he did."

In closing, he reminded the jury about the need to bring closure to the victim's family once again. "Justice in this case has been a long time coming."


Billy McNeal had wanted to hear Murphy's closing, but he ended up missing it. He and his fiancée caught the defense's closing instead, and in the process, got a good look at Eric Naposki. Knowing that Nanette's upcoming trial would be somewhat similar, Billy wanted to get "a taste and feel for what the trial was going to look like."

He never really had an idea of Nanette's "type," because he hadn't seen any of her men but John Packard, who was quite a bit older than she was. When he saw Eric, he wasn't very impressed with the looks of him. Eric reminded him of Butterbean, the professional wrestler and super-heavyweight boxing champion. Billy thought Eric certainly fit the part, with his "tats, the shaved head, bouncer, tough guy."

Billy had been following the trial in the news, and had learned a few things along the way, but he really just wanted it to be over so he could move on with his life. He was so sure that Eric and Nanette would be found guilty it was beyond him "how Rosie stuck around. That just blows me away."


Gary Pohlson and Angelo MacDonald decided that Pohlson should do the closing argument because he seemed to have a good relationship with the jury. Also, when two attorneys work as co-counsels in a murder trial, one will often do the opening and leave the closing to the other.

Pohlson started his four-hour closing argument—his longest ever—right after lunch and finished the next morning, claiming that Murphy had switched his theory midstream to the "aiding and abetting" notion, which he'd never even mentioned in his opening.

Pohlson told the jury that after two hundred and forty minutes of talk, Murphy hadn't presented any real proof that Eric Naposki was guilty. All the instances Murphy presented about Eric's activities and behavior were simply just examples of how the prosecution *thought* Eric should have acted.

First of all, he said, Eric talked with the police without an attorney, and told them he had an alibi. "I would suggest to you that's exactly how an innocent man would respond."

Pohlson tried to repair the damage Murphy had done to James Box during his cross-examination and again in Murphy's closing, switching the focus back to the NBPD's mistakes. Why hadn't the detectives talked to Mike Tuomisto back in the 1990s when he still remembered what happened the night of the murder?

"If Box could do it, then any of these police officers could do it," he said. After working in law enforcement for so many years, on hundreds of murder cases, "you think he's going to come in here and lie? . . . Why? Why would he do that and perjure himself?"

The reason Box and Julian Bailey didn't show the prosecutor the phone bill in 1995, he said, was because prosecutor Debbie Lloyd wasn't being cooperative. And they didn't keep the bill all these years because they thought it was a moot point.

"They thought this thing was dead and gone," he said.

Pohlson gave Murphy back some of his own, pointing out to the jury that the prosecutor also used tactics to try to weaken the defense witnesses' credibility in the jury's eyes.

"MacDonald is the New York bully, and Pohlson is the class clown. Mr. Murphy, help me out here. I'm kind of confused. 'I'm not jumping on you, but you are lying, aren't you, Mr. Box?' Everyone has their style, it doesn't mean anything."

Pohlson said he really did believe that his client was innocent. He joked that his wife thought he was shallow, but in reality, "I do care. I take this as serious as I take anything in my life. If the McLaughlin family thinks I don't take it seriously, then I apologize to them."

Pohlson contended that Eric had never been violent before, so "why would he all of a sudden become a murderer? . . . Is he all of a sudden going to go from zero to ninety and blow [Bill McLaughlin] away six times?"

The defense was sticking with its theory that Eric wasn't the shooter, he said. They didn't have to prove that Nanette was the shooter. They were simply arguing that there was more evidence that she did it than Eric did."

"She doesn't need Eric Naposki to commit a murder," ohlson said. "He's the perfect patsy, okay?"

Regardless of what Murphy and his investigators claimed their multiple time trials, Pohlson said, "Minutes are im- ortant, but in terms of what's actually proven in this case is at there was an eight fifty-two phone call from the Denny's. here is no time trial in this case that gives Naposki time nough to commit this crime."

Calling the prosecution's "double-tap" interpretation of uxton's described pattern of shots "misdirection," he said e killer got close enough to the victim to leave stippling arks because the shooter was someone he knew.

"Also, if you're a trained killer, you're going to shoot him the head, like GI Joe told us," he said, referring to Stolt- an. "But that wasn't done because Nanette Johnston is able walk up to Mr. McLaughlin, get up close to him, and oot him."

Pohlson said the prosecution's case had so many holes in that he couldn't even understand why the DA had ulti- ately filed it. "It would be a horrible, horrible tragedy to onvict a man for something he didn't do," he said. "Mr. aposki should absolutely be found not guilty. There's not e piece of evidence that conclusively shows that he com- itted this crime."

In a particularly emotional moment, Pohlson told the ry that he'd never wanted anything more than to see this articular client acquitted.

During his hour-long rebuttal, Murphy pounded on Eric ome more, and made fun of Pohlson for being melodra- atic at the end of his closing. That day, Pohlson had rought in his young daughter, who was working as an tern in his office, to sit next to the defendant. Viewing this

as a ploy to make Eric seem benign, Murphy decided h
needed to expose these maneuvers for what they were.

When he heard Pohlson claim that he'd never wante
anything more than to get his innocent client off, Murph
believed that Pohlson had stepped over the legal line of wha
was allowed in court and had committed what is known a
"vouching" for his client.

Rather than object, Murphy decided he would "fir
back" and call him out. So, Murphy told the jury that he'
been moved the first time he'd heard Pohlson make thi
same remark during another trial, but he realized wha
Pohlson was up to when he heard him say it again in thi
courtroom.

When Pohlson heard the accusations that he was bein
disingenuous, he felt as if he'd been stabbed in the back, be
cause he'd sincerely meant what he said.

"I've never said that before," Pohlson said later. "Nobod
has ever heard me say that."

Outside of court, Pohlson told Murphy that his commer
had been hurtful, and Murphy apologized. But Murphy late
said he did so mostly as a way of saying, "Hey, I hope w
can move on from this."

"That said, I really did feel bad that Gary did have ba
feelings about it because there really is no one I respec
more than Gary Pohlson," Murphy said.

The two men eventually smoothed things over.

"He has apologized to me," Pohlson confirmed in lat
2012 as the two of them were preparing for yet anothe
match in court the following week. "We reconciled."

The jury, which included several college students and
couple of teachers, began its deliberations at 12:05 P.M. o
July 13. And as soon as the jurors sat down, they took

traw poll: eight voted to convict, two voted not guilty, and
wo were unsure.

Adrianne Reynolds, a fifty-year-old machinist who had
one into the trial with an open mind, was one of the eight.
he was surprised she'd been picked to serve because she'd
dmitted during voir dire that her brother had been sen-
enced to ten years in prison on a drug charge in Arizona,
ut she figured she was chosen because she said the police
nd the court system had treated him fairly.

By the third or fourth day of the trial, she was already
eaning toward a guilty verdict. And as the trial went on, she
nly became more convinced. Matt Murphy told her later
hat he could tell that he'd had her in his pocket from the
ery first day of trial.

"The evidence, in my mind, was really overwhelming,
ven though it was circumstantial," she said recently.

At twelve-thirty, the jury took an hour for lunch, then
tarted discussing the primary areas of evidence the panel
ad flagged for discussion.

"The biggest thing was the timeline and his supposed
all and blah, blah, blah," Reynolds said. "Suzanne Cogar
vas also a big thing. I mean, how stupid is this guy? [Telling
er] that he wanted to blow up the plane, I mean, come on.
'hat right there is an indication of where the man's mind is."

Some of the jurors wondered, what if he really had made
he 8:52 P.M. call? So, at 2:17 P.M., the jury submitted a note
o the judge asking if Julian Bailey's letter to prosecutor
)ebbie Lloyd was in evidence. The judge responded, "No,"
o the jury asked to hear Bailey's testimony again.

The next request—for a transcript of the stipulations to
e read—came at 2:46 P.M.

"But the important thing that really seemed to hit with us
vas that the defense stipulated to the fact that Eric Na-
»oski's boss never paged Eric Naposki," Reynolds said.
They stipulated to that!"

Then, around four o'clock, the jury asked to hear th
testimony from Larry Montgomery about his time trial
from Diamond Bar to Eric's apartment, to Jomsky's house
and on to Denny's. The jury quit for the day at 4:20 P.M.


The next morning, the panel listened to the testimon
about the time trials, then took a fifteen-minute break. Fo
Reynolds, it didn't make sense that Eric would drive in th
opposite direction from work to stop by Jomsky's house i
he was in such a hurry to leave the soccer field to get to
meeting.

"Maybe my three-year-old nephew of mine might bu
that one," she said. "I didn't."

Her fellow jurors, she said, also thought it was ridiculou
to claim that the phone bill was so important, and yet neithe
Bailey nor Box had saved it. But after going over the time
line in great detail, the jury realized that it didn't reall
matter whether he made the call or not. The jurors believe
the prosecution's argument that Eric still had time to commi
the crime.

"Realistically, listening to his statements to the police
and his phone call to Jenny, I mean you can't sit here an
tell me that this guy didn't buy everything that [Nanette
was saying and everything that she was doing . . . and tha
this guy wasn't picturing these millions and millions o
dollars going into his pocket."

At eleven-fourteen, the jury asked to hear Suzann
Cogar's testimony about Eric's "maybe I did, maybe
didn't" remarks after Bill's murder.

The panel took a ninety-minute break and resumed de
liberations for one last hour before notifying the bailiff a
2:35 P.M. that it had reached a verdict. After fourteen day

f trial, the jury took seven and a half hours to reach a nanimous decision.

Froeberg gave everyone about an hour to get back to court.

Once all the attorneys were assembled at 3:38 P.M., the ourt clerk read the jury's verdict aloud. As Eric heard he words come out of her mouth, he shook his head in isbelief: "'We the jury in the above entitled action find he defendant guilty of Penal Code 187(a)—murder—in he first degree as to count number one of the original in- ormation.'"

The jury also found the special circumstance of murder or financial gain to be true, and that Eric "personally dis- harged a firearm during the commission of the offense."

Eric looked shocked, exchanging looks of disappoint- nent with his attorneys. As Eric was being led out with his ands cuffed behind his back, he turned toward the galley, vhere his fiancée, Rosie, was crying.

"I love you. Don't worry, babe," Eric told her. "Everyone nakes mistakes, including these twelve."

For Pohlson, the verdict came as a devastating blow.

"I was so incredibly disappointed by that verdict," he re- alled eighteen months later. "It was a very hard verdict to ake. I've lost a lot of big cases. I've had my ups and my lowns. But this was a very frustrating case. I just felt they ,ot it wrong."

"All of the defense team believes that Naposki was not he guy who pulled the trigger," Pohlson said. "I think we ll believe that . . . still today. . . . That's not to say that Naposki wasn't involved."

Kim McLaughlin cried with tears of relief and joy as she ugged her sister. She then went over to Rosie—apparently eeing her as another victim in this tragedy—and tried to comfort her with a hug, a true sign of the benevolence, charity, and grace that Bill McLaughlin had taught his children.

Even Detective Tom Voth's eyes welled up as it hit him how many years it had taken Bill's daughters—with the family's cumulative level of tragedy heightened by Kevin's severe brain injury, caused by a drunk driver, and then his subsequent drowning—to win the justice they deserved.

But for the McLaughlin sisters, this case was not over yet. They still had to sit through another trial, hoping that Nanette Packard would also get what she deserved.

The same was true for juror Adrianne Reynolds, who had lived with this case for three and a half weeks, finding it difficult not to be able to discuss it with anyone.

This case was different from her last jury trial, when a defendant faced charges of grand theft auto a decade or so earlier. This one had captured a place inside her. It was important for her to see the McLaughlin family get the justice, closure, and peace they'd been waiting to get for so long.

"I still think of Kim and Jenny, how horrible it was that they had to endure this for [seventeen] years," Reynolds said in late 2012.

It was a shame, she said, that Suzanne Cogar hadn't gotten "a little braver, a little earlier," and that Kevin McLaughlin had not only died before the case was resolved, but was also accused of being the killer by an audacious defense team. "Those are the things that really irritate and stick with me."

Reynolds said she would never forget the experience of serving on this jury. Knowing "how hard everybody worked, and all the tests," she said, "it really took me over and I had to see the whole thing come to a complete close for me to be okay."

# CHAPTER 41

Within a couple months of the verdict, Eric Naposki [as]ked to speak to Matt Murphy. He said he had some impor[ta]nt information to convey about who had *really* killed Bill [M]cLaughlin.

On September 8, Murphy went to the jail to meet with [Er]ic, whom he'd named "the Superbouncer." He brought [al]ong DA Investigators Larry Montgomery and Susan [Fr]azier, paralegal Dena Basham, Detective Tom Voth, and [tw]o other NBPD detectives. Representing Eric were Gary [Po]hlson and his investigator, Tom Gleim.

Apparently expecting a one-on-one with the prosecutor, [Er]ic seemed surprised and uncomfortable at the number of [pe]ople who crowded into the room. Murphy said they spent [th]e next eighty minutes listening to Eric essentially say, "I [kn]ow who did it, but I'm not going to tell you."

Eric told the prosecution team that Nanette had paid [so]meone to kill Bill. He said he knew the man, but he didn't [w]ant to disclose the name because he was worried for his [fa]mily's safety back east. They got a little more of the [st]ory—although still not enough—after Murphy told Eric

to give up some more details without naming the guy. E
refused.

Frustrated, Murphy's team started packing up to lea
Pohlson had been getting upset too. He'd promised Murp
that Eric would reveal the full story, and now his client w
playing games.

"You need to come clean with what you said you we
going to tell them," Pohlson said.

With Eric still reluctant, Pohlson asked for a time-o
He talked softly with Eric in the corner for a few minut
after which Eric finally agreed to disclose the man's nan
Juan Gonzales (pseudonym).

"I am one hundred percent sure my gun was used," E
said, explaining that the last time he'd seen his Beretta w
about a week before the murder, when it was under the s
of his car. Nanette was the only person who could ha
taken it.

He also said that the killer must have switched out t
bullets with Hydra-Shoks, because he always stacked h
gun with alternating soft-tipped and hard-tipped bullets, n
the deadly hollow points.

After the meeting, Detective Voth went home to sear
his files for any evidence that would confirm or dispro
this new story. As he looked through the pages they'd copi
from Eric's notebook in December 1994, Voth discover
the only reference to this alleged hit man that he could fi
anywhere. In the journal, where Eric kept track of money
owed and had received, he'd written *$2,000* next to t
name *Juan*.

"So . . . why's he paying [Juan] two thousand dollars
wondered Voth, who showed the page to Murphy and Mo
gomery.

Eric claimed that the presence of Juan Gonzale

umber on Nanette's phone records for December 8, 13, and
4, 1994, supported his story. Although the detectives
pparently didn't explore this connection in their original
nvestigation, Montgomery subsequently did look into it.
Ie learned that Gonzales had that number in 1995, but it
vas also used by a man named Ira Chroman, who told
Montgomery that he had it for a few months when he lived
n North Hollywood. However, he couldn't remember exactly
vhen that was. And, besides, he didn't know Nanette or
Gonzales.

Detective Scott Smith called Gonzales, who had since
moved to Arizona, for a taped interview while Voth listened.
After Montgomery reviewed the tape, he was satisfied that
Gonzales wasn't involved in the murder. Gonzales didn't try
o delay the interview, nor did he sound evasive, as a guilty
man might have. In fact, he seemed genuinely cooperative.

As soon as Montgomery heard Gonzales's response to
Smith's first question, he felt confident that Gonzales didn't
now anything about the case.

"Eric was murdered?" Gonzales asked.

As a matter of course, the NBPD and the prosecution
eam had been monitoring Eric's visits, phone calls, and
orrespondence since he'd been in jail. In reviewing Eric's
tatements to Rosie, Montgomery found even more reasons
o believe that Eric's new story was false.

On August 27, 2011, Eric wrote to Rosie, *It's now my
urn to show all the mistakes. Right the wrongs, speak out
n my defense and come home. I know you think I could of
[sic] done it in May '09, but it was not an option. Trust me.*

Then, three days after Eric's September 8 meeting with
he prosecution team, he wrote this to Rosie: *I'm so glad
ou know what is going on now. It's been harder than hell
o hold it all in all 27 months.*

When she came to visit him in jail on October 8 and 9 he didn't tell her he'd already released the "hit man's" name. And when he wrote her on November 6, he said he was still gearing up to do it.

*We must put this crime to bed and let everyone know I am innocent and who is guilty,* he wrote, adding that he would have his friend John Pappalardo release the information to the media and also fill in the Greenwich and Monroe Police Departments so they could watch over Rosie. *I sure hope that this person does not try anything stupid, but he is well connected and well funded.*

Warning Rosie to be careful going forward, and to keep an eye out for "anything strange," he said he felt he had no choice at this point but to release the hit man's name.

Eric wrote to his son, Eric Junior, about this as well. In a November 7 letter, Eric described how he was wrongly arrested in 2009 and said he wasn't able to prove his innocence because he'd lost his "stuff."

*The other day I told them everything I know,* he wrote. *Now they are faced with a question of what to do.*


Summing up Eric's excuses as nonsense, Murphy noted that Eric was so scared for the safety of Rosie and his family that he waited *fifty-nine days* to tell them that he'd just released the hit man's identity to the authorities, information he claimed to have kept secret all these years because it would have put his loved ones in danger.

But unlike Murphy, Eric's family was convinced that this story was true. As a result, they were living in fear of an angry hit man outed by Eric Naposki, and some said they were too scared to show their faces in the photo section of this book.

Eric told the prosecution team that he'd informed Pohlson two years earlier that Juan Gonzales was the hit man, but hlson couldn't come up with anything. However, when ohlson talked with Montgomery in October 2011, he said ney'd done no investigation into this angle because Eric adn't wanted to take his defense in that direction.

In late 2012 Pohlson confirmed that Gonzales's name ad come up within the first month of Pohlson taking the ase in 2009, but "there were reasons [Eric] wouldn't allow s to bring it up. In the end, there were still going to be reories that Naposki was involved. The only value to that ould have been if Naposki wanted to make a deal, to plead uilty, and to testify."

Citing attorney-client privilege, Pohlson said he couldn't ay anything more than this: "We didn't pursue that."

When Montgomery ultimately confronted Eric about the elay in the disclosure to his family, Eric said he was refer- ng to his worries about revealing the information *to the nedia.* But that excuse held no water for Murphy and the eam of investigators.

After looking into Eric's claims, they concluded that he vas, once again, lying to save his own skin. He told a sim- ar story to *48 Hours,* which aired a rare second show on ne case. McLaughlin family advocates saw both shows as verly sympathetic to Eric Naposki, but many viewers who idn't know the players personally stated on the *48 Hours* acebook page that they believed or wondered if Eric was nnocent.


Voth and Montgomery went on their own to meet with ric a second time, on December 23, 2011.

This time, Eric said that he'd actually parked his truck at is friend Leonard Jomsky's house—where he'd said during ne 2009 interview that he was living, not at his own apart- nent in Tustin—before the soccer game on the night of the nurder. Montgomery said he believed this new story could actually be true, because it fit with the theory that rather than dropping Eric off at his apartment, as Nanette and Eric told police from the beginning, that she'd actually dropped him off at the Newport Boulevard Bridge near Balboa Coves so he could use the key to get through the pedestrian gate, kill Bill, and run across the bridge to work at the Thunderbird.

Following that theory further, Montgomery said Eric must have paged Nanette after work that night because he wanted her to pick him up and drive him to get his truck at Jomsky's. If she and Eric had told the truth in the first place about Eric leaving his truck at Jomsky's, Montgomery said, they ran the risk of Jomsky telling police that Eric's truck had been sitting outside his house until late that night, thus contradicting the couple's initial claims that he'd driven it to work after Nanette dropped him off at his apartment.

Bottom line: Voth and Montgomery just didn't believe the hit man story.

"I think it tells volumes as to his last and final story to us, to the DA's office, and to the police department," Voth said. "It's just another lie and maybe he was trying to wiggle out of it, and if he was, he put himself right in the middle of it. Since when do hit men borrow guns?"

# CHAPTER 42

As I was researching and writing this book, I wanted to look Eric Naposki in the eye and hear this hit man story for myself. So I made arrangements to visit him at the Theo [?]acy Facility in the city of Orange on December 2, 2011.

Anticipating that we would only get to talk for the regular hour-long visiting slot, I was surprised and pleased that the deputies, with whom he apparently got along well, let me stay for two hours after Eric asked them if I could stay longer.

"Things are not always what they seem," Eric said as soon as I sat down on the cold round seat, using one of my hands to hold the phone receiver, which was attached to the wall with a metal cord like the old-school pay phones, and the other hand to scribble in my notebook. "I told them what happened. I told them I'm not responsible for the murder in any way. . . . I'm doing someone else's jail time."

I always find it fascinating and important, if I can, to speak directly with the killers I write about, so I can convey my impressions to my readers. Through my books, my hope is for all of us to learn lessons of inspiration and strength from the victims, and also to educate ourselves in how to

identify the bad guys (and women, in this case) before w
become victims ourselves.

One thing I want to say right off the bat is that Eric, sin
ilar to other convicted killers I've interviewed in jail or i
prison, was very charming, convincing, and didn't seem a
all threatening. He was also just as big as everyone said h
was. And, as I'd heard, he talked about himself in the thir
person, a key indicator of narcissism.

Granted, we had a pane of glass or plastic between u
but I went into the interview, as usual, with an open min
I didn't want him to think I was passing judgment or h
wouldn't open up to me. But even my one remark that
thought Matt Murphy had done a good job in court wa
enough to convince Eric that I already thought he wa
guilty. I didn't argue with him. I simply told him I wante
to tell the truth and reveal both sides of what happened.

Essentially, what I heard that day was yet another ne
version of the Eric Naposki story and a revisionist-historic
account of his relationship with his codefendant.

Nanette, he said, was a "pathological, fucking liar," an
the instigator of Bill McLaughlin's murder, because it wa
her "big mouth" that had gotten him killed.

Eric claimed that she'd come to him, all shaken up, i
October 1994, with her arms bruised and a fat lip, sayin
that Bill had "beat[en] her up and forced her into a sexua
encounter" the night before. When Eric told her to mov
out, she said she didn't have to, because Bill was moving t
Las Vegas. But she must have told someone else, who kille
Bill for abusing her, Eric said, someone who wasn't as goo
with guns as he was.

"I'm a better shot than that," he said, adding that
wouldn't have taken him six bullets to kill Bill. "I could
a Dixie cup from fifty yards away."

No, he said, the shooter was a hit man to whom she

aid something like $30,000. And the police had never
ound any such sum in any of Eric's bank accounts because
 had gone to the real killer.

Nanette called Eric from jail in April 1995 "to bail her
s out," he said, but he knew "zero" details about her em-
zzlement charges. After the police told him about the
eft and forgery allegations, and that she'd had a sexual re-
tionship with Bill, he confronted her.

"Is what they're saying about you and Bill true?" he asked
r. "Because if it is, they have every right to look at me."

But she claimed it was all a big mistake. "She looked me
raight in the face and said, 'No,'" he said.

Eric said he guessed the killer's identity after the fact and
vent to the people responsible. They couldn't *not* admit it.
 had proof."

But he said he hadn't told anyone until now because the
ller had threatened him: "If I hear that you're talking . . .
· doing anything like that, there's going to be problems, a
t of problems." And because of this, Eric was scared for
s family's safety.

"That killer is out there," he said. "I can solve the crime.
m the only guy who knows the truth."

He told me he'd started having trust problems with
anette in October 1994, so he asked a buddy to trail her,
d that's how Bill's license plate number ended up in his
otebook. (This was a very different story from what he'd
iginally told police, which was that he'd gotten the number
ter Bill's murder because he was trying to determine if his
rl was in danger.)

I listened, thinking that much of what he said was ques-
onable "woe-is-me" stuff. When he finally let me get a
ord in, I asked him, if his story was true, then why not
·ing it up *before* his trial?

Eric told me his attorneys knew all about the hit man

story, but they didn't bring it up in court because they didn think the prosecution had enough evidence to convict him As a result, they decided to go "straight for the win. The didn't tell me because I never would have agreed."

Eric said his attorneys also wouldn't let him testify, an "I blew it by not forcing the issue."

So, I asked, if he knew that Nanette had hired a killer murder Bill, then why did he stay with her for months aft the murder, living with her on Seashore Drive in Newpo Beach and later that summer on Foxhollow in Dove Canyor

Despite what came out at his trial, he still claimed h really wasn't *with* her all that time.

"I didn't want nothing to do with that fucking girl aft I found out what happened," he said.

But what about the photo the police took of his Pathfind parked at the Dove Canyon house? I asked.

That didn't mean he was living there, he said. He cam back to town to pick up the car in September 1995.

"I was never going to live there," he said. "I'm the on who called the guy in Lake Forest to tell him we weren taking the house." (Eric did call the owner, but he said th he and Nanette still wanted to buy the house. They ju couldn't do it until after the controversy had died down.)

In spite of such indignation, I had to ask him half-a dozen times for details about the timing and reasons fo his breakup with Nanette. Eric repeatedly tried to evade th question, then, as if I were his confidante, he acknowledge that it took him a while to pull away.

"You keep your friends close and your enemies closer he said.

At one point, he told me that he and Nanette weren't to gether again after he left to train for the June 1995 seaso Then a few minutes later, he acknowledged that he went visit her at the "farm." I found out later that the six month

he served at that detention facility didn't even start until
May 1996 or I would have asked him to clarify that.

Still trying to keep his ego in tact, Eric claimed he was
the one "who broke it off, not Nanette. She wanted me to *be*
with her. She wanted the relationship to continue."

I told him I'd be back to talk some more after Nanette's
trial.

# CHAPTER 43

On the morning of January 9, 2012, when opening statements were set to start in Nanette Packard's trial, there was a full moon in the cobalt blue sky, which slowly lightened as the sun rose over Santa Ana.

Outside the courthouse, several satellite trucks from Orange and Los Angeles Counties were parked along the street for this high-profile media event, which was also being covered by *Dateline* and *48 Hours*. The coverage proved that a greedy and diabolical woman charged with murder was considered just as, if not more, interesting to the American public than an NFL-playing pseudocelebrity such as Eric Naposki.

True to form, Nanette's appearance had changed dramatically since she'd gone to jail two and a half years earlier, only this time it wasn't by choice. Her dyed and chemically straightened blond hair had grown out and was now back to its natural state: long, very dark, and wavy to the point of frizz. She wore it pulled back tightly into a ponytail or braid, with a few blond skunk-stripe highlights. Her hairstyle, reminiscent of jailhouse gang fashion, exposed her thin face and reportedly cosmetically altered cheekbones.

Sitting behind the McLaughlin family were Nanette'

ather and stepmother, Nanette's daughter Lishele and her
usband Shawn. Nanette's ex-husbands Billy McNeal and
. Ross Johnston were there too, but the bailiff ordered them
to leave the courtroom and said they couldn't come back
until the closing arguments. Nanette had made sure of that.

Her attorney, Mick Hill, followed them into the hallway
to explain. "She's making it a point that you and K. Ross
aren't in there for the opening or for the trial," he told Billy.
Hill added that because they were prosecution witnesses,
Nanette didn't want them to be present while the other witnesses were testifying.

Knowing how vindictive Nanette was, Billy wasn't surprised. He also didn't mind, though, because he hadn't
planned to come back until the closings anyway, when the
whole case would be summarized. K. Ross, on the other
hand, was quite upset. He'd attended every day of Eric Naposki's trial as a walk-up to the main event, where the fate
of his children's mother would be decided.

"I can't believe this," K. Ross told Billy in their first
conversation ever, complaining that "his rights were being
violated" because he couldn't observe the proceedings.


Now that Nanette's accomplice had been found guilty,
the McLaughlin family and the prosecution team felt more
confident about their case, knowing that much of the same
evidence and witnesses had already persuaded the first jury.

This time, both sides gave their openings at the start.
Speaking to the primarily female jury, Murphy's two-hour
presentation not only incorporated many points from the
first trial, it was strikingly similar in some ways to the one
that Eric's defense team had delivered, alleging that Nanette
was the real culprit because she was the instigator behind
the murder.

Given that this was a conspiracy-to-murder case, some

of Murphy's job was already done. Judge Froeberg didn't prevent the jury from knowing that Eric had already been convicted, which likely bolstered the believability of Murphy's theory about how the murder went down.

Describing Eric Naposki's dire financial straits, Murphy called the defendant's "deadbeat dad status" a "milestone in fatherhood" that prevented him from getting a driver's license in Massachusetts. Nanette had no assets or income of her own either, he said. She owed Bill McLaughlin $35,000, and "she had no job, no profession, no college degree, no formalized skill set."

He said the owner of the hardware store where Eric had keys made just weeks before the murder would testify that he could tell from looking at the key the killer had left in the front door that it had most likely come from his high-quality key-cutting machine.

"He thinks he cut that key," Murphy said.

The prosecutor explained that the detectives drove from the soccer field to Eric's apartment and on to Balboa Coves in forty minutes, proving that Eric had a ten-minute window to commit the murder while Nanette hightailed it over to Crate & Barrel.

"Detectives have driven this route repeatedly," he said.

The evidence was going to show that "Eric Naposki was at [Nanette's] side every step of the way." She knew Bill would be home the night of the murder. She drove Eric toward the murder scene, where Eric got the key stuck in the front door. He fumbled around and dropped the other key, shot Bill, and walked across the bridge to work. Then, later in the evening, Nanette paged Eric as soon as the police left her at the beach house. She had him watch her kids the day after Bill's funeral, and she asked Eric to move into the house on Seashore Drive while she was in jail. Eric owned a Beretta F-series 9-mm gun, and used the same Hydra-Shok bullets in his Jennings .380 that the killer had used.

Eric had Bill's license plate number in his notebook. They both lied about guns. Eric prevented Kevin McLaughlin from trying to change the locks at the beach house. And Nanette sued the McLaughlin family for half the estate, the beach house, and a monthly stipend.

"I have every confidence you're going to hold this woman accountable for what she did and convict her for murder."


Mick Hill's opening statement included points from both the defense's and prosecution's cases from Eric's trial, but attempted to spin Nanette's behavior in a whole new way. Hill claimed that seventeen years of delayed prosecution and the loss or destruction of exculpatory evidence made it difficult for his client to get a fair trial. He also character-ized the NBPD detectives as aloof and incompetent.

The jury already knew Eric was responsible for pulling the trigger, he said, "the question is why." The evidence, he said, would show that Eric murdered Bill out of jealousy and greed, to eliminate the competition so he could have Nanette to himself.

"Nanette was not involved in this case, so why are we here?" he asked rhetorically. Because her ex-husband showed police the singles ad she placed to meet Bill McLaughlin, he said.

Nanette placed a great importance on money, he said. "She wants a rich man to take care of her. . . . She always had a lover on the side. Does that mean she's a killer? No." She would never murder Bill McLaughlin "for someone who had no money," because her MO was to have sex with men on the side.

Using Bill's money, she bought these men presents, took friends to concerts, and told everyone that she was success-ful, he said. She also adopted Bill's life story as her own.

But, he said, "she never, ever, ever leaves Mr. McLaughlin for all of these people," because he was worth more to her alive than dead.

Eric, on the other hand, was a deadbeat dad who wrote in his journal that his goal was to get out of his financial mess. He owed money to everybody and "he saw Nanette as this way to get out."

As Joseph Stoltman Jr. would testify, he said, Eric became suspicious of Nanette two months before the murder and wanted to hire him to tail her. But instead, Eric asked Todd Calder to do the job, which is how he got Bill's license plate number in his notebook.

It was Eric, not Nanette, who made copies of the keys, he said, and one of them jammed in the lock. "She wouldn't give him a key that would jam," he said, and "the fact that he had a silencer made is indicative that he was planning something."

"We know that Eric did the planning and the murder on his own," Hill said, adding that he even "boasted about the murder to Suzanne Cogar."

And it was Eric, not Nanette, who knew that the gun used to kill Bill was a nine-millimeter. He changed his story to incorporate the Denny's call at 8:52 P.M. and said he had the phone bill. But "the bill never surfaces . . . and that's because he never made that call."

At that point, Hill switched gears to focus on his client, acknowleding that she was a "horrible person." But at the same time, he said, she was also a "loving mother," a school volunteer, and a soccer mom.

"She was really engaged in her children's lives . . . and she wanted the best for them."

Because money was her primary motivator, he said, she wasn't "going to kill the golden goose to be with the pauper."

She would not have done this to her kids," certainly not two weeks before the Christmas gift-giving season.

From there, Hill explained the importance of Bill's lawsuit with Jacob Horowitz: Nanette knew that Bill had finally won the protracted legal battle and was about to get $10 million more in the coming months, one more reason to keep him around.

Nanette wrote the $250,000 check while she was on a spending spree, he said, but "the fact that she files a palimony suit is far more indicative of her *not* being involved in the murder than of her being involved in the murder," because ending up with a $220,000 settlement would not be anywhere as lucrative as that $10 million.

Eric did this murder, he said, but he did it on his own. "You're going to realize she has her perfect life."

As the prosecution witnesses discussed Nanette's lies, the defense piled on during cross-examination until the extent of her general bad behavior was cumulatively astounding. The heartbreaking testimony of her first and third ex-husbands, who clearly had once loved her dearly, showed how incredibly skilled she'd been at seducing and manipulating men into giving her more love *and* money than most people see in a lifetime. And yet, here she was, indigent enough to qualify for a public defender, with nothing to show for her years of deceit.

Nanette scribbled furious notes, which she showed to her attorney. This trial moved much more quickly than the first one, because Hill didn't spend anywhere near as much time as Angelo MacDonald cross-examining witnesses. But in a strategy that baffled some observers, Hill, nicknamed "Columbo" by Judge Froeberg, brought out more of her scheming and nasty behavior than the prosecutor.

Hill admitted at the start that he was going to spend a lot of time showing what a bad person Nanette was, but that didn't make her a killer. Yet, as he continued to highlight his client's negative traits, his claims that she was a good and loving mother—with a pattern of cheating on Bill but never leaving him—left virtually no room for sympathy.

"Did Nanette have expensive tastes?" Hill asked for the zillionth time, prompting annoyed utterances from one of Bill's friends who had been watching every day.

"Yes," K. Ross Johnston replied.

"You kept a pretty thick file on Nanette?"

"Very," K. Ross said. "My son is twenty-six."

"She burned you numerous times. Would that be fair to say?"

"I wouldn't say it's all of them, just the ones I know of," K. Ross said, referring to her affairs.

"Do you think she's motivated by money?"

"Yes, that's a fair statement."

Turning K. Ross's testimony his own way, Matt Murphy got him to say that even though Nanette followed a general pattern with her lovers, she broke it with Eric. And that although Nanette went on cruises and skiing with other men, to K. Ross's knowledge, Eric was the only one she introduced to her family.

Reminding the jury that Nanette had asked K. Ross not to tell police that Eric was with her at the game, Murphy asked, "Are you telling the truth about that?"

"Absolutely," K. Ross said.


On the morning of day three, Murphy was about to play one of Eric's interviews with police when Mick Hill renewed his motion to keep the jury from hearing it. Judge Froeberg had already denied the request once, ruling that Eric was a co-conspirator, but Hill contended that Murphy still "has failed to present any evidence there was a conspiracy."

The judge disagreed. While the jury was absent, Froeberg recited a compelling list of points and evidence that bolstered the prosecution's conspiracy theory, signaling that he appreciated the merits of Murphy's case:

1) The boot salesman had testified that when Nanette bought lizard skin boots she said they were for her boyfriend who played in the NFL.
2) Eric called Jason Gendron and threatened him, trying to get the Cadillac back for Nanette.
3) K. Ross Johnston testified that Eric and Nanette said Eric had to leave the soccer game because he had an appointment at eight o'clock. Then Nanette asked K. Ross not to tell police Eric was at the game.
4) Sharon Hedberg, the real estate agent, said Eric and Nanette had been shopping for a home in July 1994, but they couldn't purchase it until the next spring.
5) Brian Ringler, Bill's accountant, detailed all the sums of money that Nanette had misappropriated.
6) And Detective Voth had talked about the keys the killer had left in the door and on the doormat, noting that Nanette didn't have one for the pedestrian-access gate on her key chain.

Hill tried to argue one last time. "I don't believe any of that evidence is indicative of a conspiracy at all," he retorted. Insisting that Murphy's theory was "innuendo" and "stretched" at best, he said that allowing the jury to hear Eric's interview would be prejudicial for his client because Hill couldn't cross-examine Eric.

Murphy disagreed. "Every single one of those things [the judge listed] independently is enough to introduce Mr Naposki's [statements]," he said.

Froeberg sided with Murphy again, and the jury heard the tape.

Knowing he was about to testify, Nanette's third husband, Billy McNeal, stopped in the bathroom, where, to his discomfort, he ran into Nanette's father. Billy hadn't talked to the Maneckshaw family since the summer before her arrest in 2009, and yet her father acted as if no time had passed. It was almost as if they were running into each other at the grocery store.

"Hey, Billy," Adi Maneckshaw said in a friendly voice.

Billy politely returned the salutation, but he had no interest in prolonging the conversation. "Hey," he said, then proceeded with his business, thinking, *Dude, you're crazy, man.*

Putting the awkward encounter behind him, Billy walked with confidence to the witness stand, where he sat down and stared at Nanette, giving her the "dead eye." This silent confrontation sent the typically unemotional and expressionless defendant into an instant fury.

"Fucking bastard," she said loud enough for Billy—and presumably the jury—to hear.

Billy watched her seethe as Mick Hill scolded her for the outburst. Billy then turned to the jury box to see if any of them noticed the exchange. He was shocked to see how little self-restraint Nanette had when it counted the most.

Anxious because there was so much he wanted to say, Billy hoped to demolish her with his testimony. Therefore, he was a bit disappointed that Murphy didn't probe any deeper than the quick, straightforward questions about the lies she'd told and how much money she'd made Billy spend n her. It seemed like Murphy had "left a lot of artillery in he gun."

Under cross-examination, however, Billy was pleased to see that Mick "did all of Matt's work for him," and was equally pleased when this "opened up a whole can of worms."

"It totally backfired [for the defense]," he recalled. "Matt s taking notes, waiting for Mick to finish," then the prosecutor stood up and piled on some more.

By the time Billy got off the stand, he felt good. Unburdened. "I was pretty pumped up," he said.

Contrary to the defense's point of view, Billy said later, he didn't think Nanette was a great mother, because she had two small children who could have lost their mother to prison if she'd been convicted of Bill McLaughlin's murder in the 1990s.

And yet, he said, "she made that horrible decision two more times with Jaycie and Cruz, bringing in two more children, knowing there was a possibility that she could leave them motherless, and leave the fathers fending as single parents, and that the children and the fathers and the McLaughlins didn't have a choice in the matter. None of us had a choice."

# CHAPTER 44

Once the defense presented its case, Nanette's attorney only put on a few character witnesses, including Bill's housekeeper, Mary Berg; Nanette's second husband, John Packard; and her older daughter, Lishele, who was several months pregnant. In total, defense witness testimony lasted about an hour and twenty minutes.

During his brief time on the stand, John Packard looked entirely annoyed and uncomfortable, responding with the shortest answers possible.

"I thought it was very odd that he acted that way," Detective Tom Voth said later. "Maybe because he didn't want to say anything bad. . . . It just seemed like it was just an imposition for him to be there."

Voth was also surprised that K. Ross had been less forthcoming as a prosecution witness. In fact, Voth thought K. Ross even seemed to downplay Nanette's behavior, a marked contrast to their many conversations in the early years.

"I was still getting calls from him five or six years" after the murder, Voth said.

\* \* \*

Lishele teared up during her brief time on the stand. Although she tried to describe Nanette's maternal traits in glowing terms, she still managed to paint her mother in a bad light as she recounted the story of Jaycie's fashion show and talked nostalgically about Nanette's enormous collection of sparkly clothes and shoes. Even so, Lishele's testimony was the *only* time during the entire investigation and trial that Voth saw Nanette soften and look at all emotional.

As the months after the arrest went by, Nanette's house in Ladera Ranch went into default and then foreclosure. When friends from church came over to help Lishele box up Nanette's designer wear, Lishele testified it took them two days to fill twenty or thirty boxes. She thought they'd finished—until she looked in the closet.

"It didn't even look touched," she said.

Lishele said she didn't really think of Nanette as her mother.

"She's always been my best friend. If we were ever upset, we'd go shopping. . . . We called it 'retail therapy.' Some people turn to drugs. We shop."

Lishele had a dance recital the night her mother was arrested in 2009. When Nanette didn't show up, her daughter knew something was wrong. Nanette had never missed any of her performances.

After Nanette went to jail in the 1990s, Lishele said, she and her brother, Kristofer, went to live with K. Ross and Julia. She said she still remembered how K. Ross took away the photo album of Bill McLaughlin that Nanette had made for them, and she never saw it again.

Lishele said disapprovingly that she'd always thought her father and his wife had "a disturbing obsession" with Nanette, the way they helped police and spoke so ill of her on *Hard Copy*. It upset Lishele to talk about the case, and she wasn't happy with her father for "kind of, like, airing it to everyone."

"I think he wanted people not to like her," she said.

Earlier in the trial, I'd asked Lishele if she would agree to an interview for this book, even if she wanted to say only positive things about her mother.

"I'll pray on it," she said.

Ultimately she didn't grant an interview, and K. Ross didn't want to either, for fear of further upsetting his daughter.

# CHAPTER 45

Just before the closing arguments began that afternoon, Judge Froeberg announced that the court was entitled to take "judicial notice" of certain facts, which the jury could consider as evidence in this case.

On March 22, 1996, Nanette Johnston pleaded guilty to one count each of theft and forgery, the judge said. She'd signed the plea agreement and declared under the penalty of perjury that everything in it was "true and correct," specifically that on December 14, 1994, *[she] forged another name on a $250,000 check with the intent to pass the check and defraud.*

The statement certainly didn't set a hopeful tone for Nanette's future. To say she seemed doomed was no understatement.

Saying he'd been waiting four years for this day, Murphy started his closing with one of his favorite analogies: one ingredient alone does not make a chicken salad, just as one piece of evidence alone does not make a guilty verdict.

"It's when you consider every piece of evidence in light of every other piece of evidence," he said.

Pointing out that Hill had elicited more witness testimony about Nanette's bad behavior than he had, he tossed aside the defense's entire case—that she was a bad person but a great mother and not a killer—with one swoop.

"To a very large extent, I don't care," he said. "I'm not asking you to convict her because she's a bad person . . . [or if she's promiscuous, because she is. . . . I'm asking you to convict her because she's a murderer.

"That woman is responsible for the murder of Bill McLaughlin," he said, pointing at Nanette. "She could be Mother Teresa or Adolf Hitler, I don't care. The question is did she aid and abet Eric Naposki in this murder?"

Murphy also dismissed Hill's strategy—to try to cheapen Nanette's relationship with Eric, to make it seem that she didn't care about him enough to leave Bill. "Unfortunately, the evidence doesn't bear out his theory," he said.

"That woman," as he continued to call her, had more than just the $1 million life insurance "chump change" payout coming to her once Bill was dead, because he'd made her a trustee to his estate.

"People have killed other people for a lot less," he said, noting that she'd purposely set up the Krishel corporation to launder "large amounts of stolen money," as evidenced by the $250,000 forged check, most of which she deposited into the newly formed corporate account in January 1995.

"How do you get the man you really want and keep the money you so dearly love? There's only one way to do that. Hope that Bill McLaughlin gets struck by lightning—or you kill him." How else, he asked, could Nanette think she could get away with marrying Bill when she'd introduced Eric as her boyfriend at her sister's wedding in November?

"She knows Bill McLaughlin is going to die," he said.

Bill treated Nanette well, Murphy said. "He was a good

man. Just like Jenny and Kim, just like Kevin. She used him. She took him for everything he was worth, and then when he wasn't good enough, she murdered him with Eric Naposki. . . . They were together in the murder. Now, that woman is responsible for that man's death, no matter how you look at this. . . . You have the opportunity to make it right."

That evening, John Packard brought Jaycie to dinner at California Pizza Kitchen, along with Lishele and her husband, Nanette's father and stepmother, and one of Nanette's friends, who had come to both trials. Just like Nanette had looked the night before Bill's memorial service, these people sat and chatted with each other as if it were any random evening out for pizza. If you hadn't known they'd spent the entire day at a murder trial for the woman who connected them all, you never would have guessed.

It was, in a word, surreal to sit right next to them. Thankfully, they didn't even notice me.

The next morning, Mick Hill, wearing a dark suit and a serious expression, began his closing argument by contending that this was actually an "anticonspiracy" case.

Nanette and Eric did nothing to hide that they were a couple, he said. They showed up at the soccer game together in front of fifty or sixty people. They went shopping at the mall, and they flew to San Francisco.

"A conspiracy, by definition, is something secret," he said.

But there were no witnesses, no incriminating statements, and no real evidence that Nanette was the killer, he said, and no witnesses who could testify that she didn't drop Eric at his apartment before going shopping at the mall.

"Not a single witness who ever saw or heard her and Eric Naposki conspire in any way."

Hill criticized the NBPD for its "disgraceful lack of effort," and for not gathering important evidence during the 1990s, such as videotapes from security cameras at the mall, which could have proven that Nanette was telling the truth about where she was at the time of the murder, show how long she'd been shopping, and illustrate whether she'd acted anxious or upset.

Because now that seventeen years had passed, that evidence had been destroyed, which meant that he couldn't prove where his client was or show her state of mind. "That is incredibly important."

The NBPD also never interviewed Eric's previous wives, such as the one who filed a restraining order against him, to flesh out his history of aggressive behavior, he said.

But after countless hours of more recent investigation, Hill said, he and his staff found evidence that Nanette didn't do the crime. She started spending money after Bill was killed, he argued, because she simply panicked that her money stream was going to get cut off.

"Eric Naposki acted by himself," he said.

Eric was the one who saw Nanette as the golden goose. Hill maintained that Nanette had no intention of marrying him, "because Eric is a deadbeat loser, pauper," and her pattern was to lie, cheat, and steal, but never to leave Bill.

Eric was the one fired because of his bad temper, the one using steroids, and the one making threats, such as "I'm going to get that guy. I'm going to blow up his plane." And he was the one cursing angrily at police and engaging in countersurveillance tactics. Not Nanette.

"Bill was worth more to Nanette alive than he was dead," he said. "Hate her as much as you want for being a thief, a liar, and a cheat, slut—whatever you want—but you can't vote guilty based on that."

As a father who had coached his daughter's soccer team for eight years, Hill couldn't see Nanette and Eric screaming at the sidelines and thinking, "We'd better leave soon. . . . We've got to kill a guy," he said, tapping his watch to illustrate. "It just doesn't make sense."

Then, in a blustery and self-congratulatory epiphany, Hill told the jury that he'd just discovered a huge detail that the prosecution had overlooked: The key left on the doormat was not stamped "do not duplicate." Therefore, it couldn't have been Nanette's.

At this point, some observers were confused about why this was such an important detail for the defense, just as they were about earlier explanations of how and why only certain keys in evidence were stamped, and by whom. However, Hill made it sound as if he was sure this "new" information was going to shed some light on all of that—and also win the case for Nanette.

While Hill went on with his argument, Murphy sat at the prosecution table, shaking his head as Hill told the jury that the prosecutor had been wrong all along.

Because "if she's part of a conspiracy, she's going to give [Eric] keys that work," Hill said.

His voice dripping with drama as he held up the key in its evidence envelope, Hill walked over to Murphy, looking him in the eye, and said, "How did she have a key that says 'do not duplicate,' but the killer didn't?"

Matt Murphy practically leapt out of his chair to respond in his rebuttal argument, quickly pointing out the defense attorney's fatal gaffe, which, ironically, was to claim that he'd caught the prosecution in a mistake.

Noting that this was his 114th trial, he said, "I've never heard a defense attorney invent his own Perry Mason moment, but that's what he just did. . . . It's extraordinary."

Hill may have just learned that the key didn't say "do not duplicate," Murphy said, but the prosecution team had known that since they started looking at the case again four years ago. "That's never been an issue."

Everyone in the McLaughlin household had a key to the pedestrian-access gate, because no one wanted to walk all the way down to the main entrance to get to the peninsula, or to use the jogging path, especially Nanette, an avid Rollerblader, whose key chain was missing one of those keys, he said.

"She can shake her head all she wants," Murphy said, his arms crossed and his dander up as he called attention to the defendant's gestures at the defense table as she tried to negate what he was saying. "I'm so fired up. I don't want to put in my PowerPoint yet."

Claim by claim, Murphy rebutted each explanation Hill had given for Nanette's lack of involvement in the murder. Murphy also defended the NBPD, mistakes and all, saying that Hill wanted the jury to believe that the detectives did a "sloppy job" because they didn't interview all the kids on Kristofer's soccer team.

"It's a dumb argument, and I ask you, don't buy it," he said, adding that the NBPD was one of the finest law enforcement agencies in Orange County, which showed "no ego . . . no politics, zero," when it asked DA Investigator Larry Montgomery to pick up this cold case and reexamine it.

Hill was wrong when he said all the pertinent records had been destroyed and that this had prevented him from building a proper defense, Murphy said. The records from the bank, mobile and home phones, beach house, and bank account had all been presented in court, so the only missing records were those from Eric's alleged alibi call from the Denny's pay phone.

"So, for the purpose of assessing *her* guilt, what is the point?" Murphy asked.

Although Murphy noted that Hill kept saying, "I know where my client was at the time of the murder," Murphy argued that point was irrelevant, because "she's not the shooter. We know she's not the shooter. Eric Naposki was the shooter."

Mocking Hill's "anticonspiracy" claim that Nanette wouldn't have tried to call attention to herself, Murphy said, "Hey, if they committed a murder, and then they're stupid about it, then that means they couldn't have done it. Gang members all over California will be relieved about that."

Murphy said he also didn't understand the logic behind the defense that Nanette was a good mother, "ergo not the killer."

"She's not 'Mother of the Year,'" he said, noting that she taught her eight-year-old girl how to scam money out of their neighbors and then lie about it.

Hill had also made a huge deal out of the soccer game, Murphy said, but the defense attorney didn't address one important point. Why were Nanette and Eric in such a rush to leave the field, even before the medal ceremony?

"There's a closing window of time," Murphy said, answering the question. "Eric has got to get in there while Kevin is at his AA meeting."

Murphy pushed to the inevitable finish, turning up the volume of emotion by playing the excruciating 911 tape once more, reminding the jury of who the real victims were here. As it played, Kim McLaughlin bent over in her chair, resting her forehead against the seat in front of her, and put her fingers in her ears. Her foot shook as Kevin's voice sounded throughout the courtroom.

"That's what we're doing here. This is real. This woman put that together," he declared, pointing at Nanette once again. "This woman is responsible for that moment, sure as I'm standing here right now. The evidence is all there."

By this time, Kim was crying and trembling in the

gallery as her husband kept his arm tightly and lovingly
wrapped around her.

"I'm going to ask you from my heart," Murphy told the
jury. "You take care of business. You do what needs to be
done and hold that woman accountable for what she's done."

Kim dabbed the tears from her eyes with a tissue her
husband had handed her. Jenny wiped her eyes and nose
as well, but she was smiling. Murphy's closing was palpa-
bly painful for the family to hear, but they seemed to know
that it would help the jury come to the right decision when
they saw how much Nanette's actions had hurt them.

The jury filed into the deliberation room at 2:42 P.M., and
took a break after only fifteen minutes. The panel resumed
talks until four-thirty that afternoon, and was back at it at
nine-ten the next morning.

At 9:33 A.M., the jury issued two requests, one for some of
K. Ross's testimony to be read back, and two for a search
through the trial record for any mention—outside of the closing arguments—of the words "duplicate" or "duplication."

After a search by the clerk, at 11:07 A.M., the jury was
told the words were not mentioned, and neither was the
phrase "do not copy." Ten minutes later, the jury announced
it had reached a verdict, after barely three and a half hours
of deliberations, most of which seemed to be spent waiting
to confirm Murphy's rebuttal argument that Hill's "key
moment" was nothing but theatrics.

Calls went out right away to alert the attorneys, the
families of the victim and defendant, and the media that the
verdict was in.

Donna Hakala, the sister of Bill McLaughlin's college
buddy Don Kalal, had attended many days of both trials

as had her brother. After getting a call from him at 12:45 P.M., she rushed as fast as she could to get to the courtroom on the wet roads, which were clogged with lunchtime traffic. It does rain in Southern California, but not often enough for the locals to get used to driving in it.

The courtroom was packed. Nanette's daughter Lishele, who was three months pregnant, had told a McLaughlin family member that she didn't want to attend the entire trial for fear of traumatizing her baby. But she was there that day, bracing herself for the outcome. Her father, K. Ross Johnston, and her most recent stepfather, Billy McNeal, were also there, waiting to see justice served on the woman who had lied to and taken advantage of both of them.

At 1:41 P.M., the judge signaled for the jurors to come in. Their faces somber, they walked single file into the jury box.

As the clerk read the guilty verdict and confirmed the finding of the special circumstance of murder for financial gain, Nanette sat stoic, motionless, and silent, staring straight ahead as her attorney put his arm around her to offer comfort.

Reminiscent of Bill's funeral, Lishele was the one who broke down sobbing as the reality struck her.

"It's just a hard thing for her to take," Hakala speculated. "The sadness is that all these things were in the paper. Maybe it was the best thing for this young girl. . . . She will not be a mother like her mother was."

Judge Froeberg announced that Nanette would be sentenced on May 18. Lishele left before the jury was dismissed.

Matt Murphy had done it again, raising his extraordinary homicide trial stats to 39 and 0.

The judge, who was smiling ear to ear, told the jurors they'd made a good intellectual and conscientious decision. He ordered them not to talk to any media for profit for ninety days.

Jenny and Kim, crying happy tears, thanked Murphy. Kim hugged Billy, who had brought his fiancée. Then she hugged K. Ross as well.


Billy McNeal felt relieved that the whole ordeal was over, and that he wouldn't have to fight this vengeful woman for custody of his son. He'd had a tiny concern that the jury wouldn't convict her, but as soon as he learned that the panel had deliberated for such a short time, he knew she was going down.

He also felt grateful for the opportunity to get a fresh start, and "to be happy again, not to have that dark cloud hanging over [me] . . . thankful that God had given me the strength to get through the whole thing and keep my wits."

And he was pleased to see the McLaughlins get the satisfaction and closure they deserved. Here he'd been complaining about going through his own nightmare for two years, he said, when they'd been suffering for more than seventeen.

"I couldn't imagine," he said. "I was glad for them. Good people."

The one lesson he'd learned from all this: Trust your gut. If your significant other tells you something that doesn't sound quite right, or conflicts with something he or she said before, confront that person about your doubts.

Looking back, he said, he'd felt such twinges many times, but he'd never pursued them because they'd never seemed important enough to start an argument. But even if he had, he still couldn't be sure it would have changed anything, because Nanette was such a good liar. He figured that her siblings had never exposed her because they didn't want to deal with any more conflict after what they'd been through with their mother and stepfather.

"They were afraid of [Nanette]," he said. "All the har

imes they'd had with the family, the last thing they wanted
vas to stir up the past . . . so they were all paddling the same
oat. And I think Kris and Lishele didn't want to bring up
he past. They were afraid [too, and were probably think-
ng,] 'I'm not going to rat my mom out.'"

The jury requested a special elevator to get downstairs
nd safely away from the reporters, who were gathered on
he second floor, where news conferences were held.

In front of a dozen news cameras, Matt Murphy, Tom
oth, and Larry Montgomery stood with the McLaughlin
isters, as the winning prosecutor described how Nanette
ad blown through all kinds of money after Bill's death,
hen had the gall to sue his family for more. And today that
noney was all gone.

Kim and Jenny thanked the police, Murphy's team, and
he jury, saying that the system had worked. They felt as if
heir father had been at the proceedings in spirit.

"He was a wonderful man, who was always loving his
amily . . . and caring for his family tremendously," Hakala
emarked later, noting that the verdict must have lifted a
uge burden from Bill's daughters.

"It was a lot of peace" for the family, she said, adding
hat at the same time "our hearts went out to Nanette's
aughter, who was pregnant. . . . You can't understand the
amage this woman [Nanette] has done."

That evening, the McLaughlin family and friends, detec-
ves, and the prosecution team celebrated a victory long in
oming at the Yard House on Fashion Island, where Kim
xpressed her gratitude to everyone once again.

The next day, on January 24, a family court judge con-
irmed the custody award of Cruz to Billy McNeal, stating

that Nanette "shall have no contact with the parties' son, unless specifically provided by court order."

The judge ordered Nanette to repay Billy the $5,000 he'd paid to attorney Al Stokke, as well as the $24,290 partial payment he'd made to cover Nanette's obligation of the $150,000 loan. The judge also said that neither party had to pay spousal support. Ever.

# CHAPTER 46

On March 23, 2012, Larry Montgomery finally received the "package" of information from Eric for which he'd been waiting since their first meeting in September 2011. Eric had also promised to send over his "notes" after their subsequent meeting.

If Eric really was telling the truth that he was innocent, was the DA investigator's job to make sure the prosecution didn't send an innocent man to prison. But try as he might, Montgomery just couldn't find any truth to Eric's story.

It was highly unusual for a convicted man to come up with a story like this *after* his trial, but as Montgomery wrote in a letter to the defense's private investigator, Tom Gleim, he'd still *[put in] months of time, effort and investigation into trying to determine if Naposki's "new" story is inconsistent with innocence and [Gonzales's] guilt.*

Montgomery told Gleim that he'd gone through Eric's police interviews and reviewed all his past actions, *considering the totally __different mindset__ he would have if his new story is true.* Bottom line was that Montgomery had found

nothing that made Eric look innocent, but he had *found eve*
*__more__ things that are consistent with his guilt.*

On April 23, Montgomery completed his report o
the information that Eric had provided in Septembe
Two days later, Gleim delivered yet another package fro
Eric, but the new information didn't change Montgomery
viewpoint—or Matt Murphy's—one iota.

# CHAPTER 47

My second interview with Eric Naposki lasted nearly five hours, in May 2012. This time, he was even more charming as he made self-deprecating jokes about the "pretty toupee" he'd worn in the 1990s.

Nanette never responded to the letter I sent before her sentencing in which I said I wanted to hear her side of the story. So much for her claim to want to tell everything when the case was "all over."

After being bombarded with Eric's explanations for "mistakes" in the prosecution's case, I walked out of the Theo Lacy Facility almost believing his story, which was exactly what Matt Murphy said he'd been worried would happen if Eric had testified: He sounded so confident and sure of himself, a juror just might believe him. I was also curious to read the thick stack of papers he kept holding against the glass during our lengthy interview.

Since his trial, Eric said, he'd gone through six thousand pages of discovery to which he hadn't had access before his trial, and that was why he'd taken so long to come out with his new version of what happened. And that, he said, was why he was now able to provide documentation for his

claim that Nanette had used Bill's own money to put a h
out on him.

Eric pointed to certain calls on her car phone bill, sayin
these showed she was making arrangements with th
guy in the final days before Bill's murder. He said he'd als
tabulated all the smaller amounts of money she'd take
throughout 1994 to come up with a payment of approx
mately $30,000 for the hit man.

"To hear Matt Murphy try and use the [SWAT] trainin
as a precursor for killing Bill with an unknown teachin
called 'double tapping' was one hundred percent absurd an
ridiculous," he said. "I never thought in my wildest dream
that my assistance in helping law enforcement would rend
me an expert assassin."

Holding a photo of his two younger children against th
glass, he told me, "I swear on my babies" that he was tellin
the truth.

This time, he told me the name of the "hit man": Jua
Gonzales, whose identity I'd already learned through oth
sources. Eric said he was going to announce it at his ne
court hearing.

He said he'd known Gonzales for about a year before th
murder, and they'd been putting together Midnight Moo
Productions with Nanette's help. While they were meetin
to talk business, Nanette brought up the story that Bill ha
raped her, and Gonzales offered his help.

"I've got people to handle rapists," Gonzales reported!
said.

"I'm not interested in help," Eric told Gonzales. "I'
fine. I'm handling it with Nanette."

Ultimately, he said, Gonzales went ahead on his ow
with Nanette, but it was over Eric's protests. Eric insiste
that he personally had nothing to do with the shooting.

"I don't know who [Juan] had shoot Bill, or if he did

imself. What I do know is it was sloppy and deliberate," e said.

Eric pointed to a statement from one of Bill's neighbors, ho told police that she'd seen "an expensive white-over-lack sports car parked just outside the gate" at Balboa oves the night of Bill's murder. Eric said the reflection of street light must have caused the car to look two-toned.

He then pointed to a police report that quoted a Thunder-rd valet saying that *"[a club employee] would sometimes rrive with Naposki in the Pathfinder, or, about the same me, in a 1989 or 1990 black BMW. . . . A male white, 25 yrs., '11", 200 lbs., full-face, with black hair."* Eric said this was onzales. (I subsequently checked with police, and Gonza-s was never an employee there.)

The details of Bill's alleged rape of Nanette had escalated nce our last interview. Looking back later, I wondered if e thought his earlier story about the "rape" hadn't been iocking or salacious enough to convince the prosecution am or the media, so he had to take it up a notch. The new etails were that Nanette had told him that Bill was a drinker ith sexual performance issues, and that he'd raped her with ie of his guns. (His attorney Angelo MacDonald later ld me that the gun-rape detail actually wasn't new; Eric id described this to him and Pohlson from the very begin-ng. But based on Eric's next statement to me, this seemed ore likely to be one of Nanette's concoctions.)

"There's a reason why Suzanne Cogar and I had that onversation," Eric said. "I had a reason to hate Bill. . . . Nanette's] intent was to incite me." (This is the same con-ersation that Eric had previously denied having with ogar.)

So, I asked, why not turn in Nanette during the police terview in Greenwich when he was arrested in 2009?

Eric said he kept quiet in that interview because he was

sure that Julian Bailey was "going to go down to the DA
office within twenty-four hours and get me out."

"Do you regret doing that now?" I asked.

"Do you think?" he replied facetiously. Then he quickl
went back to discounting the prosecution's allegations. Bu
"when you tell me something I know is wrong, you call m
a murderer . . . and I have proof that I'm innocent, I'm goin
to tell you to go fuck yourself."

I asked him about his steroid use, and he said he wasn
using them around the time of Bill's murder or anytime afte
college, for that matter. In a surreal but telling show of hi
personality, Eric smiled as he flexed his biceps for me, poin
ing out that even after three years in jail he was still ver
muscular. Swearing again on his children's lives, he saic
"I'm two hundred sixty pounds. I've got twenty-two-inc
arms. I don't need steroids. I'm just naturally a big guy."

I asked him what it was about Nanette that had draw
him and all these other men to her. He said she tended t
have "highly sexual relationships" that didn't last long
When he and Nanette were just friends, she used to tell hir
"about the size of a man's penis, if it was unusually large c
unusually small. You lie to the person you're with, bu
you're honest with your friends, because there's nothing a
stake. . . . She had no reason to lie to me."

Over time, they found they had a lot in common and de
cided to give dating a shot. "I didn't fall head over heels fc
Nanette," he said. "She grew on me and she was cool. . .
I loved her kids and that's how she gets you. . . . To me
Nanette was a single mom, just like my mom."

He said he loved Nanette's kids as well, and what the
did together typically revolved around Kristofer's games. "
had Lishele in my arms, my baby," he said. "She wrote m
a letter here that I was her favorite boyfriend that her mor
had. I loved that girl."

He showed me a photo of Nanette shooting a rifle at

arnival booth, with Kristofer's arm resting on Eric's back.
You can't make kids lie," he said. "Bill McLaughlin had to
now about me in some respects."

While he, Nanette, and her kids were on the East Coast
n November 1994, he said, they spent ten days together—
vith no mention of Bill. "She talked about how we were
oing to be a big, fat family and live in California, maybe
ne day move back."

He said he was shopping for rings around Christmas in
994, and also applied for a $10,000 loan. "Why would I
eed a loan for ten thousand dollars if I'm about to become
Mr. Rich' and my girlfriend has hundreds of thousands of
ollars in the bank? Isn't that silly?"

Yes, Eric Naposki was very convincing that day, so I
vaited to write these last chapters until I could do more
esearch and look deeper into his claims, just as Larry
Montgomery and the NBPD had.

But after I'd spent nearly two years going through all the
vidence and documentation myself, after I'd sat through
oth trials, interviewed witnesses, detectives, and the pros-
ution team, and after I'd compared the various versions of
ic's evolving story, I have to say that I, too, found a whole
t of discrepancies.

For me, the final point that really undermined Eric's
edibility was this: I checked the California secretary of
ate's website for Midnight Moon Productions and saw that
wasn't registered as an LLC until June 1995. The business
lan that police found on Nanette's computer during the
earch of her home in Dove Canyon, where Eric insisted
e wasn't living but his truck was parked, was dated August
4, 1995—eight months *after* the shooting. Even if he truly
vasn't living there, why would he go into business with
Nanette and a guy who he knew was a killer and had report-
dly threatened him? And, as Voth and Murphy had pointed
ut, why would a hit man need to borrow Eric's gun?

When I talked with Suzanne Cogar about Eric's lates[t] story, she summed it up like this: "He's throwing stuff o[n] the wall and seeing what sticks."

"My gut feeling is that he pulled the trigger," she said. "[I] guess it's the circumstantial evidence that convinces me[.] The fact that he worked close to Bill's house, the timelin[e] of him not having an airtight alibi, because I know how fas[t] you can get from that apartment to that part of town [i[n] Newport Beach]—ten minutes!"

After living in that same apartment complex in Tustin fo[r] six and a half years, she said, "I didn't drive it and time i[t] like the cops did, but at nine o'clock at night, traffic wasn'[t] an issue."

To this day, Murphy and investigators involved in thi[s] case remain quite confident that Eric was the shooter.

If you're going to get yourself an alibi during a murde[r]-for-hire, Murphy said, "You're going to be in Vegas, sippin[g] a piña colada with an Elvis impersonator—on video. That'[s] what somebody does when they get a hit man."

As an investigative journalist trained to be objective, I'[m] not here to make judgments, so I will let the readers weig[h] both sides for themselves. But facts don't lie. Killers do.

# CHAPTER 48

In the last days before the May sentencing date, Eric's attorneys decided they needed more time to work on their motion in light of the "new evidence" that Eric had brought forth about the hit man. Even so, the dynamic duo of Eric and Nanette were going to be in court together for the last time, a key draw for the media and other observers who were curious to see whether sparks would fly or knowing glances would be exchanged between them.

Fittingly, May 18 was a warm sunny day in Santa Ana. As Kim McLaughlin Bayless chatted with her father's college friends in the hallway outside the courtroom that morning, an expression of relief and anticipated closure played like soft light across her face. Now that the emotional heaviness caused by so many years of grief and frustration had been lifted from her petite shoulders, she walked with more bounce to her step. The pain of sitting through the trials had dissipated from her eyes.

"This is like icing on the cake for us," Kim said, smiling at Sandy Baumgardner and Sandy's father, Ken. "Gives us such hope, such inspiration," she added, explaining that the authorities never gave up on this case—a sharp contrast to the lack of justice that her brother received after the drunk driver hit Kevin on his skateboard all those years ago.

Hugging Adrianne Reynolds, the faithful juror from Eric's trial who had come to watch the proceedings, Kim said, "She gave five weeks of her life to us. We're grateful."

It was like a family reunion for Bill's daughters and his friends, the crew of detectives and prosecution team, all of whom had been waiting so long for this day to arrive— some for many more years than others. It was also a day of justice, serenity, and peace, of reminiscing about Bill McLaughlin, and of satisfaction knowing that his killers were finally going to get what was coming to them.

"I knew she wasn't who she said she was," Ken Baumgardner said of Nanette.

Tom Reynolds, Nanette's ex-boyfriend who had found her "Wealthy Men Only" singles ad while they were living together, came to watch as well. He wondered whether she would exhibit any emotional reaction.

"The 'Ice Queen' has got to melt sometime," he said.

Asked how Nanette had drawn in and manipulated him and the other men, he made an analogy to the recent bestselling erotic novel.

"You've heard of *Fifty Shades of Grey*? Well, this was *fifteen hundred*."

Inside, the courtroom filled with many of the same people who had attended the two trials, although this time Nanette's family was noticeably absent. The only recognizable supporter was a pretty friend named Laura, whose well-groomed hair had gone from light brown to red and now to highlighted blond during the course of the court proceedings.

The bailiff led a grim-faced, handcuffed Nanette to the corner of the jury box at the judge's right, where she sat with her back to the single TV pool camera behind her. The bailiffs seated her there to keep her separated from Eric, who, in previous courtroom appearances, had sat at the defense table in front of the judge.

Her hair was pulled back into a long ponytail. Her blond skunk stripe cut across her dark waves and her thin face looked even more drawn than before. Wearing a long-sleeved pale pink sweater over the same simple black dress she'd worn at trial, she kept her gaze trained straight ahead, where no one could look her in the eye.

Nanette had been so tight-lipped about her past that she'd even been unwilling to speak in her own defense to the probation officer who had prepared her sentencing report, which typically includes a social history and any abuse, criminal acts, and other personal details. She'd been so guarded that even her own attorney, Mick Hill, said he didn't know that much about her. Because this was not a death penalty case, he'd never had to research her family background or look for mitigating factors to try to save her life.

"Beyond her just growing up in Arizona, and then hooking up with K. Ross Johnston, I don't know anything," Hill said later, adding that he didn't think she had a very good relationship with her first husband.

Hill took the chair next to Nanette, which blocked even a side view of her from the gallery and made it just as difficult for the print photographer to get a decent shot of her face.

That's when the drama started.

\* \* \*

Eric had announced to his attorney, Gary Pohlson, that he didn't want to come out of the holding cell, knowing, perhaps, that no one was going to make him. If the judge granted more time for the due process motion, Eric wouldn't be sentenced that day. The attorneys filed into the judge's chamber, apparently to discuss how to handle this, given that Eric had a right to be present at the proceeding and to hear the discussion, which, at least theoretically, could affect his case.

When the group emerged from the powwow, Hill returned to his seat in the jury box. The bailiff opened a little wood-framed door that served as a window into the eight-foot-by-eight-foot holding cell, where defendants were kept until they were brought into the courtroom. Pohlson, who had been seated at the defense table, stood up so Nanette and her attorney could move and sit there. But when the head bailiff motioned to Nanette and Hill to sit at the table, they didn't budge. The bailiff punched in a code and opened the regular door to the holding cell, allowing Eric, who had no speaker or microphone in there, to hear the judge and vice versa.

"Mr. Naposki," Judge Froeberg said without looking in Eric's direction, "you don't want to be out here in court?"

"No, thank you, Your Honor," came a disembodied voice from the cell, from which Eric was unable to see into the courtroom, even with the window and door open.

"You have the right to," Froeberg said.

"No, thank you, Your Honor."

As Pohlson told the judge he needed more time to finish the new trial motion, the judge expressed his displeasure that they were ten months past Eric's conviction and yet the defense was still asking for another postponement. He said he wasn't inclined to give any additional delays, making this the last one he would grant. Eric's new sentencing date was set for three months out, on August 10.

Commenting on the "due process" portion of the motion, Murphy summed up the prosecution's position that the issues had already been adjudicated, the missing records for the alleged 8:52 P.M. call in particular. Eric had told police that Nanette had dropped him at his apartment and he'd then driven by Leonard Jomsky's house before making that call, a story that Murphy deemed physically impossible.

After hearing the evidence presented at both trials, Froeberg agreed, saying he was even "less convinced than ever that the receipt [for that phone call] ever existed," and that he believed his current reading of the situation only reinforced the accuracy of his original ruling, which was to deny Eric's due process motion. Froeberg also denied Nanette's motion for a new trial, which was based on similar grounds.

If Murphy couldn't force Eric to come out to face the family of the man he'd killed, allowing them to avoid making another set of victim impact statements down the road, then he was going to verbally skewer him for it. But by this point, one of the bailiffs, who had not been informed of the plan, had already returned Eric to the bus that would take him back to jail.

Murphy was left to state his thoughts about Eric for the record.

"Mr. Naposki is a coward . . . for not facing these people today to hear what they have to say," he said, summing up Eric's behavior as "a final blaze of no-class cowardice."

With that, Jenny McLaughlin began reading her statement, describing the scene she imagined in the kitchen the night her father's killer pointed a gun at him while he was helpless to defend himself. He must have felt sickened, shocked, and horrified, she said.

She talked about the sadness she'd felt being deprived of her father's presence at her wedding, how she'd cried through Kim's entire marriage ceremony as well, and that she was also sad that her husband had never gotten to meet her father.

"'I feel very grateful for having such a wonderful father in my life for as long as I did,'" she said. "'I wish he could have stayed with us longer and that God would have chosen his time to leave rather than a person with a gun and a greedy heart.'"

Then it was Kim's turn. Disappointed that Eric wouldn't hear the statements she'd prepared for him and Nanette, she walked to the podium, and edged it over to the right a few inches, trying to get to a vantage point—beyond the obstruction of Nanette's face by Hill's self-admittedly large head—where she could look directly into the eyes of the woman who had orchestrated her father's murder. But Nanette kept slinking behind Hill.

Kim started off by reading her take on a poem, "Imagine a Woman," originally written by Patricia Lynn Reilly. Kim had written Reilly for permission to use parts of the original, informed her that she was going to read it to her father's killers, and had even sent her a copy of it. Kim had written her own version about the positive qualities her father had instilled in her—qualities she felt that Nanette lacked entirely.

She aimed to make her words poignant and from the heart. But unsure of what Nanette would take in, she hoped that Nanette wouldn't just shut out her message. Kim and her sister ultimately decided that these statements were more important for them to deliver, regardless of Nanette's response, as a way of carrying out their father's legacy and of challenging Nanette to be "a woman of integrity."

The first line of her poem was this: *Imagine a woman who others aspire to be.*

What followed was a long list of this woman's good qualities, such as being compassionate and tenderhearted someone who told the truth and refused to surrender. Kim ended the poem by telling Nanette that this woman was everything Kim's father had taught her to be: *Everything you are not.*

The schoolteacher then launched into the vile and astounding "destructive trail of deceit" Nanette had left in her wake.

"'Your web of lies has caught up with you finally and your true nature has been revealed by this team of law enforcers,'" she said. "'Your trial revealed what an abomination your life has been. We are appalled and repulsed.'"

Kim said Nanette had no right to do this horrible deed to a man who had been so good to her for four long years—let alone do this to her own children, Lishele and Kristofer.

"'What a despicable, disgraceful disappointment you are to your family and the children you dared to bring into this world,'" Kim said. "'Your one life, Nanette Johnston Packard McNeal, has been a complete and utter waste.'"

While Kim was speaking, Nanette remained expressionless until Kim mentioned her children. Only then did Nanette shake her head in disagreement—a reaction that went largely unseen except by those sitting nearby at the prosecution table.

Kim concluded by saying that she hoped and prayed that while Nanette sat in prison for the rest of her life, she would eventually own up to her part in the murder of Bill McLaughlin.

The last of three speakers was Bill's friend Don Kalal. Reading a letter written by Bill's brother Patrick, who could not make it out from Chicago for the hearing, Kalal was the most overtly emotional. His voice cracked as he read the short missive, which labeled Nanette as "a true black widow" who had ruined the lives of everyone with whom she'd come into contact.

After the statements were done, the judge promptly sentenced Nanette to the expected LWOP term. Asked if she had any questions about appealing her case, Nanette said the only word she spoke the entire hearing: a soft-spoken "no."

Froeberg rose abruptly from his chair and walked out of the courtroom without saying another word. As the bailiff cuffed the disparaged femme fatale once more and led her back to the holding cell, her face remained blank and she looked at no one.


Downstairs on the second floor, a throng of cameras gathered for a news conference as Kim and Jenny rode down in the elevator with Gary Pohlson.

"My client is a jerk," he said to them apologetically.

Pohlson later acknowledged that he'd communicated that same sentiment to Eric.

"For him not to come out that first time during their victim witness statements was appalling to me, and I told him that," he said. "I like Eric Naposki, but I was embarrassed by some of the things he did at the end."

During the news conference, Murphy smiled as he made his typical cutting remarks, with Detective Tom Voth and DA Investigator Larry Montgomery on one side, and Jenny and Kim McLaughlin, who stood with their arms around each other, on the other.

Noting Nanette's haggard appearance, Murphy said, "Jail clearly hasn't been good to her. Today she got what she ultimately deserved."

Everyone agreed that the victim's family shouldn't have to make more than one set of victim impact statements, he said. Everyone except Eric Naposki, who was "afraid to come out of his cell and face these two women. He was a gigantic coward. . . . He threw his binky down today."

"He did it. He knows he did," Murphy said, and maybe that's why he didn't come out, because he had "some sense of shame."

Nanette was the most pretentious of nouveau riche defendants, he said, but now, instead of going to lavish salons to color her dark hair blond, she had to settle for the best of what the Orange County jail system had to offer. Nanette now had to stoop to getting "contraband dye for her hair and grind[ing] up magazines for her makeup."

"She leaves a trail of destruction and shattered lives everywhere she goes," Murphy said. "Today is the end of her rip-offs and con games."

Asked why Eric's sentencing was delayed, Murphy said Eric had blamed Jacob Horowitz, Kevin McLaughlin, Nanette Packard, and random drug dealers for the murder and now he was blaming someone else. The defense wanted more time to investigate those claims, which Murphy characterized as "story number five." But as far as he was concerned, he said, "none of it has borne any truth."

On June 18, 2012, Nanette Packard, inmate #WE4559, was sent to the Central California Women's Facility in Chowchilla, where she joined another murderess successfully prosecuted by Matt Murphy: Skylar Deleon's now ex-wife Jennifer, who goes by her maiden name, Henderson.

And in July, Billy McNeal married the woman he began dating after Nanette was in jail, a new law-abiding mother for his son, Cruz.

# CHAPTER 49

On August 10, 2012, the final chapter of this saga was set to take place, nearly eighteen years after the fatal shooting in Balboa Coves.

True to form, Eric was all hepped up for his sentencing hearing and unwilling to go to prison without a fight. Because the prosecution team hadn't believed him or found any substance to his newest story, Eric had alerted the media as he'd threatened, but that had done him no good either. He was still behind bars. Had he really thought the DA would drop the charges against him in the wake of a successful conviction?

Now that the main event—Nanette's sentencing—had passed, the throngs of McLaughlin family and friends coming to watch the proceedings had thinned out, as had the number of media outlets and detectives who had worked the case.

Kim McLaughlin Bayless and her husband sat with Jenny's longtime friends Krissy and Jason Gendron, along with the family's former housekeeper, Mary Berg, Bill's college friend Ken Baumgardner and his daughter, Sandy. Tom Voth and Larry Montgomery came as well, as did former juror Adrianne Reynolds. Jenny McLaughlin, who had been battling an illness, was too sick to attend.

None of Nanette's people or ex-husbands were there, and neither was John Pappalardo, Eric's lawyer friend. The only identifiable person there for him was his fiancée, Rosie Macaluso, whose face reflected the strain of fatigue and anxiety as she sat with defense attorneys Angelo MacDonald and Gary Pohlson.

Both networks had already run their episodes, but the *48 Hours* and *Dateline* producers were there to catch the last hearing for updated reruns in the future. Both producers had pregnant bellies, evidencing the passage of time since the trials, when they were both in court with flat stomachs.

When the *48 Hours* episode aired its second interview with Eric, the producers ran a tease by intimating that they would release the name of the alleged hit man. However, they ultimately chose not to mention it, presumably because the prosecution had dismissed the story as ridiculous.

Eric came out of the holding cell in a long-sleeved pink shirt and mouthed a greeting to Rosie in the gallery. After sitting down at the defense table, he smiled and nervously riffled through papers as he chatted with Pohlson.

The hearing started off as routine. MacDonald went over the high points of the defense motion to dismiss the guilty verdict and to ask for a new trial on the constitutional grounds of due process, jury misconduct, error of law, and prosecutorial misconduct, based on the "unnecessary and unjustified prosecution of Mr. Naposki."

Setting aside the verdict, he said, "would not be a popular thing to do . . . but it would be the just and right thing to do."

Judge Froeberg, noting that he'd already indicated he hadn't changed his mind about the due process motion, officially denied it.

"After reviewing the extensive testimony in this case, I

did not find anything—any evidence—presented at trial that would change the court's position," the judge said.

The defense's main issue dealt with the "phone call that was supposedly placed from the Denny's at eight fifty-two," he said. Siding with the prosecution, Froeberg said it was clear from the numerous time trials that it would have been "impossible" for Eric to have been dropped off at his apartment in Tustin, go by Leonard Jomsky's house, and then make the call from Denny's by 8:52 P.M. The jury didn't believe the claim, and neither did he.

"It defies logic," Froeberg said, adding that the only way the call could have been made was on Eric's way from the soccer field to Newport Beach.

Froeberg then listed the allegations in the motion and his corresponding responses:

Jury misconduct: Juror number one was reported to have said to another juror that Eric "creeps her out." When the judge questioned her about the comment, she said Eric was "too serious and should smile more." Froeberg stood by his decision to let her stay on the jury.

Prosecutorial misconduct: Murphy demonized the defendant as a bully and improperly called attention to MacDonald's being an out-of-towner from New York City, a dynamic to which the judge contributed. Froeberg countered that he was trying to "lessen the tension that was rampant in the courtroom," and dismissed the "us versus them" remarks by Murphy as pretty tame. The court and the prosecution "have said a lot worse things than that," he said, and they haven't been overturned.

Froeberg noted that Eric had filed a declaration stating that he was no longer in fear for his life and was now willing to name the contract killer who murdered Bill McLaughlin. The judge explained that the key requirement to grant a new trial motion was evidence that wasn't known *before* trial. He looked at this offer with suspicion because

Eric had provided so many variations of the truth during this case. Evidence supporting the claim that the NBPD had failed to follow leads had already been presented, he said, and "the jury was free to accept or reject that."

Was there sufficient evidence to support the guilty verdict? Yes, the judge said, and he wasn't going to go through the "mountain of circumstantial evidence" at the hearing, but in his view it was "overwhelming."

Then, in a highly unusual scene more reminiscent of a TV courtroom drama than a real-life hearing, the judge allowed Eric to make a statement. What was perhaps most surprising was that Froeberg let Eric vent without interruption, even as his voice grew louder and he admitted that he was getting angry. Froeberg also didn't stop him from making audible comments while the victim's friends and family read their statements into the record.

This was high courtroom drama at its best as Eric went on a freestyle rant, the back of his neck turning bright red like a thermometer, just as it had at the preliminary hearing in 2009. After complaining seventeen years earlier about the media cameras documenting the police's reputation-damaging allegations against him, Eric now appeared to be trying to use those same cameras for his own purposes.

He said he'd written a statement, but he had changed his mind at the last minute and decided to improvise. But, clearly, he'd been practicing this speech *for months*.

"What happened in this courtroom a year ago is about the worst thing the justice system can do," he began.

Referring to his inch-thick stack of papers, he proceeded to repeat many of the same points he'd made to me during our jailhouse interviews.

He admitted that he had lied and "made some bad decisions. Did I lie to protect myself, Nanette, her children, and my children? Yes, absolutely. But I won't sit here and be scapegoated," he said, proclaiming his innocence.

"Guilty by association, Your Honor, is not guilty. There's a big difference, Your Honor, between sleeping with someone and committing murder for them."

Although Nanette was the orchestrator and "catalyst" for this murder, he said, he wasn't the shooter.

"I was never, ever convinced by Nanette Johnston to commit a murder. . . . I did not do the crime and I will prove it," he said. (It was unclear, however, what more proof he thought he was going to get if this statement didn't work its magic to free him.)

He said he couldn't come forward with proof before his trial because he didn't have access to the discovery materials until afterward: "I didn't have that information until . . . when, Gary? . . . January."

Eric said he knew he was seventeen years late in admitting that it was the "hit man," Juan Gonzales, who had carried out the murder. "I apologize to the McLaughlins for that."

But blaming everyone but himself, Eric claimed that perpetuating this "scam"—i.e., labeling Eric as the shooter— was, in effect, "robbing the McLaughlins of the most important thing—[the ability] to solve the crime."

"It was a sloppy investigation, Your Honor," he said. "I'm innocent and that will never change. Those twelve people made a mistake."

Following up on Eric's indignant and righteous performance, Sandy Baumgardner led off the victim impact statements, responding to Eric's remarks as though she'd heard them in advance.

As she charged him with making "an absolute spectacle of himself" and touting the "flagrant lie" that Bill McLaughlin was a rapist, Eric smiled and shook his head.

"'Prosecutor Matt Murphy's numerous points on what an "innocent Eric Naposki" would have done seventeen years ago are now a matter of record,'" she said. "'What the now "guilty Eric Naposki" has done since his arrest in 2009 has been no better. His stories changed numerous times as he exhausted every possible avenue to avoid accountability. And even after the verdict last July, he continues to weave his tall tales of innocence.'

"'It's an established phenomenon that many a convicted murderer goes to his own grave feverishly denying his guilt, and Mr. Naposki is certainly no exception. His recent attempts to occlude the facts that led to his conviction last summer are absolutely ridiculous and frankly callous.'"

As the next speaker took to the podium, Eric toned down his facial expressions, stopped smirking, and looked down as Krissy Gendron, Jenny McLaughlin's childhood friend, read into the record the same statement that Jenny had read at Nanette's sentencing.

But Eric's behavior changed when Kim McLaughlin Bayless got up to read her statement, drawing attention to himself in a display that came off as disrespectful for the grief and loss the McLaughlin clan was still feeling, surely heightened even more now that Jenny was in ill health.

Just as Kim had done during Nanette's hearing, she turned the podium so she could look the convicted killer in the eye. But, unlike Nanette, Eric turned his chair toward her so he could meet her gaze from about ten feet away—and with bravado, no less. His apparent lack of humility and compassion came off as arrogance and insensitivity—the epitome of narcissism.

Kim started off by saying that it was important for Eric to hear how close she'd been with her father, and what a "very sweet friendship" they'd shared. They met on weekends, she said, and he brought her on business trips to train her how to sell his products.

As she continued, Eric shook his head and smiled again.

"'Eric,'" she said, "'you have no idea of the far-reaching devastating effects'" of this murder.

Speaking up for her brother Kevin, fingered by Eric's defense team as the likely killer of his own father, Kim's voice broke with emotion.

"'My dad's murder really messed with him. He was so angry and so frustrated. Kevin never got over the image of his dad lying on the kitchen floor, lying in a pool of blood in the house that we grew up in.'"

Kim said her family was grateful that Kevin was upstairs in his room at the time of the shooting, "'or we're sure you would have taken him from us as well.'"

As for the claim that Eric had never set foot in the house, she said, "'That's a lie.'"

"It's not a lie," Eric interjected. "Your father knows."

Crying now, Kim continued. Whatever the motive was for the murder—jealousy or anger or greed—she couldn't grasp it. But the one thing Eric couldn't take away from her and her family was the "intense" and "abundant amount of love" that Bill McLaughlin had given them, and the way he'd taught them to do random acts of kindness for others.

Eric looked away as Kim challenged him to honor Bill McLaughlin, the man he murdered, to change his "horrific ways" and to live by the same credo.


With that, Judge Froeberg pronounced the only sentencing option for Eric based on the charges and conviction before him: life without the possibility of parole for murder in the first degree with the special circumstance of financial gain, as well as the additional weapons charge, which added four more years.

After the bailiffs had cuffed Eric's hands behind his back, he stood up from the defense table and leaned his shaved head toward prosecutor Matt Murphy to deliver one last message.

"You blew it," Eric said. "You fucking blew it."

Murphy, who always enjoyed an opportunity to spar with a defendant, spoke right up. "Bye-bye," he said from his chair.

"I'll see you again," Eric fired back.

Afterward, spectators in the gallery shook their heads with disbelief. "The Eric Show" had been remarkable, even to the most veteran court watchers.

Murphy and Pohlson said later that they were shocked by Eric's behavior, and Pohlson was embarrassed, to boot. Neither attorney had ever seen a defendant challenge a victim's family member while he or she was reading a statement at sentencing.

"I did support Eric Naposki, but I did want him to have some class," Pohlson said. "No matter what happened, those people deserved the utmost respect."

Angelo MacDonald said he wasn't surprised, but "I was not happy about it. We repeatedly told him not to say things, not to react." But in this case, "I think [Eric] felt he needed to respond. 'I've got to let them know I didn't do this.' That's who he is."

MacDonald said he didn't believe that Eric meant to be disrespectful, however, he noted that such outbursts are much more common in Eric's birth state of New York, where people are more vocal and animated in general.

But, thankfully for the McLaughlin family, this was the last they would have to see of Eric Naposki—other than in his TV interviews.


Outside the courtroom, a reporter asked MacDonald why the defense never presented any information about the alleged hit man, Juan Gonzales.

"Didn't come together," the attorney said. Back in 1994, "[Gonzales] was a young guy with a lot of contacts."

Downstairs during a quick news conference, Murphy made a few comments to address the media's questions about Eric's story. The prosecutor dismissed it once again as "lie after lie after lie after lie," which had no truth, no corroboration, and no relevance.

"We investigated it," he said. "I have absolutely no doubt that it's complete crap."

Even if the story were true, Murphy said, Eric's own admissions made him guilty of murder: Eric had said that Gonzales used Eric's gun in the murder, that Eric introduced Gonzales to Nanette, and that Eric and Gonzales were across the street from Bill's house the week before the murder.

Clearly, Murphy said, "Naposki hasn't researched conspiracy law," because given these self-proclaimed facts, Eric would still be guilty of murder. It would only "take ten years off his LWOP sentence. He would still be a murderer for financial gain."


On September 5, 2012, Eric Naposki was transferred to a state prison in Wasco, a reception center where corrections officials would decide which institution was best suited for his life term. They also would likely take into account that he was a somewhat high-profile prisoner due to his multiple TV appearances and his brief time in the NFL.

As inmate #AM2598, the forty-five-year-old prisoner was finally placed at the High Desert State Prison in Susanville in December—presumably just as muscular, if no more so, in anticipation of protecting himself from other convicted killers.

* * *

In January 2013, Investigation Discovery host Aphrodite Jones aired a show on the case in which she said she received a jailhouse letter from Nanette and also spoke on the phone with her. After all these years of silence and claims that she didn't think Eric had anything to do with the murder, Nanette finally had decided to change her story too.

She said she'd never told Eric that Bill had raped her. Yet, somehow he'd found out about her engagement to Bill, planned the murder on his own, and killed Bill "in a fit of jealous rage."

"I'm a victim of Eric's jealousy," Nanette told Jones.

It just wasn't Nanette's style to let an ex-boyfriend get away with blaming her or having the last word. That's how she took care of her men.

# ACKNOWLEDGMENTS

I want to thank the following people for helping me put this book together. I couldn't have done it without you: Dave Byington; Tom Voth; Joe Cartwright and Scott Smith, of the NBPD; Matt Murphy, Larry Montgomery, Susan Frazier, and Dena Basham, from the Orange County DA's office; Laura Hoyle; Eric Naposki's attorneys Gary Pohlson and Angelo MacDonald and friend John Pappalardo; Nanette Packard's attorney, Mick Hill; Debbie Lloyd; Jeff Stempien, of the Greenwich Police Department; Brian Ringler; Sandy Baumgardner; Kim McLaughlin Bayless; Patrick and Jenny McLaughlin; Barbara LaSpesa; Billy McNeal; Tom Reynolds; Suzanne Cogar; Adrianne Reynolds; Patricia "Tricia" Stearns; Rebecca Allen, Frank Mickadeit, and Michele Cardon, of the *Orange County Register*; Don Kalal; Donna Hakala; Chris Fiore; Angie Naposki; Terry Thornton; Michael Signora; Carole Levitzky; Susan Ludwig; Mike Matteson; Susan Leibowitz and Allen Larson.

I also want to thank Michaela Hamilton at Kensington, along with my agent, Peter Rubie, for helping me keep the dream alive.

Special thanks to my readers, and also to those who have graciously supported and helped keep me sane while I wrote this book: Carole Scott, Susan Gembrowski, Géza Keller, Samuel Autman, Rachel Ingersol, Carlos Beha, Bob Koven, Myra Chan, and the crew at Einstein Bros Bagels #3048.